Blackstone's

Police Investigators' Workbook

Blackstone's

Police Investigators' Workbook

2009

Paul Connor

With contributions from

David Pinfield, Neil Taylor, and Julian Chapman

OXFORD
UNIVERSITY PRESS

OXFORD
UNIVERSITY PRESS

Great Clarendon Street, Oxford OX2 6DP

Oxford University Press is a department of the University of Oxford.
It furthers the University's objective of excellence in research, scholarship,
and education by publishing worldwide in

Oxford New York

Auckland Cape Town Dar es Salaam Hong Kong Karachi
Kuala Lumpur Madrid Melbourne Mexico City Nairobi
New Delhi Shanghai Taipei Toronto

With offices in

Argentina Austria Brazil Chile Czech Republic France Greece
Guatemala Hungary Italy Japan Poland Portugal Singapore
South Korea Switzerland Thailand Turkey Ukraine Vietnam

Oxford is a registered trade mark of Oxford University Press
in the UK and in certain other countries

Published in the United States
by Oxford University Press Inc., New York

British Library Cataloguing in Publication Data

Data available

Library of Congress Cataloging in Publication Data

Data available

Typeset by Laserwords Private Limited, Chennai, India
Printed in Italy
on acid-free paper by
Legoprint S.p.A.

ISBN 978-0-19-955296-2

10 9 8 7 6 5 4 3 2 1

Acknowledgements

Thanks must go to all the Trainee Investigators from West Midlands Police, West Mercia Constabulary, and Essex Police who provided me with feedback about the content and style of the Workbook.

Many thanks to all the team at OUP, especially Peter Daniell, Lindsey Davis, and Jodi Towler.

Contents

Contents

Introduction to the Workbook

This Workbook has been custom-written to assist the Trainee Investigator who is revising for any of the National Investigators' Examinations (NIE), due to take place in 2008.

In order to make this publication as beneficial as possible, officers studying for the NIE have examined each section of the Workbook and have provided feedback on the content and style of the material. The feedback received enabled the Workbook to be tailored to suit the needs of the Trainee Investigator.

The Workbook does not cover every single subject mentioned in the text of the *Blackstone's Police Investigators' Manual 2008* (the Manual). This is because subjects dealt with in the Workbook are approached in a different manner to that of the Manual. The Manual, by necessity, covers the entire syllabus of the NIE, whereas the Workbook is selective in its coverage. In order to ensure that you understand a subject you will be asked to complete a variety of tasks such as answering multiple-choice questions, completing written exercises, and examining flowcharts. This approach means that a subject dealt with in a matter of five pages in the Manual can take 20 pages to deal with in the Workbook.

Before you begin, I must make two important points clear:

1. It is important that you do not use the subjects covered in the Workbook as a predictor of the content of the NIE. *Any* subject contained in the Manual can be tested in the examination and that subject might not be covered in the Workbook.
2. The questions you will answer in the NIE are based *solely* on the text contained in the Manual. If there is ever any contradiction between the Manual and the Workbook (or indeed any other text), remember: *'The Manual is always right.'*

A lot of effort has gone into writing this Workbook. I hope that you will benefit from that effort and that it makes a positive contribution to your revision.

How to use this Workbook

Whether it is for an examination, an interview, a new skill at work, or for any other purpose, we all have different approaches to learning. Because we are all so very diverse there is no set formula for revision that will suit us all. What works for me may not work for you.

For those who have successfully used a particular style or approach to revision in the past and believe that it will work when revising for the NIE—stick with it. I am sure you will adapt the Workbook to suit your needs.

For those who do not fall into this category, you might want to try the below method to get the most out of the Workbook. Please remember that this is only a *suggested* way for you to use the Workbook. How you use the Workbook is a choice only you can make.

1. Identify what sections of the Manual have a corresponding section in the Workbook (we will use 'Theft' as an example).
2. Begin your revision by answering the multiple-choice questions on 'Theft' contained in the Workbook (it does not matter if you have no knowledge whatsoever of the subject you are being tested on—your best guess will be fine).
3. When you have answered the multiple-choice questions, read the section on 'Theft' contained in the Manual (once only).
4. After you have read the 'Theft' section in the Manual, complete the Workbook section on 'Theft'.
   To get the most out of the Workbook you **must** try to complete any written exercises you are asked to. If you do not know the answer to a question do not worry as all of the exercises have an explanation. Do not fall into the trap of telling yourself 'I know that' when you do not and then not bothering to write anything down in the space provided. Practising self-deception with regard to the level of your knowledge might make you feel secure when you are reading the Workbook, but it will not help you to learn. Being honest with yourself about your own knowledge level will be far more beneficial in terms of passing the NIE.
5. Attempt the 'Recall Questions' at the end of the 'Theft' section.
6. When you are satisfied with your answers, return to the Manual and read the section on 'Theft' for the second time.
7. When you have finished reading the 'Theft' section for the second time, return to the Workbook and make your second attempt at the multiple-choice questions. When you have finished, check your answers.

After checking your answers, you could choose to answer other multiple-choice questions on the subject you are revising if they are available to you.

Be prepared to perform badly at first but do not give up because of this performance; it is quite normal. Your knowledge and ability will steadily increase as you move through the stages, and if you follow the above instructions I am confident that you will finish the process with a good level of knowledge. Remember that this process will provide you with a good *foundation* of knowledge, but in order to maintain that level you should briefly revisit the subject from time to time.

PART ONE

Evidence

1 | State of Mind and Criminal Conduct

Aim

The aim of this section is to identify and explain some of the major issues regarding state of mind (*mens rea*) and criminal conduct (*actus reus*).

Objectives

At the end of this section you should be able to:

1. Explain how a court may infer intention.
2. Outline the meaning of recklessness.
3. Describe what is meant by the term 'chain of causation'.
4. Apply your knowledge to multiple-choice questions.

Introduction

Examining state of mind and criminal conduct will provide you with valuable information that you can relate to all the offences you will study while revising for your National Investigators' Examination. This is because every crime in your *Investigators' Manual* will involve some form of guilty knowledge and some form of action (there are no strict liability offences in your Manual). There is no need to go into great depth with regard to these subjects and for that reason this section of the Workbook concentrates on three areas: (i) intention, (ii) recklessness, and (iii) the chain of causation.

Multiple-choice Questions

Begin this section of the Workbook by answering the below multiple-choice questions. Mark your answer in the 'First Attempt' box. Then read and complete the exercises in the 'State of Mind and Criminal Conduct' section. Once you are satisfied that your knowledge is of a good standard, return to these questions and mark your answer in the 'Second Attempt' box. The answers to these questions can be found in the 'Answers Section' at the rear of the Workbook.

MCQ 1.1   MERCER (an 11-year-old) and HOWDEN (a 14-year-old with the mental age of a nine-year-old) enter the back yard of a shop. They set fire to some newspapers and throw the papers underneath a plastic wheelie-bin before leaving the yard. MERCER and HOWDEN both believe that the newspapers will extinguish themselves on the concrete floor. However, the newspaper fire sets fire to the wheelie-bin, which spreads fire to the shop and some adjoining buildings, causing damage estimated at £1 million. MERCER and HOWDEN are arrested and state that they did not appreciate the risk that the wheelie-bin, let alone the shop and its adjoining buildings, would be destroyed or damaged by fire.

With regard to the meaning of 'recklessness', which of the below statements is correct?

A MERCER and HOWDEN could be prosecuted for an offence of arson as their state of mind would constitute objective recklessness.

B As MERCER and HOWDEN have failed to consider an obvious risk, their actions would be considered reckless.

C MERCER and HOWDEN were unaware that the risk existed or would exist, and would not be reckless in these circumstances.

D As MERCER is under 14 years of age, he will not be considered to be reckless. As HOWDEN is over 14 years old, he should have foreseen the consequences of his actions and will be considered reckless.

First Attempt	
Second Attempt	

MCQ 1.2   GRICE and LOVATT play for rival football teams. During a football presentation evening a fight between the two men begins. In the course of the fight GRICE stabs LOVATT twice with a knife. LOVATT is seriously injured and falls to the floor. GRICE picks LOVATT up and tries to carry him to a nearby hospital, but trips over several times during the short journey, dropping LOVATT onto the floor and further injuring him on those occasions. When LOVATT arrives at the hospital, a nurse examines him but misses the fact that one of the wounds has pierced a lung and caused a haemorrhage. The nurse gives LOVATT treatment that is negligent and affects his chances of recovery. LOVATT dies from his injuries a short time later. It is later established that the medical treatment LOVATT received was primarily responsible for his death.

Considering the law with regard to causal links and intervening acts, which of the below statements is correct?

A If the medical treatment, which the victim is given, results in his/her ultimate death, the treatment itself will not normally be regarded as an intervening act.

B GRICE is not responsible for LOVATT's death because the primary reason for his death was the poor medical treatment received from the nurse.

C Poor quality and/or negligent medical treatment will never break the chain of causation.

D The fact that LOVATT was dropped and injured several times during the journey to the hospital and was given poor medical treatment will break the chain of causation.

First Attempt	
Second Attempt	

MCQ 1.3 There is a significant amount of case law regarding what will and will not be seen as an 'intervening act' which breaks the chain of causation.

Which of the below comments is correct with regard to that case law?

A   JERROM is a drug dealer who supplies heroin to REED, who later kills himself by taking an overdose of the heroin. JERROM is liable for the death of REED.

B   WALTER stabs KERR during a fight. KERR requires a blood transfusion as a consequence but refuses this as he is a Jehovah's Witness. KERR bleeds to death from his injuries as a result. WALTER is not liable for KERR's death.

C   FOSTER and STORK are passengers in a car being driven along a motorway by CURTIS. STORK tries to rape FOSTER, who jumps from the car to escape and is killed in the process. STORK is liable for FOSTER's death.

D   BERESFORD is a pensioner who has a serious heart condition and is of a very nervous disposition. STATHAM robs BERESFORD of her handbag and, because of the fright caused by the incident, BERESFORD immediately has a heart attack and dies. STATHAM is not liable for BERESFORD's death.

First Attempt	
Second Attempt	

MCQ 1.4 DC HAWK and TI PORTER are having a general discussion about *mens rea* (guilty knowledge). Several comments are made by the officers during the course of the discussion but only one of them is correct.

Which comment shows a correct understanding of the concepts relating to *mens rea*?

A   DC HAWK states that there have been some instances where the courts have held that an offence does not require any *mens rea* to be proved.

B   TI PORTER states that there is no situation in which 'absolute liability' can be imposed.

C   DC HAWK states that there is a specific legal definition of the word 'intent'.

D   TI PORTER states that recklessness can be objective or subjective.

First Attempt	
Second Attempt	

MCQ 1.5 In order to prove the *actus reus* of an offence, the prosecution are required to prove two elements.

What are those two elements?

A   That the defendant's conduct was voluntary and that he/she realized the consequences of his/her actions.

B   That the defendant brought about a consequence as a result of his/her actions and that this consequence was a realistic possibility when the act took place.

C   That the defendant's conduct was voluntary and that it occurred while the defendant still had the requisite *mens rea*.

D   That the defendant knew what was likely to occur and he/she had the requisite *mens rea* for the act at the time of the offence.

First Attempt	
Second Attempt	

Intention

E

EXERCISE 1.1

The word 'intent' is mentioned in many of the offences you will study as part of your revision for the National Investigators' Examination.

What is the definition of 'intent'?

_____

_____

Explanation 1.1

When you actually thought about this exercise you may have struggled to remember where you have read the definition of intent. That would not be surprising as there is no such definition. To keep things as simple as possible it is best to consider 'intent' from a common sense point of view. If you intend to do something then you want it to happen and set out to see that it does; it is your purpose.

One of the reasons why it would be difficult to provide a definition of intent is that it is ever-changing according to the offence. The intention for murder is the intent to kill or cause grievous bodily harm, whereas for theft it is to act dishonestly, intending to permanently deprive.

Proving intention is not easy unless the defendant provides an admissible confession, perhaps during interview, where he/she states that his/her intention was to bring about a certain result, *'I wanted him dead because he was having an affair with my wife'*. But what happens when such evidence is not available?

E

EXERCISE 1.2

Read the below scenario and answer the question that follows it.

DICKSON and STONE work with each other on a machine in a car factory. The machine presses metal into car parts and exerts high pressure on the metal in order to do so. The machine is extremely dangerous and both men are aware of this fact as there have been several serious accidents involving the machine in the past, one of which was fatal. An argument begins between the two men while they are operating the machine, culminating in DICKSON pushing STONE into the press which closes and crushes him to death. DICKSON is arrested for murder and during his interview he denies the offence. He maintains that he wanted to frighten STONE and teach him a lesson and that he did not intend to kill or seriously injure him. He is charged with murder and the case goes to trial. There is no confession evidence to readily establish DICKSON's state of mind.

There are two ways that a jury may be able to infer intent from the circumstances. What are they?

1. _____

2. _____

Explanation 1.2

The two ways that a jury may be able to infer intent are by way of

1. case law, and

2. s 8 of the Criminal Justice Act 1967.

We will deal with each of the above methods in turn.

Case law states that *foresight of a probability of a consequence does not amount to an intention to bring that consequence about, but may be evidence of it.*

The jury/court considers:

*   At the time of the criminal act was there a probability of a consequence?
*   The greater the probability, the more likely it is that the defendant foresaw that consequence.
*   If the defendant foresaw that consequence, the more likely it is that the defendant intended it to happen.

E

EXERCISE 1.3

Now apply case law to the circumstances. How would case law assist a jury/court to infer DICKSON's intent?

_____

_____

_____

_____

_____

_____

_____

_____

_____

_____

Explanation 1.3

It is best to deal with each word in turn and then consider its meaning in light of the evidence at your disposal.

Foresight   =   What did DICKSON see

Probability   =   was likely to happen

Consequence   =   as a result of the action

So *foresight of a probability of a consequence etc.* means

you saw what was likely to happen as a result of your actions and while it doesn't prove you intended it, it may be evidence of it.

At the time of the criminal act was there a probability of a consequence?

(When DICKSON pushed STONE into the machine, was it likely that he saw that STONE would be killed or seriously injured?)

the greater the probability, the more likely it is that the defendant foresaw that consequence

(there was a very high chance of death or serious injury and therefore it is likely that DICKSON saw what the result of his actions would be)

if DICKSON foresaw that consequence, the more likely it is that he intended it to happen

(DICKSON knew what would happen—it is highly likely he intended it)

Section 8 of the Criminal Justice Act 1967 states that a court/jury, in determining whether a person has committed an offence

(a) shall not be bound in law to infer that he intended or foresaw a result of his actions by reasons only of its being a natural and probable consequence of those actions; but

(b) shall decide whether he did intend or foresee that result by reference to all the evidence, drawing such inferences from the evidence as appear proper in the circumstances.

Let's say that the following additional information was available to the police.

DICKSON and STONE have never got on with each other and have had several arguments. The relationship between the two men has been getting progressively worse and last week the foreman of the factory had to step in to break up a fight between them when blows were exchanged in the factory canteen. Another worker at the factory, PARVIEW, overheard a conversation between DICKSON and another man in a pub several days ago. During the conversation, DICKSON was heard to say, *'Don't you worry, when the little shit's dead I'll make it look like an industrial accident.'*

E

EXERCISE 1.4

Using the additional evidence at your disposal, explain how s 8 would assist to allow a court/jury to infer intent.

_____

_____

_____

_____
_____
_____
_____
_____
_____
_____

Explanation 1.4

What s 8 of the Criminal Justice Act 1967 says is that pushing STONE into the press machine would quite obviously cause his death. However, just because this is obvious does not mean to say that the jury/court can infer that DICKSON intended to kill or cause GBH as a result. *However,* they can look at the evidence as a whole and by looking at that evidence infer intent if it appears proper to do so. The more evidence there is available that supports that inference, the more likely it is that DICKSON intended the result.

See *Investigators' Manual*, para 1.1.4.1

Recklessness

> **EXERCISE 1.5**
>
> You will see the word 'recklessness' in a large number of the offences you will study. Do not worry about a precise legal definition just yet; instead, write down what you think it means.
>
> _____
> _____
> _____

Explanation 1.5

There will be a wide variety of responses to this exercise. You may have included the following: acting without caution, an act marked by a lack of proper caution, without thought or care for the consequences of an action, an act marked by a lack of thought about danger or other possible undesirable consequences, doing something dangerous and not caring about the risks and the possible results, completely heedless of dangers or consequences, or rash.

All of these (and more) would be a fair response to the question.

Now that you have considered the word from a common sense perspective, you need to move on to consider it from a legal perspective.

E

EXERCISE 1.6

Examine the below scenarios and see if you agree or disagree with the statements that follow them.

1. PALMER is a 23-year-old who has learning difficulties; his mental age is that of a five-year-old. He is out shopping with his mother and the two are inside a jeweller's shop. PALMER is looking at a display stand containing a glass decanter and glasses and, thinking that the stand is 'earthquake proof', he shakes the stand violently. The glass decanter and glasses fall to the floor and smash to pieces.

   In these circumstances PALMER would be considered 'reckless' and could be convicted of criminal damage. This is because the term 'recklessness' in criminal damage means *objective recklessness*.

   Do you agree or disagree with this statement?

   Agree / Disagree

   Why/Why not?

   _____

   _____

   _____

2. BAREHAM is hired to repair a large section of roof on a three-storey house. He needs to remove a large section of the existing roof before he can begin, and places a skip at the front of the house at ground level to throw roof tiles and other debris into as he demolishes the existing roof. BAREHAM does not bother to place a chute leading from the roof to the skip and realises that there is a slight chance that flying debris could injure someone. However, he believes that he is accurate enough to ensure that all the debris will land directly in the skip as he throws it from the roof. BAREHAM begins work, but the first tile he throws towards the skip misses and hits CASSWELL on the shoulder as she walks past the house. The blow breaks CASSWELL's collarbone.

   In these circumstances BAREHAM would be considered 'reckless' and could be convicted of a s 20 assault. This is because the term 'recklessness' in assaults means *subjective recklessness*.

   Do you agree or disagree with this statement?

   Agree / Disagree

   Why/Why not?

   _____

   _____

   _____

Explanation 1.6

Recklessness is similar to intent insofar as it changes with the nature of the crime. This is illustrated in the two examples above and they will be explained shortly. What is important for you to remember is that historically there were two types of recklessness: *objective* and *subjective* recklessness.

Objective recklessness is dead!

Objective recklessness primarily related to offences of criminal damage and involved the jury or court making a decision from the perspective of the reasonable man. It did not matter that the defendant was a child, had learning difficulties, or did not appreciate the risk, etc. because the reasonable man would have. Therefore, the defendant was reckless because a reasonable man would have appreciated the risk. This approach was reversed by the decision in *R v G & R* [2003] 3 WLR 1060. Subjective recklessness remains.

1. PALMER is not reckless (he would have been under the old law). Recklessness in criminal damage has been defined on the following basis:

   A person will be 'reckless' as to circumstances when he/she is aware of a risk that existed or would exist. A person will be 'reckless' as to a result or consequence when he/she is aware of a risk that it would occur and it is, in the circumstances known to him/her, unreasonable to take the risk.

   In other words either

   • the defendant has got to know there is an actual risk or that one will be created; or
   • know that by doing something (in whatever current circumstances there are) an unacceptable risk will be created.

   PALMER does not know that by shaking the display stand there will be a risk that the decanter and glasses will fall and smash.

2. BAREHAM is reckless. You should remember that recklessness in assaults is *subjective*, i.e. the defendant saw there was a risk of harm but went on to take that risk anyway.

The simple approach to recklessness is this:

Recklessness is subjective. If the defendant *did not* see the risk, then he/she *is not reckless*.

See *Investigators' Manual*, para 1.1.4.2

The Chain of Causation

EXERCISE 1.7

Read the below scenario and answer the questions that follow it, providing reasons for your answers where appropriate.

TULLAH and McDOWELL are involved in an argument inside a pub. Members of the pub door staff eject both men from the pub and the argument between the two men continues outside. The argument escalates and TULLAH punches McDOWELL in the face, intending to cause him actual bodily harm. The force of the blow knocks McDOWELL backwards and he trips on the kerb, causing him to fall over onto the pavement. McDOWELL's head hits the pavement and he loses consciousness. An ambulance is called to the scene and McDOWELL is taken to the Accident and Emergency (A & E) ward of a nearby hospital. The A & E ward is extremely busy as it is Saturday night and there have been a large number of serious incidents, adding pressure to the already overworked staff. A nurse quickly examines McDOWELL and, believing that he has sustained a very minor concussion, leaves him and goes to deal with another patient. In fact, McDOWELL has fractured his skull and has sustained life-threatening brain damage from the fracture. Thirty minutes later, McDOWELL dies without receiving any treatment. A post-mortem reveals that McDOWELL had a rare medical condition meaning that a slight blow to his skull could cause it to fracture and consequently cause his death. The blow that caused McDOWELL's skull to fracture would have left only bruising to the skull of the average person.

1. If you were dealing with this case, what offence would you charge TULLAH with?

   _____

   Why?

   _____

   _____

   _____

   _____

   _____

2. McDOWELL had a rare medical condition that contributed to his death. Did this affect your reasoning?

   Yes / No

   Why/Why not?

   _____

   _____

3. McDOWELL received negligent treatment when he arrived at the A & E ward. Did this affect your reasoning?

   Yes / No

   Why/Why not?

   _____

   _____

Explanation 1.7

1. You would probably charge TULLAH with murder or manslaughter, but how did you justify this charge based on the fact that TULLAH only intended to cause McDOWELL actual bodily harm?

The chain of causation is all about cause and effect and is sometimes called the 'but for' test, e.g. 'but for the actions of the defendant this would not have happened'. A connection between the act(s) of the defendant and the final consequence must exist; this must be an unbroken chain of events. It is sometimes better to begin with the final link in the chain and work backwards.

McDOWELL is dead

What was the cause of death?

Brain damage

What caused the brain damage?

A fracture to his skull

What caused the fracture to his skull?

His head hitting the pavement

What caused his head to hit the pavement?

He tripped on the kerb

What caused him to trip on the kerb?

A blow to the face that knocked him backwards

Who struck the blow?

TULLAH

BUT FOR *the fact that TULLAH struck McDOWELL, he would still be alive.*

TULLAH is responsible for McDOWELL's death.

2. The fact that McDOWELL has a rare medical condition meaning that his skull is exceptionally weak does not matter. Defendants must 'take their victims as they find them'. McDOWELL's thin skull may well have been a contributory factor leading to his death, but the reason it made a contribution was because of the chain of events that TULLAH set in motion by striking the blow.

3. Negligent medical treatment *will not normally* be regarded as an intervening act that will break the chain of causation. There are some exceptions to this rule, but it is best to consider these exceptions for what they are: 'exceptional'.

See *Investigators' Manual*, paras 1.2.4 to 1.2.5

Conclusion

Having completed this section of the Workbook, you should be able to see how *mens rea* and *actus reus* connect to form part of nearly every crime you deal with. As such, the importance of these subjects should not be underestimated and you should remember to pay attention to other areas of the subjects that were not covered in this part of the Workbook, e.g. omissions and the **DUTY** mnemonic.

Now that you have finished the Workbook section on 'State of Mind and Criminal Conduct', you should attempt the 'Recall Questions' before re-reading the relevant section in the Manual and making your second attempt at the multiple-choice questions. The answers to these questions are printed in the 'Answers Section' at the rear of the Workbook.

Recall Questions

Try and answer the questions below. Do not allow yourself to continue until you have answered the questions to your satisfaction.

- What is an offence of 'specific intent'?
- There is one offence on your syllabus that can be committed by 'negligence'. What is it?
- Summarize s 8 of the Criminal Justice Act 1967.
- How does case law allow us to infer intent?
- What is the most important thing to remember about 'recklessness'?
- What two factors must you show when proving *actus reus?*
- What does the mnemonic **DUTY** stand for?
- What is the 'chain of causation' all about?
- What is the state of mind required of an accessory?
- Can a company commit a criminal offence?

2 | Incomplete Offences

Aim

The aim of this section is for you to comprehend the offences of conspiracy, and attempts and their respective exceptions.

Objectives

At the end of this section you should be able to:

1. State what constitutes a statutory conspiracy (s 1 of the Criminal Law Act 1977).
2. State what constitutes an attempt (s 1 of the Criminal Attempts Act 1981).
3. List the exceptions to the offences of incitement, conspiracy, and attempts.
4. Apply your knowledge to multiple-choice questions.

Introduction

Offences involving conspiracy, and attempts (sometimes called inchoate offences) all relate to the preparation undertaken by a defendant prior to the commission of a substantial offence. As the defendant moves closer to the commission of an offence, he/she may commit some or all of these offences. As it is not always desirable to allow an offence to take place, it is important to know at what stage an incomplete offence has been committed. For the purposes of your examination, you must be able to understand and distinguish between these types of offences.

Multiple-choice Questions

Begin this section of the Workbook by answering the below multiple-choice questions. Mark your answer in the 'First Attempt' box. Then read and complete the exercises in the 'Incomplete Offences' section. Once you are satisfied that your knowledge is of a good standard, return to these questions and mark your answer in the 'Second Attempt' box. The answers to the questions can be found in the 'Answers Section' at the rear of the Workbook.

MCQ 2.1   John BURCOTT plans to rob a bank. He asks his wife, Alison BURCOTT, if she will assist him in the robbery and she agrees. He also asks SALE (who works as a security guard at the bank) to assist him and SALE agrees. Alison BURCOTT and SALE do not know that each of them will play a part in the robbery.

Is this an offence of statutory conspiracy (contrary to s 1 of the Criminal Law Act 1977)?

A   No, because BURCOTT's wife and SALE do not know of each other's existence.

B   Yes, but if the agreement is later abandoned the offence will not be committed.

C   No, because one of the conspirators is John BURCOTT's wife.

D   Yes, a husband and wife can commit conspiracy if they conspire with a third party.

First Attempt	
Second Attempt	

MCQ 2.2   BLACKMAN decides he is going to break into a garden centre and steal gardening equipment. He goes out and buys a jemmy to force the lock on the store door. Late at night he goes out of his house wearing a pair of gloves and a balaclava. He climbs over the fence surrounding the garden centre and walks towards the store doors. He takes out the jemmy and tries to break the door lock but is disturbed by a security guard. BLACKMAN panics and runs home.

At what point, if at all, does BLACKMAN commit the offence of attempted burglary (contrary to s 1 of the Criminal Attempts Act 1981)?

A   When he leaves his house with the jemmy and wearing the gloves and balaclava.

B   When he climbs the fence and walks towards the store doors.

C   When he takes out the jemmy and tries to break the door lock.

D   He does not commit an attempt in these circumstances.

First Attempt	
Second Attempt	

MCQ 2.3   MYCROFT goes to some garages at the rear of his house with an aerosol can containing orange spray paint. He intends to spray graffiti on several garage doors (belonging to his neighbours), causing a few pounds worth of damage. However, when MYCROFT tries to use the aerosol paint on a garage door, it does not work as it is blocked and therefore no damage is caused.

Which of the below statements is correct with regard to MYCROFT's activities?

A   He commits the offence of attempted criminal damage.

B   He cannot commit attempted criminal damage, as 'simple' criminal damage is a summary only offence and you cannot attempt a summary only offence.

C   You cannot attempt the impossible; as the aerosol spray will not work, MYCROFT commits no offence.

D   MYCROFT has not committed attempted criminal damage, as he has not 'embarked on the crime proper'.

First Attempt	
Second Attempt	

MCQ 2.4   BULLMAN wishes to commit a robbery at a supermarket. He originally intended to commit the offence alone, but realizes that to escape capture he needs somebody to act as his getaway driver. He approaches FLINTOFF and suggests that he assists him as the getaway driver; FLINTOFF does not want to get involved in the offence and refuses BULLMAN's request.

In relation to offences under the Criminal Attempts Act 1981 alone, which of the below statements is correct?

A   BULLMAN is guilty of attempting to conspire with FLINTOFF.

B   BULLMAN is guilty of attempting to counsel FLINTOFF to commit the offence.

C   BULLMAN commits no offence under this legislation.

D   BULLMAN is guilty of attempting to procure the commission of an offence.

First Attempt	
Second Attempt	

MCQ 2.5   MUNN falls out with her neighbour, JARROW, and decides to take revenge on JARROW by causing criminal damage to JARROW's car. MUNN waits until 3am when she sneaks out of her house and approaches JARROW's car. It is MUNN's intention to get into the car and slash the seats inside. She reaches the car and tries the driver's door handle but the car is locked. She decides to cause damage to a trailer attached to JARROW's car instead and lifts the cover of the trailer and slashes a tent stored in the trailer.

In respect of the offence of interfering with vehicles (contrary to s 9 of the Criminal Attempts Act 1981), which of the following statements is correct?

A   MUNN has not committed the offence.

B   MUNN has committed the offence but only in respect of her attempt to open the car door.

C   MUNN has committed the offence but only when she lifts the cover of the trailer.

D   MUNN has committed the offence when she tries the car door and also when she lifts the cover of the trailer.

First Attempt	
Second Attempt	

Statutory Conspiracy (s 1 of the Criminal Law Act 1977)

Complete Exercises 2.3 and 2.4, before referring to their joint explanation 2.4.

E

EXERCISE 2.1

Examine the below situations and decide whether they would constitute a statutory conspiracy. Give a short reason for your decision. (The explanations are given after the exceptions to the offence.)

1. HORNER and his wife plan to break into a pub. They recruit DAVIES to act as the getaway driver.

   Statutory conspiracy?

   Yes / No

   _____

   _____

   _____

2. GRISDALE agrees with SPENCER that they will damage FAULKNER's car, as FAULKNER has been sleeping with GRISDALE's wife. Before they damage the car it is stolen, making the commission of the offence impossible.

   Statutory conspiracy?

   Yes / No

   _____

   _____

   _____

3. MAJOR asks his friend MOSS (who works in a breaker's yard) to crush his car so he can claim for the car on the insurance; MOSS refuses.

   Statutory conspiracy?

   Yes / No

   _____

   _____

   _____

Explanation 2.1

The definition of statutory conspiracy provides two points for you to consider:

1. Was there an agreement between at least *two* people, and, if so,

2. if the agreement was carried out, would it lead to the commission of an offence by one or more of the parties?

If the answer is 'Yes' to both questions, then you have a statutory conspiracy. The fact that the commission of the offence is impossible is immaterial.

E

EXERCISE 2.2

There are three instances where a defendant will not commit statutory conspiracy. There will be no statutory conspiracy where the only other party is:

1. _____

2. _____

3. _____

Explanation 2.2

There is no statutory conspiracy where the only other party is:

> **H** His/her spouse (or civil partner)
>
> **A** A person under ten years of age
>
> **T** The intended victim

Please note that a husband and wife or civil partners can conspire if there is a third party involved in the conspiracy.

1. This is a statutory conspiracy. Although two parties to the conspiracy are husband and wife, a third party (DAVIES) is involved.

2. This is a statutory conspiracy. The fact that the car has been stolen, making the commission of the offence impossible, does not matter.

3. This is not a statutory conspiracy as there is no agreement between two or more parties.

See *Investigators' Manual*, para 1.3.3.1

Attempts (s 1 of the Criminal Attempts Act 1981)

E

EXERCISE 2.3

When you consider 'attempts', what comes to mind?

_____

_____

```
_____
_____
_____
_____
```

Explanation 2.3

You may have answered the question using the words 'more than merely preparatory'. You may also have mentioned the fact that the *mens rea* required is an intent to commit an offence, that you can attempt the impossible, and some of the exceptions to the offence.

'More than merely preparatory'

EXERCISE 2.4

LEE sacks PARK from his job as a security guard at a supermarket. To get revenge against LEE, PARK intends to burn down LEE's house. As the below sequence of events unfolds, decide if an attempt has been made by PARK and, if so, at what stage the attempt is made.

1. PARK makes some enquiries to find out where LEE lives.

2. PARK visits LEE's house to check if there are any security devices present.

3. PARK buys some rubber gloves to avoid leaving any fingerprints.

4. PARK puts a petrol bomb in his car.

5. PARK buys a lighter.

6. PARK drives to LEE's house.

7. PARK puts on the rubber gloves.

8. PARK picks up the lighter and petrol bomb and walks towards LEE's house.

9. PARK stands outside LEE's house with the petrol bomb in his hand.

10. PARK lights the lighter and moves it towards the petrol bomb, but extinguishes it on seeing that he is being watched by one of LEE's neighbours.

Explanation 2.4

Ask yourself two questions:

1. At any point, has the defendant embarked on the crime proper? If the answer is 'Yes' then,

2. At what point did he/she go beyond mere preparation?

In the above example, points 1 to 9 would be considered mere preparation. At point 10, PARK would be liable for an attempt. Whether the defendant has gone beyond mere preparation will be a question of fact for the jury/magistrate(s).

Attempting the impossible

A defendant would be guilty of an attempt even if the facts were such that the commission of the offence is impossible. For example, a defendant decides to steal a wallet from a jacket left in a changing room. However, the fact is that there is no wallet in the jacket pocket. When the defendant puts his hand into the empty jacket pocket he would still be guilty of attempted theft.

As ever, there are certain offences that cannot be attempted:

1. conspiracy;
2. aiding, abetting, counselling, or procuring an offence; and
3. offences of assisting an offender and accepting or agreeing to accept consideration for not disclosing information.

See *Investigators' Manual*, paras 1.3.4 to 1.3.5

Conclusion

> Now that you have completed this section of the Workbook, you should be able to identify when an incomplete offence has been committed. You should realize that although these offences are relatively straightforward, the exceptions to the rule could cause some difficulty.

Now that you have finished the Workbook section on 'Incomplete Offences', you should attempt the 'Recall Questions' before re-reading the relevant section in the Manual and making your second attempt at the multiple-choice questions. The answers to these questions are printed in the 'Answers Section' at the rear of the Workbook.

Recall Questions

Try and answer the questions below. Do not allow yourself to continue until you have answered the questions to your satisfaction.

- What is the definition of incitement?

- What type of offences cannot be incited (can you remember the mnemonic)?

- What are the two points you need to consider for an offence of statutory conspiracy?

- Who can't you conspire with (can you remember the mnemonic)?

- What are the two questions you need to ask yourself when considering an offence involving an attempt?

- What offences cannot be attempted?

3 | The Regulation of Investigatory Powers Act (RIPA) 2000

Aim

The aim of this section is to provide you with an understanding of the issues surrounding the use of Covert Human Intelligence Sources and surveillance.

Objectives

At the end of this section you should be able to:

1. Outline the purpose of RIPA 2000.
2. Describe what a C.H.I.S. is.
3. State the authorization levels related to C.H.I.S. activity.
4. Describe what Intrusive Surveillance is.
5. Describe what Directed Surveillance is.
6. State the authorization levels related to surveillance activity.
7. Demonstrate your knowledge by completing the exercises in this section.
8. Apply your knowledge to multiple-choice questions.

Introduction

The Regulation of Investigatory Powers Act (RIPA) 2000 governs the way in which the police and other public authorities utilise their ability to carry out surveillance and use Covert Human Intelligence Sources (C.H.I.S.). Apart from the Act there are specific Codes of Practice that relate to RIPA along with guidelines produced by the Office of Surveillance Commissioners. Add to this individual force practices and policies and RIPA becomes a very complex piece of legislation to deal with. In this section of the Workbook you will only be dealing with the Act, which provides an outline of how this legislation works. For particular issues you should seek guidance from your force specialist departments.

Multiple-choice Questions

Begin this section of the Workbook by answering the below multiple-choice questions. Mark your answer in the 'First Attempt' box. Then read and complete the exercises in the RIPA 2000 section. Once you are satisfied that your knowledge is of a good standard, return to these questions and mark your answer in the 'Second Attempt' box. The answers to these questions can be found in the 'Answers Section' at the rear of the Workbook.

MCQ 3.1   BARKER (who works as a cashier for a building society) is looking out of her window when she sees WIDDOWS acting suspiciously on a street corner outside her house. As BARKER watches WIDDOWS it becomes plain that he is dealing in drugs. BARKER contacts the police and speaks to DC GAMER and tells him about what she has seen. The next day, BARKER observes WIDDOWS when he enters the building society where she works and places a large amount of cash into an account in the name of John OGDEN. Once again, BARKER speaks to DC GAMER and tells him what she has seen. DC GAMER asks BARKER to keep a close eye on the 'John OGDEN' account and to keep a note of when WIDDOWS enters the building society and with whom he enters, if anyone.

At what point, if at all, does BARKER become a Covert Human Intelligence Source (C.H.I.S.)?

A   When she provides information to DC GAMER about WIDDOWS dealing drugs on the street outside her house.

B   When she provides information to DC GAMER about WIDDOWS entering the bank and placing money into the 'John OGDEN' account.

C   When DC GAMER asks her to keep an eye on the 'John OGDEN account and WIDDOWS' activities when he enters the building society.

D   BARKER does not become a C.H.I.S. in these circumstances.

First Attempt	
Second Attempt	

MCQ 3.2   DC JAKKAN wishes to obtain authorization for TREWER to become a C.H.I.S. He approaches the appropriate officer for authorization and it is granted. TREWER contacts DC JAKKAN and tells him that he can provide information about crime taking place across the United Kingdom and also in France.

Could the C.H.I.S. authorization cover TREWER's activity in these areas?

A   No, a C.H.I.S. authorization can only cover TREWER's activity in the force area where it was granted.

B   Yes, but only for activity carried out in the United Kingdom.

C   No, a C.H.I.S. authorization can only cover TREWER's activity in England and Wales.

D   Yes, a C.H.I.S. authorization can cover activity in the United Kingdom or elsewhere.

First Attempt	
Second Attempt	

MCQ 3.3 TI LITTLER approaches DS SALE for some advice in respect of HARDEY who has contacted TI LITTLER and told her that he wishes to provide information to the police about a gang of operating armed robbers, who frequent a gym that HARDEY owns.

In normal circumstances who would authorize HARDEY to become a C.H.I.S. and for how long?

A Authority would have to come from an officer of the rank of chief constable; the authority would last for 12 months.

B Authority would have to come from an officer of the rank of superintendent or above; the authority would last for 12 months.

C Authority would have to come from an officer of the rank of superintendent; the authority would last for three months.

D Authority would have to come from an officer of the rank of inspector or above; the authority would last for three months.

First Attempt	
Second Attempt	

MCQ 3.4 DC MADDALENA receives information that GARDEN is selling drugs from inside a small factory unit that he rents. DC MADDALENA wants to set up a surveillance operation that will involve placing a video camera inside GARDEN's factory unit to watch and record what is going on.

With regard to the Regulation of Investigatory Powers Act 2000, which of the below statements is correct?

A This activity would be classed as intrusive surveillance because the activity is taking place inside premises.

B This activity would be classed as directed surveillance.

C This activity would be classed as intrusive surveillance as the operation is using a video camera to watch and record GARDEN's activities.

D This activity would not be covered by the Act as it does not involve the presence of an individual on the factory premises to watch GARDEN's activities.

First Attempt	
Second Attempt	

MCQ 3.5 BUCK witnessed MENDIS breaking into his house and reported the matter to the police. TI YARD arrested MENDIS for the offence; MENDIS was charged and bailed for burglary. BUCK contacts TI YARD and tells him that he is receiving threatening telephone calls at his home address stating that if he does not retract his statement his house will be burnt down. TI YARD asks BUCK if he would consent to a recording device being placed on his telephone to record the threats and attempt to identify the offender. BUCK states that he does not mind what the police do to try and catch the person responsible.

Which of the below statements is correct in relation to this situation?

A This activity would require an authorization for directed surveillance.

B This would be an interception of a communication and requires the authorization of the Home Secretary.

C   Recording telephone conversations is only permissible in the investigation of offences relating to terrorism.
D   As this is taking place inside MENDIS's house this would require an authorization for intrusive surveillance.

First Attempt	
Second Attempt	

MCQ 3.6   DC McVEIGH is part of an enquiry team investigating a series of serious sexual assaults. During the course of the investigation, the team receives information that the offender, who is unknown, is going to carry out an attack in a nearby park. The team requires urgent authorization to carry out directed surveillance in the park and DC McVIEGH is tasked with obtaining that authorization.

Which of the below statements is correct?
A   DC McVEIGH could approach an officer of superintendent rank or above for urgent authorization. The authorization can be written or oral and will last for a period of one month.
B   DC McVEIGH could approach an officer of superintendent rank or above for urgent authorization. The authorization must be written and will last for a period of seven days.
C   DC McVEIGH could approach an officer of the rank of inspector or above for urgent authorization. The authorization can be written or oral and will last for a period of five days.
D   DC McVEIGH could approach an officer of the rank of inspector or above for urgent authorization. The authorization must be written and will last for a period of three days.

First Attempt	
Second Attempt	

MCQ 3.7   DC TOXTEN is part of a team investigating the kidnap and murder of a child. Intelligence is received regarding the identity of the offenders but in order to gain further intelligence and evidence, it is decided that non-urgent intrusive surveillance should be carried out against the suspects.

If an intrusive surveillance authorization is granted as above, how long will it last?
A   72 hours.
B   seven days.
C   one month.
D   three months.

First Attempt	
Second Attempt	

The Purpose of RIPA 2000

You may consider that RIPA does not affect you in your day-to-day police duties but it is incredibly easy to find the Act having some kind of involvement in your investigations. RIPA is not necessarily just about surveillance relating to major investigations—in fact it is the opposite as it relates to ordinary run-of-the-mill investigations on a far more regular basis. Therefore, it is important that you know what the Act regulates along with the consequences of breaching the Act.

E

EXERCISE 3.1

1. What do you think the purpose of RIPA 2000 is?

_____

_____

_____

2. What three types of police activity does RIPA 2000 regulate?

   i. _____

   ii. _____

   iii. _____

3. Would the Act apply to a journalist?

Yes / No

Why/Why not?

_____

_____

4. Breaching RIPA 2000 will have three potential consequences—what are they?

   i. _____

_____

   ii. _____

_____

   iii. _____

_____

5. How long does a person have to make a claim relating to a breach of the Act?

three months / six months / one year or five years?

6. What independent group monitors and supervises the application of the Act?

_____

Explanation 3.1

1. You may have said that the purpose of the Act is to regulate police activity in covert investigations but the Act does not just apply to the police. The purpose of the Act is to control the use of surveillance and Covert Human Intelligence Sources (C.H.I.S.) operations by public authorities (not just the police).

2. The type of police activity the Act regulates is:

    i.   Covert Human Intelligence Sources (C.H.I.S.)
    ii. Intrusive surveillance, and
    iii. Directed surveillance.

3. The Act would not apply to a journalist—this is because the Act only applies to *public authorities* and not to private companies or private individuals.

4. Breaching the Act will have three consequences:

    i.   Evidence obtained may be excluded by any court or tribunal
    ii. A breach may give rise to proceedings under police conduct regulations
    iii. A person may take a claim to the Investigatory Powers Tribunal.

5. 1 year.

6. The Office of Surveillance Commissioners (or OSC).

See *Investigators' Manual*, paras 1.4.2 and 1.4.3

What is a C.H.I.S.?

You have already come across this acronym several times in this section so you should be aware that C.H.I.S. stands for:

C	Covert
H	Human
I	Intelligence
S	Source

That is what C.H.I.S. stands for but *what exactly* is a C.H.I.S.? Rather than come up with a lengthy definition try answering the below questions in Exercise 3.2.

E

EXERCISE 3.2

1. Is the activity of the C.H.I.S. carried out in an open fashion for everyone to see?

    _____

2. What does a C.H.I.S. establish or maintain?

    _____

3. With whom?

    _____

4. For what purpose?

_____

Explanation 3.2

1. Of course not, what would be the point? A C.H.I.S. carries out his/her activity in secrecy—their activity is *covert*.

2. A C.H.I.S. establishes or maintains *a relationship*.

3. The relationship is with *another person*.

4. For the covert purpose of obtaining information/providing access to information or covertly disclosing information obtained by the use of such a relationship.

E

EXERCISE 3.3

1. What is a covert purpose?

_____

_____

2. RAFER is walking his dog when he sees BOYD dealing drugs outside a school. He telephones the police to inform them of BOYD's activities.

Is RAFER a C.H.I.S.?

Yes / No

3. PESSLEY is a window cleaner. On his round he is cleaning LAKE's bedroom windows when he sees over 50 boxes containing computer equipment in LAKE's bedroom. PESSLEY thinks they are stolen and contacts the police to inform them.

Is PESSLEY a C.H.I.S.?

Yes / No

4. If you believe that neither RAFER nor PESSLEY are C.H.I.S. what would it take to change that opinion?

_____

_____

_____

Explanation 3.3

1. A purpose is covert if the relationship (and subsequent disclosure) is conducted in a manner calculated to ensure that one of the parties is unaware of that purpose (it is a secret purpose).

2. No. There is *no relationship* between RAFER and BOYD so RAFER cannot be a C.H.I.S.

3. No. Once again, there is *no relationship* between PESSLEY and LAKE.

4. If the police direct the actions of either person then they could become a C.H.I.S. For example, RAFER contacts you about BOYD. You note the information provided and then ask RAFER if he will approach BOYD the next time he sees him to find out what he is selling and for how much. It might not seem a great deal to ask but what you are doing is 'tasking' RAFER. Imagine that RAFER does as you ask and then reports back that BOYD is selling cannabis for £20.00 per bag. Consider the following:

   i.   Has RAFER established a relationship with BOYD? The answer is 'Yes'.
   ii. Was it for the covert (hidden) purpose of obtaining information? The answer is 'Yes'.
   iii. Is one of the parties (BOYD) unaware of RAFER's true purpose i.e. to provide information to the police. The answer is 'Yes'.

RAFER is now a C.H.I.S.

See *Investigators' Manual*, para 1.4.5

Authorization for C.H.I.S. Activity

One area that always causes problems for police officers is trying to remember who authorizes C.H.I.S. activity and for how long.

$\boxed{\text{E}}$

EXERCISE 3.4

1. A C.H.I.S. can be authorized to carry out activity in any part of the United Kingdom or elsewhere.

   True / False

2. What is the relevant rank for C.H.I.S. authorization in normal circumstances?

   _____

3. In normal circumstances how is that authorization given?

   _____

4. In normal circumstances how long will that authorization last?

   _____

5. DC JAMES is contacted by DAVIS who tells him that he can provide information about drug smuggling. DAVIS states a shipment of cocaine is arriving at an airport in 1 hour's time and wants to know if he should try to find out more about the shipment. DC JAMES needs to obtain *urgent* authorization for DAVIS to act as a C.H.I.S.

   (a) Who are the two officers who could provide this authorization?

      i. _____

      ii. _____

(b) How could this authorization be given?

i. _____

ii. _____

(c) How long for?

i. _____

ii. _____

6. The next day DC JAMES is contacted by MARSTON (aged 16 years) who tells the officer that he can provide information about the same gang of drug smugglers.

Can juveniles become C.H.I.S.?

Yes / No

7. If 'Yes' who could authorize this?

_____

8. For how long?

_____

9. What is the difference between DAVIS and MARSTON?

_____

_____

_____

Explanation 3.4

1. True.

2. In normal circumstances an officer of the rank of superintendent or above.

3. In normal circumstances it is given in writing.

4. In normal circumstances authorization lasts for 12 months (beginning on the day it was granted).

5. (a) i. A superintendent or above.
      ii. An inspector may give the relevant authorization.
   (b) i. A superintendent could give the authorization in writing or orally.
      ii. An inspector may give the authorization but ONLY in writing.
   (c) i and ii. The time limit for an urgent authorization is the same for both authorizing ranks—72 hours (three days).

6. Yes.

7. ONLY a superintendent can authorize a juvenile to become a C.H.I.S.

8. The authorization time limit for a juvenile C.H.I.S. is reduced from 12 months to one month.

9. Juvenile C.H.I.S. activity can only be authorized by a superintendent and for one month not 12. An inspector COULD NOT provide urgent C.H.I.S. authorization for a juvenile.

EXERCISE 3.5

An inspector cannot give oral authorization in any circumstances and cannot authorize the activity of a juvenile C.H.I.S.

1. What other restriction is placed on an inspector's authorization?

_____

_____

Explanation 3.5

Inspectors cannot give authorization for any type of C.H.I.S. activity where the C.H.I.S. may obtain confidential material (this is material subject to legal privilege, confidential personal material, or confidential journalistic material).

See *Investigators' Manual*, para 1.4.5.2

Why Can a C.H.I.S. be Used?

The designated person (superintendent or inspector) must believe that C.H.I.S. activity is *necessary* for the following reasons:

C   Crime and Disorder Prevention

H   Health and Tax

I   Interests of National Security

S   Specified by Secretary of State

and that an authorization is *proportionate* to what is sought to be achieved.

See *Investigators' Manual*, para 1.4.5.4

Surveillance

Before you examine intrusive and directed surveillance, you must consider exactly what the term 'surveillance' means.

EXERCISE 3.6

What do you consider the term 'surveillance' to mean?

_____

_____

_____

_____

Explanation 3.6

Like C.H.I.S. activity, any type of surveillance must be _covert_ (carried out in a manner that is calculated to ensure that people subject to it are unaware that it is (or might be) taking place). You may have included other terms when answering the question such as the use of cameras or recording equipment and watching people from observation posts. You would not be wrong as the actual term 'surveillance' encompasses activities such as:

i.   Monitoring, observing, listening to and recording people and their conversations, activities and communications,

ii. Recording anything monitored observed or listened to in the course of surveillance, and

iii. Surveillance by or with the assistance of a surveillance device.

See _Investigators' Manual_, para 1.4.6

Intrusive Surveillance

Before you examine what directed surveillance is, it is best to examine what intrusive surveillance is. This is because the definition of directed surveillance refers to intrusive surveillance. Start by examining Exercise 3.7 and deciding whether or not the activity considered by the officer would be intrusive surveillance. An explanation is given after Exercise and Explanation 3.8.

EXERCISE 3.7

DC FARMER is considering carrying out the following activities to obtain intelligence on the activity of CARMEN, a known handler of stolen goods. Decide whether the potential activities would be considered intrusive surveillance or not.

1. DC FARMER wants to place a recording device in the lounge of CARMEN's house to record conversations he has with his criminal associates who visit him there.

   Is this intrusive surveillance?

   Yes / No

2. DC FARMER also wants to place a recording device in a small storage unit that CARMEN rents to store goods.

   Is this intrusive surveillance?

   Yes / No

3. CARMEN is known to meet his criminal associates in a room at a hotel near to his house. DC FARMER wants to place a listening device in the hotel room that CARMEN uses.

   Is this intrusive surveillance?

   Yes / No

4. DC FARMER wants to place a 'tracker' device underneath CARMEN's car. This will provide the police with the geographical location of CARMEN's vehicle.

   Is this intrusive surveillance?

   Yes / No

5. DC FARMER also wishes to place a recording device inside CARMEN's car to monitor conversations he has.

   Is this intrusive surveillance?

   Yes / No

6. DC FARMER wishes to use a recording device to monitor CARMEN's conversations when he visits his brother's house. Although the device will be held by DC FARMER some 30 feet from the house, the device will provide sound recordings of the same quality as if the device were actually in the house.

   Is this intrusive surveillance?

   Yes / No

E

EXERCISE 3.8

Complete the following definition (some clues have been provided for you):

Surveillance will be 'intrusive' if it is

↓

_____ (hidden)

↓

_____ (type of premises?)

↓

_____ (type of vehicle?)

↓

_____ (involves what?)

↓

_____ (or is carried out using what?)

Explanation 3.8

Your answer should have looked something like the below:

Surveillance will be 'intrusive' if it is

↓

Covert

↓

Carried out in relation to anything taking place on any residential premises or

↓

In any private vehicle and

↓

Involves the presence of an individual on the premises or in the vehicle or

↓

Is carried out by means of a surveillance device

Now considering the definition of 'intrusive surveillance', let's return to Exercise 3.7.

Explanation 3.7

1. Yes—Intrusive surveillance (CARMEN's home is residential premises).

2. No—Not intrusive surveillance (the storage unit is NOT residential premises or a private vehicle).

3. Yes—Intrusive surveillance (this is because hotel bedrooms are considered residential premises at all times).

4. No—Not intrusive surveillance (the surveillance is taking place ON not IN CARMEN's private vehicle. But even if the device were placed INSIDE CARMEN's vehicle, surveillance carried out by means of a device purely to provide information about the location of the vehicle is NOT intrusive).

5. Yes—Intrusive surveillance (the device is inside the vehicle but is different to example 4 as it is recording/monitoring conversations).

6. Yes—Intrusive surveillance (although the device is outside the house it is providing recordings of such quality that it *might as well be in the house*. As such it is intrusive surveillance.)

Remember—Residential premises and private vehicles!

See *Investigators' Manual*, para 1.4.6.4

Authorizing Intrusive Surveillance

Like C.H.I.S. authorizations, this is another problem area and therefore often one questioned by examiners.

| E |

EXERCISE 3.9

1. What is the relevant rank for an intrusive surveillance authorization in normal circumstances?

   _____

2. In normal circumstances how is that authorization given?

   _____

3. In normal circumstances how long will that authorization last?

   _____

4. Who else needs to be told about the application before it is actually approved?

   _____

5. BRAWN has been kidnapped and it is believed his life is in danger. The incident room dealing with the investigation receives information that KING might be responsible. The SIO in charge of the investigation wishes to carry out *urgent* intrusive surveillance in KING's house.

   (a) Who are the two officers who could provide this authorization?

      i. _____

      ii. _____

   (b) How could this authorization be given?

      i. _____

      ii. _____

   (c) How long for?

      i. _____

      ii. _____

Explanation 3.9

1. Chief constable/commissioner or designated deputy.

2. In normal circumstances it is given in writing.

3. In normal circumstances authorization will last for three months.

4. The authorization will not go 'live' until the *Office of Surveillance Commissioners* has been notified of the application (after approval by the chief constable/commissioner the OSC is notified. When it approves the application and that approval is received in the office of the chief constable/commissioner, the intrusive surveillance can begin).

5. (a) i. The chief constable/commissioner or his designated deputy.

   ii. An assistant chief constable/assistant commissioner.

   (b) i. The chief constable/commissioner or his designated deputy can give the authorization in writing or orally.

   ii. An assistant chief constable/assistant commissioner can give the authorization but ONLY in writing.

   (c) i and ii. The time limit for an urgent authorization is the same for both authorizing ranks—72 hours (three days).

Where the authorization from the chief constable, etc. is of an urgent nature, the surveillance may begin when he approves it. The application is still sent to the OSC for its approval afterwards. Should the OSC refuse the application, any surveillance activity must cease (an extremely rare occurrence).

Intrusive surveillance may not take place unless the authorizing office believes that it is necessary and proportionate and:

- In the interests of national security
- For the purpose of detecting or preventing 'serious crime'
- For the purpose of safeguarding the economic well-being of the UK.

See *Investigators' Manual*, para 1.4.6.5

Directed Surveillance

Now that you have dealt with intrusive surveillance you come to the final RIPA 2000 category covered in your Manual—directed surveillance. Before you consider the definition, attempt Exercise 3.10. An explanation is given after Exercise and Explanation 3.11.

EXERCISE 3.10

1. An overt CCTV system in a town centre which displays signs around the town centre telling shoppers they are subject to surveillance would not be caught by the provisions of RIPA 2000.

   True / False

2. The proper use of covert TV detector equipment would not amount to directed surveillance.

   True / False

3. PC KALSI is on uniform foot patrol and sees what he believes to be a drug deal taking place. He takes off his high visibility clothing and watches the suspected drug dealer for several minutes. This is directed surveillance.

   True / False

4. DC PUGH has the permission of GRANTBY to tape her telephone conversations as she is receiving telephone calls that are threatening her life. This is directed surveillance.

True / False

E

EXERCISE 3.11

Complete the following definition (some clues have been provided for you):

Surveillance will be 'directed' if it is

↓

_____ (hidden)

↓

_____ (what for?)

↓

_____
_____ (what might you get?)

↓

_____
_____
_____ (fast response?)

Explanation 3.11

Your answer should have included:

Surveillance will be 'directed' if it is

↓

Covert (but NOT intrusive)

↓

For the purposes of a specific investigation or operation

↓

Likely to result in the obtaining of private information about a person (including information about their family life)

↓

Whether or not that person has been specifically identified for the purposes of the investigation/operation and

↓

Is not carried out in immediate response to events/circumstances where it would be reasonable to seek prior authorization

Some points to note:

- Covert but NOT intrusive—which is why you must know what 'intrusive' surveillance is. Remember that one surveillance activity cannot be both types of surveillance, e.g. placing a device inside a car cannot be directed and intrusive surveillance—it must be one or the other (intrusive).
- Private information is an extremely far-reaching term. The contents of your shopping basket as you leave a supermarket; the fact you are there; what time it is; and who you are with: all constitute private information about you.
- An operation does not have to target a specific individual or individuals. Observations on a supermarket car park for unknown offenders who are robbing shoppers would be a good example.
- Immediate response—How long can an officer observe in immediate response before it is no longer an immediate response and is activity requiring authorization? The courts and OSC have not addressed this thorny problem and so your examiners will have to avoid it other than in the most basic terms.

Explanation 3.10

Based on the information in Explanation 3.11 we can state the following:

1. True. The cameras are OVERT (the signs). CCTV normally falls outside the Act. BUT if the cameras were used for a specific operation, e.g. to target drug dealers outside a pub covered by the system, then it becomes *directed surveillance*. This is because the use of the cameras is no longer 'general' but specific. The drug dealer at the door of the pub has a camera specifically focusing on him—do those signs tell the drug dealer that fact? They do not. The use of the cameras in this fashion is *covert* and the rest of the definition is satisfied.

2. True.

3. False. See the definition and points to not (above).

4. True. This is termed a 'one-sided consensual interception'. Telephone interceptions are beyond the scope of your Manual but would require the authority of the Home Secretary if carried out without the knowledge of the parties concerned. However, if ONE party to the conversation KNOWS of the police activity, i.e. recording the conversation, then this becomes directed surveillance.

One last point on specific situations—a 'tracker' device (as per the example in Exercise 3.7(4)) whilst not intrusive surveillance IS directed surveillance.

See *Investigators' Manual*, para 1.4.6.1

Authorizing Directed Surveillance

There are some similarities with the authorizations for intrusive surveillance but be careful not to confuse the two.

EXERCISE 3.12

1. What is the relevant rank for a directed surveillance authorization in normal circumstances?

2. In normal circumstances how is that authorization given?

   _____

3. In normal circumstances how long will that authorization last?

   _____

4. Information is received that VAN DURLING will be selling drugs in a warehouse in the next few hours. DC GOUGH wants to carry out *urgent* directed surveillance at the warehouse.

   (a) Who are the two officers who could provide this authorization?

      i. _____

      ii. _____

   (b) How could this authorization be given?

      i. _____

      ii. _____

   (c) How long for?

      i. _____

      ii. _____

Explanation 3.12

1. An officer of the rank of superintendent or above.

2. In normal circumstances it is given in writing.

3. In normal circumstances authorization will last for three months.
   (a) i. An officer of the rank of superintendent or above.
       ii. An officer of the rank of inspector or above.
   (b) i. The superintendent can give the authorization in writing or orally.
       ii. The inspector can give the authorization but ONLY in writing.
   (c) i and ii. The time limit for an urgent authorization is the same for both authorizing ranks—72 hours (three days).

With surveillance authorizations **REMEMBER** that **INSPECTORS** can only authorize activity in **URGENT** cases and it **MUST ALWAYS BE IN WRITING**.

- One last point to note on authorization levels. If the material sought by the directed surveillance is confidential material then the authorization level for the activity is raised to chief constable.

See *Investigators' Manual*, para 1.4.6.2

Conclusion

As you have discovered, there is a great deal to RIPA 2000 but its importance to detectives cannot be underestimated. In the practical arena there are other areas of RIPA 2000 that you will come across as well as Part III of the Police Act 1997 which has a strong connection to this legislation. The grounding you have given yourself by reading the Manual and this Workbook will assist you to deal with the more complicated issues that will present themselves to you in the workplace. From the examination angle, you have covered a great deal, if not all, of the material you are likely to be questioned on in this section of the Workbook but you should return to the Manual to ensure you have a good understanding of this subject.

Now that you have finished this section you should attempt the 'Recall Questions' before re-reading the relevant section in the Manual and making your second attempt at the multiple-choice questions. The answers to these questions are printed in the 'Answers Section' at the rear of the Workbook.

Recall Questions

Try and answer the questions below. Do not allow yourself to continue until you have answered the questions to your satisfaction.

- What are the three potential consequences for breaching RIPA 2000?
- Who oversees police activity in respect of RIPA 2000?
- What is a C.H.I.S.?
- In normal circumstances, who would authorize C.H.I.S. activity and for how long?
- What does the mnemonic **CHIS** stand for (why can a C.H.I.S. be used)?
- What is the definition of directed surveillance?
- What is the definition of intrusive surveillance?
- Who can authorize intrusive surveillance in urgent circumstances?

RIPA Flowchart—Authorization Levels

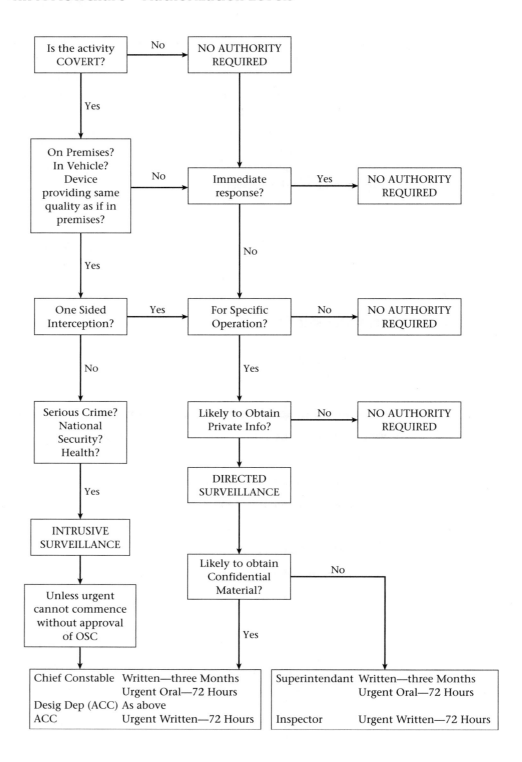

4 Code 'B', Entry, Search, and Seizure

Aim

The aim of this section is to assist you to understand the powers of entry, search, and seizure that derive from the Police and Criminal Evidence Act 1984.

Objectives

At the end of this section you should be able to:

1. Distinguish between the powers under ss 17, 18, 19, and 32 of PACE 1984.
2. Identify what an indictable offence is.
3. State your powers under s 18 of PACE 1984.
4. Explain your powers under s 32 of PACE 1984.
5. Outline your powers under s 17 of PACE 1984.
6. State your powers under s 19 of PACE 1984.
7. Demonstrate your knowledge by completing the exercises in this section.
8. Apply your knowledge to multiple-choice questions.

Introduction

There is no doubt that at some stage of your service you will have taken part in a search of premises utilizing your powers under the Police and Criminal Evidence Act 1984 (although you may not have used all of the powers that will be discussed in this section). A good knowledge and understanding of these powers is essential to any police officer but particularly detectives, as a great deal of crucial evidence could be lost if a search is carried out unlawfully. Knowing what you can and cannot do in respect of PACE searches will prevent this undesirable occurrence.

Multiple-choice Questions

Begin this section of the Workbook by answering the below multiple-choice questions. Mark your answer in the 'First Attempt' box. Then read and complete the exercises in the Code 'B', Entry, Search, and Seizure section. Once you are satisfied that your knowledge is of a good standard, return to these questions and mark your answer in the 'Second Attempt' box. The answers to these questions can be found in the 'Answers Section' at the rear of the Workbook.

MCQ 4.1 WADDILOVE has been arrested for an offence of theft from his employer and is in custody at a designated police station. The property stolen consisted of several dozen Dyson vacuum cleaners which were all recovered from a van WADDILOVE was driving when he was arrested. The officer in the case, PC LYNN, has reasonable grounds for suspecting that WADDILOVE may have electrical goods in his house that have come from other thefts from WADDILOVE's employer and wishes to search WADDILOVE's house for those goods.

Can PC LYNN use his powers under s 18 of the Police and Criminal Evidence Act 1984 to search WADDILOVE's house?

A   No, PC LYNN cannot use his power under s 18 of PACE as the property he is seeking does not relate to the offence for which WADDILOVE was arrested.

B   Yes, PC LYNN can use his power under s 18 of PACE if an officer of the rank of inspector or above authorizes it.

C   No, PC LYNN cannot use his power under s 18 of PACE as the offence of theft is not an indictable offence.

D   Yes, PC LYNN can use his power under s 18 of PACE if he obtains authorization from the custody officer.

First Attempt	
Second Attempt	

MCQ 4.2 DC AHMED wants to arrest LLOYD for an offence of burglary. He visits LLOYD's home address which is a bedsit inside a larger house. As DC AHMED approaches the front door of LLOYD's bedsit, it opens and LLOYD steps outside into the hallway holding some of the property stolen in the burglary in his hands. DC AHMED immediately arrests LLOYD for the burglary. DC AHMED now wishes to search LLOYD for anything that might be evidence of the offence as he has reasonable grounds to believe LLOYD has such evidence on his person. He is also considering searching LLOYD's bedsit and a communal lounge in the house as he has reasonable grounds to suspect that there is evidence relating to the burglary on those premises.

Considering s 32 of the Police and Criminal Evidence Act 1984 only, which of the following comments is correct.

A   DC AHMED can only search LLOYD.

B   DC AHMED can only search LLOYD and the bedsit he has just come out from.

C   DC AHMED can search LLOYD, the bedsit he has just come out from, and the communal lounge.

D   DC AHMED cannot carry out any searches under s 32 of PACE in these circumstances.

First Attempt	
Second Attempt	

MCQ 4.3   TI JACKSON (who is dressed in plain clothes) visits a house owned by LILLY to arrest her for an offence of robbery. TI JACKSON has visited LILLY's house before and knows that she lives alone. The officer rings the doorbell and steps back from the front door. As he does he sees a curtain move in an upstairs bedroom window causing him to believe that LILLY is inside the house. Several minutes later and after ringing the bell three more times and attempting to communicate with anyone inside the house, there is no answer at the door.

> Taking into account TI JACKSON's powers under s 17 of the Police and Criminal Evidence Act 1984 only, which of the below comments is correct?
>
> A   TI JACKSON cannot force entry into the house to arrest LILLY as he is not in uniform.
> B   TI JACKSON can force entry into the house to search for and arrest LILLY.
> C   TI JACKSON cannot force entry into the house unless he has communicated with the occupier who has then refused him entry.
> D   Section 17 allows TI JACKSON to force entry into the house to search for and arrest LILLY and also to search for evidence relating to the robbery.

First Attempt	
Second Attempt	

MCQ 4.4   DC DYER is making house to house enquiries in relation to a murder where the victim was stabbed with a screwdriver. He visits NICKLIN who went to the aid of the victim and was covered in the victim's blood as a result. NICKLIN invites DC DYER into his house and into the lounge where the two talk about the offence. Several minutes later, NICKLIN says to DC DYER, 'That is enough for now, I want you to leave my house. You are no longer welcome'. On his way out of the lounge, DC DYER sees a bloodstained shirt hanging over a radiator in the lounge. DC DYER reasonably believes that the shirt is evidence of the offence of murder that he is investigating.

> With regard to powers under s 19 of the Police and Criminal Evidence Act 1984 only, which of the following statements is correct?
>
> A   DC DYER can seize the bloodstained shirt as he has reasonable grounds to believe that it is evidence in relation to an offence he is investigating.
> B   Section 19 can only be used when the officer reasonably believes the item has been obtained as a consequence of an offence not as evidence of an offence.
> C   Section 19 allows DC DYER to seize the bloodstained shirt and to search NICKLIN's house for evidence relating to the offence he is investigating.
> D   DC DYER cannot use his powers under s 19 of the Act because he has been told to leave and is no longer 'lawfully' on the premises.

First Attempt	
Second Attempt	

MCQ 4.5   TI ROBERT wishes to apply for a warrant under s 8 of the Police and Criminal Evidence Act 1984 to search a house belonging to GRISHAM who is suspected of involvement in a burglary (contrary to s 9(1)(a) of the Theft Act 1968).

Which of the following comments is correct?

A If the application is successful, the warrant can only authorize entry on one occasion.

B A s 8 warrant can authorize an unlimited amount of entries to GRISHAM's house.

C Section 8 warrants will only permit a search of one specific premises, which must be clearly identified in the warrant.

D A s 8 warrant permits the large scale seizure of all material found on premises to be 'sifted' at another location.

First Attempt	
Second Attempt	

Distinguish Between the Powers Under ss 17, 18, 19, and 32 of PACE 1984

Each of these four sections at your disposal under the Police and Criminal Evidence Act 1984 provides you with different powers of entry, search and/or seizure. They also require a certain state of mind to exist on the part of the constable in order for the power to be executed. You must be aware of precisely *what* each section allows along with what you *need to be thinking* to enable the power.

EXERCISE 4.1

What does each power allow you to do? Fill the boxes with a 'Yes' or 'No' where you believe appropriate.

Section	Power to Enter Premises?	Power to Search Premises for Evidence?	Power to Seize Evidence?	Power to Search Person?	Power to Seize Evidence from Person Searched?
17					
18					
19					
32					

Explanation 4.1

Your grid should look something like this:

Section	Power to Enter Premises?	Power to Search Premises for Evidence?	Power to Seize Evidence?	Power to Search Person?	Power to Seize Evidence from Person Searched?
17	YES	NO	NO	NO	NO
18	YES	YES	YES	NO	NO
19	NO	NO	YES	NO	NO
32	YES	YES	NO	YES	YES

In essence:

Section 17 is a power of entry (for arrest—although you can search the premises to find the person you want to arrest).

Section 18 is a power of entry, search and seizure.

Section 19 is a power of seizure.

Section 32 is a power of entry, search and seizure (but you can only seize items found while searching a person!)

E

EXERCISE 4.2

We will deal with the specific state of mind required for each power later but for now just consider whether the power requires a constable to *suspect* or *believe*.

Tick or cross the box you believe is appropriate for the particular power.

Section	Officer must suspect	Officer must believe
17		
18		
19		
32		

Explanation 4.2

Your completed grid should look like the below:

Section	Officer must suspect	Officer must believe
17		X
18	X	
19		X
32		X

REMEMBER that the only power that operates on an officer's *'suspicion'* is s 18.

Indictable Offence

Sections 18 and 32 of the Police and Criminal Evidence Act 1984 require an arrest to trigger the powers—the arrest must be for an indictable offence.

E

EXERCISE 4.3

1. What is an indictable offence?

---

2. Based on your answer to question 1 of this exercise, would the following offences potentially trigger powers of search and seizure under ss 18 and 32 of PACE?

   i.   An offence of theft?

      Yes / No

   ii. An offence of burglary?

      Yes / No

   iii. An offence of robbery?

      Yes / No

Explanation 4.3

1. The Interpretation Act of 1978, Sch 1 defines what an 'indictable offence' is:
   An 'indictable offence' means an offence which, if committed by an adult, is triable on indictment, whether it is exclusively so triable (e.g. murder) or triable either way.
   In other words an 'indictable offence' also includes offences that are 'triable either way' so unless the offence you have just arrested the person for is 'summary only', you can use your powers under ss 18 and 32.

2. As a result of the above information we can say that theft (triable either way), burglary (triable either way) and robbery (triable on indictment only) are all offences that could trigger your powers under ss 18 and 32 of PACE.

Section 18 PACE

E

EXERCISE 4.4

PC SIDAWAY arrests HARTELL at the scene of a rape in a park and escorts him to a designated police station. On arrest HARTELL is wearing a distinctive green jacket. Checks on HARTELL reveal that the rape is highly likely to be the culmination of a series of sexual attacks on women in the park by an offender wearing a similar jacket. However, on the previous occasions the offender has also worn a clown mask and has sexually assaulted his victims after threatening them with a red handled flick-knife. PC SIDAWAY contacts the CID and DC KIRK takes charge of the case. DC KIRK establishes that HARTELL not only lives in a house near to the park but also rents an allotment backing on to the park. The allotment has a shed on it. DC KIRK is thinking about his powers under s 18 of PACE.

1. Before DC KIRK can use his s 18 PACE power, what must he have reasonable grounds to suspect?

---

2. Why could a search take place at HARTELL's home address?

   _____

   _____

3. Why could a search take place at the allotment rented by HARTELL?

   _____

   _____

4. Whose authority is required for this search to take place and how will it be recorded?

   _____

   _____

5. Could PC SIDAWAY have carried out a s 18 search prior to taking HARTELL to the designated police station?

   Yes / No

   If 'Yes' then why and who would you inform? If 'No' then why not?

   _____

   _____

   _____

   _____

Explanation 4.4

1. DC KIRK must have reasonable grounds for suspecting that there is evidence on the premises (other than items subject to legal privilege) that relates either to that offence (the rape) or to some other indictable offence which is connected with or similar to that offence (the sexual assaults are certainly connected to the rape but even if they were not, you could convincingly argue that they are similar to it).

2. A s 18 search can take place at premises *owned* by the arrested person.

3. A s 18 search can take place at premises *controlled* by the arrested person.

4. The authority of an inspector is required. In these circumstances the authority would be recorded in HARTELL's custody record.

5. Yes. PC SIDAWAY could have searched either of the premises (if he knew of them) and without the authority of an inspector. This can only take place if HARTELL's presence would be necessary at a place (other than a police station) for the effective investigation of the offence. For example if PC SIDAWAY knew HARTELL's address and considered that evidence might be lost if a search was not carried out immediately, he could have taken HARTELL to his home and searched it. When the search was complete,

PC SIDAWAY should inform an officer of the rank of inspector or above that he has completed it.

See *Investigators' Manual*, para 1.5.3.1

Section 32 PACE

E

EXERCISE 4.5

TI GREEN is taking a witness statement in CRONIN's house. While CRONIN is making a cup of tea, TI GREEN looks out of the front window of the house and sees HALLARD walk out of the front door of a house exactly opposite CRONIN's. HALLARD walks along the footpath to the front gate and stops at the front gate. Moments later LESTER approaches HALLARD and a drug deal takes place after which LESTER walks away. TI GREEN has witnessed the whole episode and leaves CRONIN's house and approaches HALLARD. As he approaches HALLARD, he witnesses HALLARD drop several wraps of white powder onto the floor. TI GREEN reaches HALLARD, picks up the wraps and arrests HALLARD on suspicion of supplying a controlled drug (triable either way offence).

Think about this situation in respect of s 32 of PACE.

1. There are three reasons why TI GREEN could search HALLARD. What are they?

    The officer has reasonable grounds for believing that:

    i.   _____

    _____

    ii. _____

    _____

    iii. _____

    _____

2. What three items of clothing could TI GREEN require HALLARD to remove in public?

    i.   _____

    ii. _____

    iii. _____

3. TI GREEN could search HALLARD's mouth under s 32 of PACE.

    True / False

Explanation 4.5

1. The three reasons are:

    i.   The arrested person may present a danger to himself or others, or

ii. The arrested person has something concealed on his person which might be used to assist him to escape lawful custody, or

iii. The arrested person has something concealed on his person which might be evidence relating to an offence.

2. The clothing TI GREEN could require HALLARD to remove consists of:

   i. Outer coat

   ii. Jacket

   iii. Gloves.

3. True

- Note that if a search of HALLARD's person is carried out for one of the above three reasons then there is a power of seizure for anything that TI GREEN finds that falls into any of those categories.

EXERCISE 4.6

TI GREEN searches HALLARD but does not find any drugs on his person. He asks HALLARD where he lives and HALLARD replies that lives in a flat several miles away from the scene of the arrest. TI GREEN thinks that there might be drugs in the house that HALLARD walked out of.

Could TI GREEN use s 32 of PACE to search the house that he saw HALLARD come out of moments before the drug deal and subsequent arrest?

Yes / No

Why / Why not?

_____

_____

_____

_____

_____

Explanation 4.6

Yes. TI GREEN can enter and search any premises in which the person was when arrested or immediately before being arrested for an indictable offence (provided he has reasonable grounds to believe that there is evidence on the premises in respect of that offence i.e. the supply of a controlled drug and NOTHING ELSE!)

- Bizarrely, s 32 **DOES NOT** provide a power of seizure of any item that he finds during the course of the search of the house—even if it is evidence of the offence for which he was arrested (see s 19 of PACE for a power).

See *Investigators' Manual*, para 1.5.3.2

Section 17 PACE

In essence, s 17 of the Police and Criminal Evidence Act 1984 is a power of ENTRY, by force if necessary, for the purposes of making an arrest. That entry may well be to arrest for an indictable offence but there is a long list of other offences for which the power exists e.g. to arrest a person for an offence under s 4 of the Road Traffic Act 1988 (unfit to drive through drink/drugs) or to save life and limb.

Please note the following points regarding s 17:

- Apart from when entry is to save life or limb, the officer **MUST** have reasonable grounds for believing that the person he/she is seeking is on the premises.
- When entry is to recapture a person unlawfully at large the officer **MUST** be **PURSUING** that person.
- The power of entry is open to **ANY** officer (no uniform required) *apart from two offences:*
    i. Offences under the Criminal Law Act 1977 (entering and remaining on property) and
    ii. An offence under the Criminal Justice and Public Order Act 1994 (failing to comply with an interim possession order).

    Neither of these offences are on your syllabus so the rule of thumb should be that a **UNIFORM IS NOT REQUIRED!**

See *Investigators' Manaul*, para 1.5.3.5

Section 19 PACE

EXERCISE 4.7

Consider the situation that TI GREEN might find himself in if, once he gets into the house that HALLARD was seen walking out of, he searches and finds a large quantity of cocaine.

Can he seize this cocaine?

Yes / No

Under what power?

_____

Explanation 4.7

Yes, TI GREEN can seize the cocaine BUT NOT under s 32 of PACE! He can seize it under the power provided by s 19 of PACE.

You must now consider your powers under s 19 of PACE.

EXERCISE 4.8

1. When can a constable exercise his/her powers under s 19 of PACE?

   _____

   _____

2. The constable may seize anything which is on the premises if he has reasonable grounds for believing that:

   i. _____

   _____ or

   ii. _____

   _____

3. The items may only be seized if the constable believes it is necessary to prevent the evidence from being:

   i. _____

   ii. _____

   iii. _____

   iv. _____

4. What would happen if the constable wanted to seize information stored on a computer, e.g. child pornography photographs?

   _____

   _____

   _____

   _____

   _____

5. This power can be used if the constable is a trespasser.

   True / False

6. Could a vehicle be seized under s 19 of PACE?

   Yes / No

Explanation 4.8

1. Powers under s 19 of PACE are exercisable when a constable is *lawfully* on the premises.

2. A constable may seize anything he has reasonable grounds for believing:

   i. has been obtained in consequence of the commission of an offence, or
   ii. is evidence in relation to an offence which he is investigating or any other offence.

3. The officer must believe it is necessary to prevent the item being:

   i. Concealed,
   ii. Altered,
   iii. Lost, or
   iv. Destroyed.

4. The officer can require the information to be produced in a form in which it can be taken away (e.g. a CD-ROM) and in which it is visible and legible (e.g. a print-out).

5. False—the constable must be on premises 'lawfully'. The moment he/she becomes a trespasser the power is removed.

6. A vehicle can be seized as can a tent or indeed anything which is classed as 'premises'.

See *Investigators' Manual*, para 1.5.4.1

Conclusion

> You should now possess a good understanding of what you can and cannot do in respect of your powers to enter premises, search them and individuals, and seize evidence under the Police and Criminal Evidence Act 1984. There are other areas in respect of searches that have not been covered in this section of the Workbook and you are strongly advised to read them in the Manual and also in Code B in the Appendices of your Manual.

Now that you have finished this section you should attempt the 'Recall Questions' before re-reading the relevant section in the Manual and making your second attempt at the multiple-choice questions. The answers to these questions are printed in the 'Answers Section' at the rear of the Workbook.

Recall Questions

Try and answer the questions below. Do not allow yourself to continue until you have answered the questions to your satisfaction.

- Which is the only power of search requiring an officer to 'suspect'?

- Who authorizes a s 18 PACE search?

- Could you search a garage under s 18 of PACE if you suspected that a person controlled it?

- What does a s 32 PACE search allow you to do?

- What can you seize in a s 32 PACE search?

- If you are searching a bedsit using s 32 of PACE, what other rooms/areas might you be able to search?

- Do you have to be in uniform to enter premises under s 17 of PACE?

- Why might you seize an item under your s 19 PACE power?

- What is an indictable offence?

- What is the difference between s 17 of PACE and ss 18, 32, and 19 of PACE?

5 | Codes 'C', 'D', and 'E' Case Study

Aim

The aim of this section is for you to be able to demonstrate your knowledge relating to the PACE Codes of Practice governing

i.   the detention, treatment, and questioning of persons by police officers (Code 'C');
ii. identification of persons by police officers (Code 'D'); and
iii. tape recording interviews with suspects (Code 'E').

Objectives

At the end of this section you should be able to:

1. Relate your practical knowledge of Codes 'C', 'D', and 'E' to a theoretical case study exercise.
2. Apply your knowledge to written exercises and multiple-choice questions.
3. Modify (if necessary) your practical knowledge to incorporate the specific provisions of Codes 'C', 'D', and 'E' of the Codes of Practice.

Introduction

This section of the Workbook utilizes a different methodology to the standard approach you will have become accustomed to in previous chapters. You will still have to answer multiple-choice questions and complete written exercises, but this section differs in that it combines these tasks within a case study that seeks to test your knowledge concerning many of the issues in relation to Code 'C', Code 'D', and Code 'E' of the PACE Codes of Practice. Utilizing the practical knowledge you will have gained from dealing with witnesses to offences and suspects for offences will support this process. You will be asked to think about your own experiences as the scenario unfolds and these requests are signified by a question mark.

[?] Questions relating to your experience will be asked in this space.

This section of the Workbook will take some time to complete and finishing it in one session may not be possible. Take your time and take breaks from your study where appropriate.

Although this section will not cover every single aspect of these particular Codes, it will still deal with many of the fundamental issues. The ability to comprehend and apply these

Codes is not only essential knowledge for the purposes of the examination, but also a minimum requirement for police officers dealing with a suspect interviewed in connection with an offence at a police station.

Case Study

At 10.15 hrs today, two males walk through the front door of 'Palmer's Newsagent's', 121 Green Lane. The owner of the shop, 68-year-old George PALMER, is standing behind the shop counter near to a cash till. There are no customers or other staff in the shop. One of the males remains by the front door of the shop as the other produces a knife and runs straight towards PALMER. Before PALMER can react, the male with the knife vaults over the shop counter and grabs him by the arm. He holds the knife in front of PALMER's face and shouts, 'Open the till or I'll slit your fuckin' throat!' The male lets go of PALMER's arm and a terrified PALMER tries to open the till. In fact PALMER is so frightened that his hands shake uncontrollably and he cannot do as the male with the knife has demanded. The male standing by the front door runs over to the shop counter but does not climb over it, remaining on the shop side of the counter. He shouts at PALMER saying, 'For fuck's sake open the fuckin' till or we'll stab you!' The two males make several other abusive and violent threats towards PALMER who finally manages to get the till open. The male holding the knife grabs a handful of bank notes, but as he does so Alan HEPWORTH walks through the front door of the newsagent's. HEPWORTH is a friend of PALMER's and immediately realizes that PALMER is being robbed. HEPWORTH runs towards the shop counter and the two male robbers panic and try to get away. The male standing on the shop side of the counter runs towards the rear of the newsagent's. At the same time the male holding the knife vaults back over the counter towards the oncoming HEPWORTH. As this male lands on the shop floor he slips and drops the knife and bank notes. HEPWORTH dives onto him and pins him down, shouting out to PALMER to phone the police. Although the male struggles he cannot break free from HEPWORTH's hold. His accomplice sees what has happened and, empty-handed, escapes out of the back door of the shop. HEPWORTH continues to hold on to the male until PCs OWEN and IRFAN arrive 10 minutes later. The circumstances are quickly related to the officers and PC OWEN arrests the male for an offence of robbery and cautions him. The male replies, 'OK I robbed the shop but it wasn't my fuckin' idea!' The arrested male identifies himself as Mark BOYD and tells the officers that he is 16 years old. PC IRFAN seizes the knife and cash as evidence of the offence.

?

Think of yourself as the arresting officer. Take a moment to consider what you would do with regard to the comment made by BOYD and why you would do it. If you were handing the suspect over to an interview team, would you tell them about this comment? Why?

E

EXERCISE 5.1

Would BOYD's reply to PC OWEN be classed as a 'significant statement'?

Yes / No

Why / Why not?

_____

_____

_____

What is a 'significant statement'?

_____

_____

_____

In whose presence must a 'significant statement' be made?

_____

_____

Explanation 5.1

BOYD's reply would be viewed as a 'significant statement'. This is because his reply is a direct admission of guilt. A 'significant statement' is one which appears capable of being used in evidence against the suspect (in particular a direct admission of guilt)—*Code 'C' 11.4A*. A 'significant statement' can only occur in the presence and hearing of a police officer or other police staff—*Code 'C' 11.4*.

A description of the second offender is obtained from PALMER and HEPWORTH by PC IRFAN, who circulates the description to his colleagues on patrol in the general area.

?

Do you remember an incident where you obtained a first description from a witness? What did you do? Why did you do it? Where was the first description recorded?

E

EXERCISE 5.2

Consider the obligations placed on the police under Code 'D' regarding first descriptions and decide whether the below statements are true or false.

1. Code 'D' requires that a first description provided of a person suspected of a crime (regardless of the time it was given) must be recorded.

   True / False

2. The first description must be disclosed to the defence in the pre-trial procedure in all cases.

   True / False

3. The record must be made and kept in a form which enables details of that description to be accurately produced from it, in a visible and legible form.

   True / False

4. The record of first description can be made electronically or on paper.

   True / False

Explanation 5.2

All of the above comments are true (see *Code 'D' 3.1*).

See *Investigators' Manual*, para 1.9.2.1

PC IRFAN records the first descriptions given to him by PALMER and HEPWORTH in his pocketbook. Other officers arrive at the scene and it is decided that PALMER and HEPWORTH will be driven round the immediate area of the offence to try and find the second offender.

?

Have you ever taken a witness round an area to locate an offender? You did not want your identification evidence to be compromised, so what steps did you take to ensure that this would not happen? If you have never carried out this activity, what would you do if the situation occurred at the next incident you attend?

E

EXERCISE 5.3

Carrying out a 'scene identification', i.e. taking a witness round a particular area to try and find a suspect, is an accepted practice. However, if possible this practice must follow the guidelines under *Code 'D' 3.2*. What should be considered before and during a 'scene identification'?

1. _____

_____

_____

2. _____

_____

_____

```
3. _____
   _____
   _____
4. _____
   _____
   _____
5. _____
   _____
   _____
```

Explanation 5.3

Matters to be considered include:

1. Where practicable, a record should be made of any description of the suspect given by the witness.

2. Care should be taken not to direct the witness's attention to any individual unless, having regard to all the circumstances, this cannot be avoided.

3. If there is more than one witness, they should be kept separate.

4. Once there is sufficient information to justify the arrest of a suspect, a formal identification procedure must be adopted.

5. The officer accompanying the witness must make a record in his/her pocketbook of the action taken as soon as practicable and in as much detail as possible.

Code 'D' 3.2

See *Investigators' Manual*, para 1.9.2.10

PALMER and HEPWORTH are driven round the area of the newsagent's, but the second offender cannot be found. In the meantime, BOYD is transported to a designated police station and is escorted into the custody area. PS FAGAN (the custody officer) obtains BOYD's full details (name, address, age, etc.) and, because BOYD is a juvenile, PS FAGAN asks him whom he wishes to act as his 'appropriate adult'.

? You will have arrested juveniles in the past. Think about those circumstances. In the majority of cases who normally turned up to act as an appropriate adult? What happened when that person could not or would not attend?

E

EXERCISE 5.4

There are three classes of person who can act as an appropriate adult where the person in custody is a juvenile. Who are they?

1. _____

_____

_____

2. _____

_____

_____

3. _____

_____

_____

Explanation 5.4

Code 'C' 1.7 states that in the case of a juvenile the appropriate adult is

1. the parent, guardian or, if the juvenile is in local authority or voluntary organization care, or is otherwise being looked after under the Children Act 1989, a person representing that authority or organization;

2. a social worker of a local authority; or,

3. failing these, some other responsible adult aged 18 or over who is not a police officer or employed by the police.

See *Investigators' Manual*, para 1.6.6.3

> BOYD states that his mother and father are divorced. He lives with his mother and wants her to act as his appropriate adult as he rarely sees his father. He tells PS FAGAN that his mother lives just around the corner from the police station and could get there within minutes. BOYD further states that he hates his father and would object to him acting as his appropriate adult.

MCQ 5.1 If PS FAGAN could not contact BOYD's mother, which of the below statements would be correct with regard to the use of BOYD's father as an appropriate adult?

A PS FAGAN may ask BOYD's father to act as an appropriate adult, but only if a social worker is unavailable.

B The only reason that would prevent BOYD's father from acting as an appropriate adult would be if he were involved in the investigation.

C As BOYD and his father are estranged and BOYD objects to his father acting as an appropriate adult, his father should not be asked to act in that capacity.

D   BOYD's father could be used as an appropriate adult as long as he is not suspected of involvement in the case, the victim of the offence, or a witness to the offence.

Your answer [   ]

PS FAGAN tells BOYD that he will ask BOYD's mother to act as an appropriate adult and contacts her. BOYD's mother states that she will be at the police station in a matter of minutes. PS FAGAN turns to PC OWEN and asks him to provide the circumstances of the arrest. As soon as PC OWEN finishes relating the circumstances of the arrest to PS FAGAN, BOYD says, 'It wasn't my idea, you know that someone else was involved don't you?'

MCQ 5.2   Which of the below statements is correct with regard to the action PS FAGAN should take in response to this comment by BOYD?

A   PS FAGAN should note (on the custody record) any comment BOYD makes in relation to PC OWEN's account, but should not invite comment.

B   PS FAGAN may question BOYD in respect of the comment he made in response to PC OWEN's account.

C   PS FAGAN need not make any note of the comment made by BOYD.

D   PS FAGAN should caution BOYD before asking any questions about the comment made in response to the circumstances of the arrest.

Your answer [   ]

PS FAGAN authorizes BOYD's detention and informs BOYD of his rights whilst he is in custody.

?   Think about the times that you have brought a suspect in front of the custody officer. What rights did the custody officer tell the suspect that they were entitled to?

E
EXERCISE 5.5

What three rights *must* BOYD be told about?

1. _____

   _____

   _____

2. _____

   _____

3. _____

   _____

Explanation 5.5

Under *Code 'C' 3.1*, the rights are

1. the right to have someone informed of their arrest;

2. the right to consult privately with a solicitor and to have access to free independent legal advice; and

3. the right to consult the Codes of Practice.

PS FAGAN asks BOYD if he wants someone to be informed of his arrest. BOYD replies that he does and asks that his brother, Liam BOYD, be contacted. PS FAGAN then asks BOYD if he wants a solicitor. BOYD replies that he does and asks that his family solicitor, Mr HART of Brindlewoods Solicitors, be informed. PC OWEN hears both of these requests and is concerned that Liam BOYD could be the second offender who managed to escape from the scene of the offence. Out of hearing of BOYD, PC OWEN approaches PS FAGAN and voices his concerns. PC OWEN suggests that BOYD's right to have his brother informed should be delayed.

?

Put yourself in PC OWEN's shoes. Would you be concerned? Why? What would you do about it? Have you ever faced a similar situation? What did you do?

E

EXERCISE 5.6

What do you know about the right not to be held 'incommunicado' (having the right to someone being informed of arrest being withheld)? Try answering the below questions.

1. If the police wish to keep a person in custody 'incommunicado', then the offence that they have been arrested for must be an indictable offence.

    True / False

2. What rank must a police officer be to authorize a person in custody being denied the right to have someone informed of his/her arrest?

    _____

3. What is the maximum time limit that this right can be delayed for?

    _____

4. The officer who authorizes a person in custody to be held 'incommunicado' must have reasonable grounds for believing that the exercise of the right will lead to certain consequences. What are these consequences?

    i. _____

    _____

ii. _____

_____

iii. _____

_____

iv. _____

_____

5. In addition to the above, there are two additional reasons that can be used in order to keep a person in custody 'incommunicado'. What are they?

   i. _____

   _____

   _____

   _____

   _____

   ii. _____

   _____

   _____

   _____

   _____

6. Now that you have answered the above five questions, do you think that BOYD can be kept 'incommunicado' with regard to his request to have his brother informed of his arrest?

   Yes / No

   Why / Why not?

   _____

   _____

   _____

   _____

   _____

Explanation 5.6

The right of a person in custody to have someone informed of their arrest is governed by s 56 of the Police and Criminal Evidence Act 1984 and *Code 'C' 5.1 to 5.8* (also *Annex 'B' of Code 'C'*).

1. The offence for which the person is in custody must be an indictable offence.

2. If the police wish to withhold the right of a person in custody to have someone informed of their arrest, then this activity must be authorized by an officer of the rank of inspector or above.

3. The maximum time period that the right can be delayed for is 36 hours (48 hours in cases involving terrorism).

4. The consequences are that the exercise of the right will

   i. lead to interference with, or harm to, evidence connected with an indictable offence;
   ii. lead to interference with, or physical harm to, other people;
   iii. lead to alerting other people suspected of having committed an indictable offence but not yet arrested for it; or
   iv. hinder the recovery of property obtained in the consequence of the commission of such an offence.

5. The additional grounds are that

   i. the person detained for an indictable offence has benefited from their criminal conduct (decided in accordance with Part 2 of the Proceeds of Crime Act 2002); and
   ii. the recovery of the value of the property constituting that benefit will be hindered by the exercise of either right.

6. BOYD could be kept 'incommunicado' in these circumstances (in relation to the contact with his brother).

BUT remember that a juvenile effectively has *four* rights when he/she comes in to police custody. The three rights as explained above *and* the right to have an appropriate adult informed that they have been arrested. The right regarding an appropriate adult being informed of the juvenile's arrest *cannot be denied* regardless of the nature of the offence the juvenile has been arrested for. If BOYD had been arrested for an indictable offence then his right to have someone informed (other than an appropriate adult) could be denied if the circumstances warranted and allowed it.

See *Investigators' Manual*, para 1.6.6.2

> PS FAGAN informs PC OWEN that in these circumstances BOYD can be prevented from having his brother informed of his arrest. While this conversation takes place, BOYD shouts out to the officers, 'And I want a phone call to my mate Allan YALE, I know my rights and you can't stop me from having a phone call.'

MCQ 5.3   Is BOYD right?

A Yes, a juvenile cannot be denied this facility in any circumstances.

B No, although a detained person would have had to be arrested in connection with terrorist offences for this right to be denied.

C Yes, and in addition, the police cannot listen to the telephone call.

D No, an officer of the rank of inspector or above could authorize the facility of a telephone call to be denied or delayed.

Your answer	

PS FAGAN and PC OWEN discuss whether or not BOYD should be allowed to make a telephone call. PC OWEN is concerned that YALE could be the second offender and as a result Inspector JAY is informed of the facts. The decision is made that BOYD will not be allowed to make a telephone call to YALE. As the inspector's decision is being recorded, BOYD's mother arrives at the police station and she is shown into the custody area. Mrs BOYD is informed of the circumstances of the arrest and, in the presence of his mother, BOYD is given his rights again. Mrs BOYD agrees that her son should have Mr HART act as her son's solicitor. At this point, Mrs BOYD says, 'I know a bit about the law myself so I'd like to have a look at my son's custody record please.'

MCQ 5.4   Which of the below statements is correct with regard to Mrs BOYD's entitlement to examine her son's custody record?

A Other than police officers, the only other person permitted to examine BOYD's custody record would be his solicitor.

B Mrs BOYD must be permitted to consult her son's custody record as soon as practicable and at any other time whilst her son is detained.

C Mrs BOYD can examine her son's custody record when she first arrives at the police station, but will not be permitted to do so at any other time.

D If an officer of the rank of inspector or above authorizes it, Mrs BOYD can consult her son's custody record.

Your answer	

After dealing with this issue as per the Codes of Practice, PS FAGAN authorizes PC OWEN to commence a search of BOYD's person. The search is completed and BOYD's property is recorded and retained. BOYD is placed in a Juvenile Detention Room to await interview. PCs OWEN and IRFAN place the knife and cash into the Detained Property Register and liaise with the CID. The enquiry is handed over to TI RIDDALL (a Trainee Investigator with two months' CID experience) and his Tutor, DC STYLES. PCs OWEN and IRFAN then complete their witness statements regarding the incident. A Scenes of Crime officer attends the newsagent's and examines the scene of the offence, but does not recover any forensic evidence.

After arranging for a Scenes of Crime officer to examine the knife and cash recovered by PC IRFAN, DC STYLES visits the newsagent's and obtains a statement of complaint from PALMER, TI RIDDALL visits HEPWORTH at his home address and obtains a witness statement from him. The newsagent's is fitted with a CCTV system and DC STYLES is able to obtain footage of the robbery by seizing a video cassette containing recordings of the incident. DC STYLES returns to his station and makes a copy of the original video footage. DC STYLES watches the video to obtain evidence of the offence and, although the quality of the images is excellent, he does not recognize the second offender. DC STYLES believes that there are several officers working at his station who may recognize

> the outstanding suspect. He is considering arranging for the footage of the video to be shown to these officers in order to try and establish the identity of the offender.

?

Have you ever been asked to view a video of an offence to see if you recognize the offender(s)? Where did this take place? Who was with you? What method was used?

E

EXERCISE 5.7

What does Code 'D' say about the showing of video footage to police officers?

1. _____

_____

2. _____

_____

Explanation 5.7

Code 'D' 3.28 states that if such material is shown then

1. it shall be shown on an individual basis to avoid the possibility of collusion; and

2. as far as possible, the showing shall follow the principles for identification by photographs if the suspect is not known.

See *Investigators' Manual*, para 1.9.2.2

> DC STYLES makes the appropriate arrangements for the video to be shown to a number of officers. He then joins TI RIDDALL and the two officers plan for disclosure to BOYD's solicitor and for the subsequent interview with BOYD.

At this stage of the enquiry, the evidence that the officers possess consists of

i.   the witness statement of PALMER (the complainant),
ii.   the witness statement of HEPWORTH,
iii. the knife and cash recovered by PC IRFAN,
iv.   the arrest statement of PC OWEN,
v.   the witness statement of PC IRFAN,
vi.   a copy of PC OWEN's pocket book, including the significant statement made by BOYD,
vii. a copy of PC IRFAN's pocket book,
viii. BOYD's custody record, and
ix.   the CCTV footage of the incident.

?

Think about the occasions when you have provided disclosure to a solicitor. What are they always provided with? Did you hold evidence back? If so, what did you hold back and why? How could you justify holding evidence back from a solicitor?

E

EXERCISE 5.8

Consider the above evidence in turn and decide what the officers *must* disclose to Mr HART (BOYD's solicitor) prior to an interview taking place. Give a short reason for your answer.

1. The witness statement of PALMER.

    Must this be disclosed?

    Yes / No

    Why / Why not?

    _____

    _____

2. The witness statement of HEPWORTH.

    Must this be disclosed?

    Yes / No

    Why / Why not?

    _____

    _____

3. The knife and cash recovered by PC IRFAN.

    Must this be disclosed?

    Yes / No

    Why / Why not?

    _____

    _____

4. The arrest statement of PC OWEN.

    Must this be disclosed?

    Yes / No

    Why / Why not?

    _____

    _____

5. The witness statement of PC IRFAN.

    Must this be disclosed?

    Yes / No

Why / Why not?

_____

_____

6. The copy of PC OWEN's pocket book.

   Must this be disclosed?

   Yes / No

   Why / Why not?

   _____

   _____

7. The copy of PC IRFAN's pocket book.

   Must this be disclosed?

   Yes / No

   Why / Why not?

   _____

   _____

8. BOYD's custody record.

   Must this be disclosed?

   Yes / No

   Why / Why not?

   _____

   _____

9. The CCTV footage of the incident.

   Must this be disclosed?

   Yes / No

   Why / Why not?

   _____

   _____

Explanation 5.8

You may remember that in an earlier exercise in this section of the Workbook (MCQ 5.4) you were asked who could consult the custody record. The answer to that question was that the solicitor or appropriate adult could consult the custody record as soon as practicable.

Therefore, item 8 on the list (BOYD's custody record) *must* be disclosed to his solicitor. Other than the custody record, the officers are not obliged to disclose *any other material* to Mr HART. There is no specific provision within the Police and Criminal Evidence Act 1984 or the Codes of Practice for the disclosure of any information by the police to a solicitor at a police station. The interviewing officers need to consider whether the disclosure they are providing to Mr HART is adequate for him to advise his client. In *R v Argent* [1997] Crim LR 346, the court dismissed the argument that an inference could not be drawn under s 34 of the Criminal Justice and Public Order Act 1994 because there had not been full disclosure at the interview. However, the court did recognize that it may be a factor to take into account, but it would be for the jury to decide whether the failure to answer questions was reasonable. In every case, the custody record is the starting point for disclosure. From that point onwards what is disclosed to the solicitor prior to interview is the choice of the interviewing officer(s).

See *Investigators' Manual*, para 1.7.9.7

The officers decide that they will disclose all of the evidence they have at their disposal to Mr HART and continue planning for the interview. Thirty minutes later, PS FAGAN informs them that Mr HART has arrived at the police station. The officers return to the custody area and speak with Mr HART who has examined BOYD's custody record. Mr HART is taken to a consultation room within the custody area (used for disclosure and consultations). On the way to the room, Mr HART says to TI RIDDALL, 'This is the first time I've been to this station and I have to tell you that I'm not happy about all these cameras watching my every movement in the custody area. Can you arrange for them to be turned off?' There are a number of cameras installed in the custody area and there are several notices prominently displayed within the custody area stating that the cameras are in use and recording images.

MCQ 5.5   What response should Mr HART receive?

A   Any request to have the video cameras switched off shall be refused.

B   The cameras can be switched off if Mr HART makes the request in writing.

C   Custody area cameras can be switched off with the authorization of an officer of the rank of superintendent or above.

D   Cameras within the custody area can be switched off with the authorization of the custody officer.

Your answer	

After receiving disclosure from the officers, Mr HART has a consultation with BOYD in the presence of his mother. The consultation lasts for 20 minutes, after which Mr HART informs the custody officer that BOYD is ready to be interviewed.

E

EXERCISE 5.9

What does Code 'C' of the Codes of Practice state an interview is?

_____

_____

_____

Explanation 5.9

Code 'C' 11.1A defines an interview as 'the questioning of a person regarding their involvement or suspected involvement in a criminal offence or offences which must be carried out under caution'.

TI RIDDALL is informed that BOYD is ready to be interviewed. He returns to the custody area and speaks with PS FAGAN, who tells him that two interview rooms are available. TI RIDDALL enters Interview Room 1 and ensures that there are adequate facilities for the interview to take place, before obtaining several blank tapes and relevant documentation.

TI RIDDALL, DC STYLES, BOYD, his mother, and Mr HART go into an interview room in the custody area for the interview regarding BOYD's involvement in the offence.

The interview is to be recorded via audiotape. In the interview room, TI RIDDALL checks the recording equipment, breaks open the audiotape seals, loads the tape machine, and starts recording the interview.

?

You will have taken part in numerous interviews. At the beginning of the interview you will have completed the 'Engage and Explain' section of the P.E.A.C.E. model. What did you say to the suspect, the solicitor, the interpreter, the appropriate adult, etc. at this stage? You may have used a crib sheet to assist you. What is on that crib sheet?

E

EXERCISE 5.10

At this point, TI RIDDALL must comply with the requirements laid down under *Code 'E' 4.4 to 4.6*. What are those requirements?

1. _____

_____

2. _____

_____

3. _____

_____

4. _____

_____

5. _____

_____

6. _____

_____

7. _____

_____

8. _____

_____

Explanation 5.10

At the commencement of the interview, TI RIDDALL should do the following:

1. Tell BOYD about the tape recording and say that the interview is being tape-recorded.

2. TI RIDDALL should give his name and rank, as should DC STYLES.

3. TI RIDDALL should then ask BOYD and any other party present (BOYD's mother and Mr HART) to identify themselves.

4. State the date and time of interview commencement and the place of the interview.

5. State that BOYD will be given a notice about what will happen to the tapes.

6. Caution BOYD.

7. Remind BOYD of his entitlement to free legal advice.

8. Put any significant statement or silence to BOYD.

E

EXERCISE 5.11

As BOYD is a juvenile, his mother is present in the interview. *Code 'C' 11.17* states that if an appropriate adult is present in an interview they shall be informed of what?

_____

_____

Explanation 5.11

Your answer should have said something like, 'They are informed that they are not expected simply to act as an observer and that the purpose of their presence in the interview is to advise the person being interviewed, to observe whether the interview is being conducted properly and fairly, and to facilitate communication with the person being interviewed.'

See *Investigators' Manual*, para 1.7.9.5

TI RIDDALL has followed Code 'C' and 'E' and reaches the point where he cautions BOYD. After the caution, TI RIDDALL says to BOYD, 'Do you understand the caution?' BOYD replies that he does not. At this point, Mr HART says, 'I have explained the meaning of the caution to my client and he understands it fully.'

MCQ 5.6   What action should TI RIDDALL take?

A The fact that BOYD has been told the meaning of the caution by his solicitor means that TI RIDDALL need not go on to explain it.

B If it appears to TI RIDDALL that BOYD does not understand the caution, he should go on to explain it in his own words.

C As long as the caution has been given, then TI RIDDALL may continue the interview without any further explanation of the caution.

D Providing a record is made of the fact that the solicitor has explained the meaning of the caution to BOYD, TI RIDDALL need not go on to explain it.

Your answer	

TI RIDDALL reaches the point where he wishes to put the significant statement (made by BOYD when he was arrested) to BOYD. TI RIDDALL mentions the significant statement to BOYD and presents him with a copy of PC OWEN's pocket book. BOYD examines the pocket book entry and states that he does not agree with the record because 'I didn't say that.' TI RIDDALL records the disagreement and asks BOYD to read the details and sign them to the effect that they accurately reflect his disagreement. BOYD says, 'I'm not signing anything written by you!'

MCQ 5.7   What should happen now?

A Either one of the officers present in the interview should record BOYD's refusal to sign the record of the disagreement.

B The senior police officer in the interview (DC STYLES) must record BOYD's refusal to sign the record.

C The custody officer must be called into the interview to record BOYD's refusal to sign the record.

D An officer of the rank of inspector or above must be called into the interview to record BOYD's refusal to sign the record.

Your answer	

Once the refusal to sign has been noted, the account phase (following the P.E.A.C.E. model of interviewing) is commenced.

TI RIDDALL and DC STYLES question BOYD about his involvement in the robbery. During the course of the interview, TI RIDDALL and DC STYLES put a number of questions to BOYD that are answered on BOYD's behalf by Mr HART. TI RIDDALL asks Mr HART to allow BOYD to answer the questions himself and to stop answering questions for his client. TI RIDDALL asks BOYD who the other person involved in the robbery is, at which point Mr HART states, 'Mark does not know who this other person is.'

? Has a solicitor ever interrupted your questioning during an interview? What reason was given for the interruption? What did you do?

E

EXERCISE 5.12

Code 'C' Note 6D acknowledges that a solicitor may intervene during the course of an interview. There are several reasons why such an intervention may take place. Write down as many of these reasons as you can.

_____

_____

_____

_____

_____

_____

Code 'C' 6.9 states that a solicitor may only be required to leave an interview if their conduct is such that the interviewer is unable properly to put questions to the suspect. With regard to this part of the Code, state whether the below comments are true or false.

1. Answering questions on behalf of the suspect would be an example of unacceptable behaviour.

   True / False

2. Providing written replies for the suspect to quote would be an example of unacceptable behaviour.

   True / False

3. Telling a suspect not to reply to a particular question would be an example of unacceptable behaviour.

   True / False

4. Could TI RIDDALL stop the interview in these circumstances?

   Yes / No

Explanation 5.12

You may have said that the solicitor may intervene in order to clarify a question, to challenge an improper question or the manner in which the question is put to their client, to advise their client not to reply to a particular question, or if they wish to give their client further legal advice. Examples of unacceptable behaviour include answering questions on a suspect's behalf or providing written replies for the suspect to quote. Examples 1 and 2 are unacceptable behaviour; example 3 is acceptable behaviour. In these circumstances, TI RIDDALL could stop the interview.

Owing to Mr HART's unacceptable behaviour, TI RIDDALL stops the interview.

MCQ 5.8   Which of the below statements is correct with regard to the action that TI RIDDALL should take?

A TI RIDDALL should consult the custody officer.

B TI RIDDALL should consult an officer not below inspector rank who is not connected to the investigation, if one is readily available, or otherwise the custody officer.

C TI RIDDALL should consult an officer not below superintendent rank, if one is readily available, or otherwise an officer not below inspector rank not connected with the investigation.

D TI RIDDALL should consult an officer not below superintendent rank, if one is readily available, or otherwise an officer not below chief inspector rank not connected with the investigation.

Your answer	

TI RIDDALL consults the appropriate person, who speaks to Mr HART regarding his conduct in the interview. After this conversation, it is decided that the interview should continue. The break in the interview lasted for 20 minutes, during which time BOYD was returned to the Juvenile Detention Room. All parties return to the interview room and the interview of BOYD is recommenced.

?

When you have recommenced an interview the first words out of your mouth will not have been a question about the offence. So what were those first words? What did they relate to?

E

EXERCISE 5.13

TI RIDDALL switches on the audiotape and gives the time and date of the recommencement of the interview. What else should he do?

1. _____

_____

_____

_____

2. _____

_____

_____

_____

3. _____

_____

_____

_____

Explanation 5.13

1. *Code 'C' 10.8* states that, after a break in questioning under caution, the person being questioned must be aware they remain under caution. If there is any doubt, the relevant caution should be given in full when the interview resumes.

2. *Code 'C' Note 10E and Code 'E' Note 4G* state that it may be necessary to show the court that nothing occurred during an interview break or between interviews which influenced the suspect's recorded evidence. After a break in an interview or at the beginning of a subsequent interview, the interviewing officer should summarize the reason for the break and confirm this with the suspect.

3. *Code 'C' 11.2* states that, immediately prior to the recommencement of any interview at a police station or other authorized place of detention, the interviewer should remind

the suspect of their entitlement to free legal advice and that the interview can be delayed for legal advice to be obtained.

> The interview continues and BOYD answers all of the questions put to him with the response of 'no comment.' The officers have yet to put any challenges to BOYD and have not mentioned the witness statements from PALMER or HEPWORTH or the CCTV evidence, and have only asked questions designed to obtain an account from him. They decide to conclude this part of the interview. Code 'C' is complied with when concluding the interview and BOYD has a short consultation with his mother and Mr HART before being returned to the Juvenile Detention Room. After the consultation, Mr HART approaches TI RIDDALL and says, 'I presume that's it as far as interviews are concerned, as he's not going to answer any of your questions and from your disclosure it's obvious that you have sufficient evidence to prosecute him.'

?

If you were part of the interview team would you conclude the interview at this point? Have you ever dealt with a 'no comment' interview? What did you do when faced with this response from the suspect? Did it affect the number of questions you asked the suspect? Did you stop the interview after the first few questions?

E

EXERCISE 5.14

Why is Mr HART wrong?

_____

_____

_____

_____

_____

_____

_____

_____

_____

_____

_____

Explanation 5.14

Code 'C' 11.6 provides guidance as to when an interview should be concluded. Your answer should have included the facts that the interview shall cease if the investigating officer considers that all the questions relevant to obtaining accurate and reliable information about the offence have been put to BOYD. This includes allowing BOYD an opportunity to give an innocent explanation and asking questions to test if the explanation is accurate and reliable. This has yet to be done. In addition, having 'sufficient evidence to prosecute' is not a reason to conclude the interview. The standard is that there is 'sufficient evidence to provide a realistic prospect of conviction for that offence if the person was prosecuted for it'.

See *Investigators' Manual*, para 1.7.9.14

TI RIDDALL informs Mr HART that the interview is not over because of the above reasons. Mr HART is escorted to a waiting room and TI RIDDALL and DC STYLES return to their CID office to discuss their progress so far. DS SHERWIN approaches them as they enter their office. DS SHERWIN states that he has shown the copy of the CCTV video from 'Palmer's Newsagent's' to PC VALE (the beat officer for the area that the newsagent's is situated in) and PC VALE immediately identified the second offender as Adrian JAY. JAY is 18 years old and lives next door to BOYD. DS SHERWIN and PC VALE have completed statements detailing the identification.

TI RIDDALL and DC STYLES decide to visit JAY's address to arrest him for the offence and after completing the necessary checks they attend the address with several uniform colleagues. When they arrive, JAY is standing outside his house talking to a neighbour. TI RIDDALL arrests JAY for the offence of robbery and cautions him; JAY makes no reply. JAY is escorted to the designated police station where BOYD is in custody and TI RIDDALL provides the circumstances surrounding the arrest to PS FAGAN. JAY's detention is authorized to obtain evidence for the offence and, although he does not wish anyone to be informed of his arrest, he does ask that his solicitor, Miss BAKER, be contacted to represent him whilst he is in custody. PS FAGAN contacts Miss BAKER, who states that she will be at the police station in approximately 45 minutes. After being searched, JAY is placed in a cell to await interview. Several minutes later, JAY attracts the attention of PS FAGAN and tells him that he has changed his mind and does not require the services of a solicitor.

MCQ 5.9   In these circumstances JAY may be interviewed without a solicitor, but which of the below statements is correct with regard to the procedure that should be followed?

A An interview may take place provided JAY agrees in writing and an officer of the rank of superintendent or above gives authority for the interview to proceed.

B An interview may take place provided JAY agrees on tape and the custody officer has inquired about JAY's reasons for his change of mind and gives authority for the interview to proceed.

C An interview may take place provided that JAY agrees in writing or on tape and gives his reasons for his change of mind at the commencement of the interview.

D An interview may take place provided that JAY agrees in writing or on tape and an officer of inspector rank or above has inquired about JAY's reasons for his change of mind and gives authority for the interview to proceed.

Your answer	

The appropriate procedure is followed and PS FAGAN attempts to contact Miss BAKER to inform her that JAY does not want a solicitor. PS FAGAN's attempts to contact Miss BAKER are unsuccessful. TI RIDDALL and DC STYLES are informed of JAY's decision and decide to interview him before they continue their interview with BOYD. JAY is taken into an interview room and an interview commences. After DC STYLES has followed the requirements under *Code 'E' 4.4 to 4.6*, TI RIDDALL questions JAY regarding his involvement in the offence. After TI RIDDALL's first question, JAY says, 'I'll answer your questions but there's no way I'm doing this on tape. If you keep those tapes running I'll not say a word.'

?

Has a suspect ever objected to an interview you are conducting being tape-recorded? What did you do?

E

EXERCISE 5.15

1. *Code 'E' 4.8* details the procedure to be followed when a suspect objects to an interview being tape-recorded. What is that procedure?

   _____

   _____

   _____

   _____

   _____

   _____

   _____

2. What alternative means of recording the interview should be adopted?

   _____

   _____

3. Can TI RIDDALL continue to tape-record the interview regardless of JAY's objection to the interview being tape-recorded?

   Yes / No

   Why / Why not?

   _____

   _____

4. If TI RIDDALL did continue to tape-record the interview, what should he bear in mind?

   _____

   _____

Explanation 5.15

1. *Code 'E' 4.8* requires the interviewer to explain that the interview is being tape-recorded and that the Code requires the suspect's objections to be recorded on tape. When any

objections have been tape-recorded or the suspect has refused to have their objections recorded, the interviewer shall say they are turning off the tape recorder, give their reasons, and turn it off.

2. The interviewer shall make a written record of the interview.

3. The interview can be tape-recorded regardless of JAY's objections if the interviewer reasonably considers they may proceed to do so.

4. *Code 'E' Note 4D* states that, if the interview is tape-recorded in these circumstances, the interviewer should remember that a decision to continue recording against the wishes of the suspect may be subject of comment in court.

See *Investigators' Manual*, para 1.7.9.9

TI RIDDALL decides that the interview will continue to be tape-recorded regardless of JAY's objections. He asks a number of questions about the robbery, to which JAY replies *'no comment.'*

While the interview with JAY is taking place, Miss BAKER arrives at the police station believing her services are still required by JAY. She speaks to PS FAGAN, who tells her that although he tried to contact her he was unable to do so.

MCQ 5.10   What should happen now?
A   PS FAGAN should wait either until the interview is concluded or there is a break in the interview and then ask JAY if he would like to see Miss BAKER.
B   JAY's interview must be interrupted and JAY informed of Miss BAKER's presence and asked if he would like to see her.
C   Miss BAKER should be told that her services are not required, as JAY has agreed to be interviewed without receiving legal advice.
D   Unless JAY has received legal advice over the telephone, the interview should be interrupted and JAY should be informed of Miss BAKER's presence at the station.

Your answer	

PS FAGAN follows the Codes of Practice and JAY decides to speak with Miss BAKER. After a short consultation, JAY decides that he wants Miss BAKER to represent him. TI RIDDALL and DC STYLES provide Miss BAKER with disclosure and Miss BAKER goes into consultation with JAY. Miss BAKER informs the interviewing officers that her consultation will take approximately one hour, so the officers decide to continue interviewing BOYD.

A third interview takes place with BOYD. The format of the interview follows the account and challenge phases of the P.E.A.C.E. model of interviewing using open questions to elicit a response from BOYD and referring to exhibits where necessary. The first 60 minutes of this interview consists of BOYD answering questions but denying any involvement in the offence; however, when the CCTV evidence is discussed, BOYD decides to confess. The interview progresses and BOYD provides full details of his activities prior to the robbery, including the plan to rob the newsagent's, the name of his accomplice, and details of the offence itself.

With the provision of these details the interview becomes lengthy and approaches two hours in length. TI RIDDALL is considering taking a break.

? When you have taken part in the interview of a suspect, when did a break in interviewing occur? What was the reason for the break? How long did the break last for? Have you ever delayed a break? If so, how were you able to justify delaying the break?

E

EXERCISE 5.16

1. According to the Codes of Practice, when should a break in interviewing take place?

_____

_____

_____

_____

2. When should a short refreshment break be provided?

_____

Explanation 5.16

1. Breaks from interviewing should be made at recognized meal times or at other times to take account of when an interviewee last had a meal.

2. Short refreshment breaks shall be provided at approximately two-hour intervals.

Code 'C' 12.8.

MCQ 5.11 What is the least period of time a meal break should normally last for?
A 30 minutes.
B 45 minutes.
C 60 minutes.
D 75 minutes.

Your answer	

MCQ 5.12 How long should a short refreshment break last for?
A At least 5 minutes.
B At least 10 minutes.
C At least 15 minutes.
D At least 20 minutes.

Your answer	

E

EXERCISE 5.17

Subject to TI RIDDALL's discretion, a break in the interview may be delayed if the conditions in *Code 'C' 12.8* are met. What are those conditions?

A break may be delayed if there are reasonable grounds for believing it would

1. _____

_____

_____

2. _____

_____

3. _____

_____

Explanation 5.17

A break may be delayed if there are reasonable grounds for believing it would

1. involve a risk of harm to people or serious loss of, or damage to, property;

2. unnecessarily delay the detainee's release; or

3. otherwise prejudice the outcome of the investigation.

Code 'C' 12.8.

See *Investigators' Manual*, para 1.7.9.11

> TI RIDDALL reasonably believes that the interview will conclude in a matter of minutes and that a break in the interview will unnecessarily delay BOYD's release. He continues the interview, which concludes several minutes later. BOYD is returned to the Juvenile Detention Room and the officers gather the necessary materials for the interview with JAY. TI RIDDALL informs the custody officer that they are ready to interview JAY but, when PS FAGAN goes to JAY's cell, JAY refuses to leave and says, 'I'm staying put and I'm not being interviewed!'

?

Has a suspect ever refused to take part in one of your interviews? What did you do? If this has never happened to you, what would you do in this situation? What alternative means (if any) of recording the interview are available to you?

E

EXERCISE 5.18

Consider the below statements and decide whether they are true or false.

1. JAY cannot be interviewed unless the police have obtained his consent or agreement to be interviewed.

   True / False

2. If JAY continued to refuse to be interviewed, the interview may take place in his cell.

   True / False

3. Jay should be cautioned in these circumstances.

   True / False

4. A failure or refusal to cooperate in such a manner should be recorded, but cannot be given in evidence.

   True / False

5. TI RIDDALL would require the authority of the custody officer to carry out an interview in JAY's cell.

   True / False

6. If TI RIDDALL obtained the necessary authorization to conduct an interview in JAY's cell, the interview must be recorded using portable recording equipment.

   True / False

Explanation 5.18

Code 'C' 12.5 and *Code 'E' 3.4* provide for this situation.

1. False—JAY's consent or agreement is not required.

2. True—The interview may take place in JAY's cell.

3. True—JAY should be cautioned as per *Code 'C' 10.5*.

4. False—A failure or refusal to cooperate can be given in evidence.

5. True—If the custody officer considers, on reasonable grounds, that the interview should not be delayed, the interview may, at the custody officer's discretion, be conducted in a cell.

6. False—The interview should be recorded using portable recording equipment, but if none is available the interview should be recorded in writing as per *Code 'C' 11*.

PS FAGAN tells JAY that he will be interviewed in his cell if necessary and as a result JAY decides to cooperate and accompanies PS FAGAN to an interview room. TI RIDDALL and DC STYLES begin interviewing JAY regarding the robbery in the presence of Miss BAKER.

JAY answers the officer's questions but maintains that he is not responsible for the offence. JAY disputes the identification evidence the officers possess and states that he was never at the scene of the offence. It becomes apparent to both interviewing officers that identification evidence will form a significant part of the case against JAY.

?

Think about the times when your cases have involved identification evidence. Did the suspect dispute the identification evidence? Why was there a need to hold an identification procedure? What did you do? What means of identification were chosen? What alternatives were available?

E

EXERCISE 5.19

Certain identification procedures can be used where the suspect is 'known' and 'available'. In this scenario, JAY is 'known' and 'available', but what does Code 'D' state these terms actually mean?

'Known'

_____

_____

'Available'

_____

_____

As JAY is 'known' and 'available', there are three methods of identification that could be used. What are they?

1. _____

2. _____

3. _____

Explanation 5.19

Code 'D' 3.4 states that references to a suspect being 'known' mean that there is sufficient information known to the police to justify the arrest of a particular person for suspected involvement in the offence. A suspect being 'available' means that they are immediately available, or will be within a reasonably short time, and willing to take an effective part in at least one of the following which it is practicable to arrange:

1. video identification;

2. identification parade; or

3. group identification.

See *Investigators' Manual*, paras 1.9.2.1 and 1.9.2.2

Shortly after disputing the identification evidence, JAY asks if he can use the toilet and requests a drink of water. TI RIDDALL agrees to JAY's requests, stops the interview, and turns off the tape recorder. JAY says that he will only be a minute or two and is escorted to the toilet by DC STYLES, leaving TI RIDDALL and Miss BAKER in the interview room.

MCQ 5.13   What should TI RIDDALL do with regard to the tapes left in the tape recorder?

A When a break is a short one and the interviewer remains in the interview room there is no need to remove the tapes. When the interview recommences the tape recording should continue on the same tapes.

B As this is only a short break and the suspect's solicitor remains in the interview room with TI RIDDALL, the tapes should remain in the machine. The same tapes should be used when the interview recommences.

C Regardless of the length of a break or who remains in the interview room, the procedures for the conclusion of an interview should be followed and a new set of tapes should be used when the interview recommences.

D When a break is taken and the interview room vacated by the suspect, the tapes shall be removed from the tape recorder and the procedures for the conclusion of an interview followed.

Your answer	

TI RIDDALL follows the procedures in the Codes of Practice and several minutes later the interview is recommenced. The interview continues for 30 minutes, when there is a break to allow JAY a further consultation with his solicitor and to have a meal. While this break in interviewing takes place, the officers discuss the identification evidence. The statements of PALMER and HEPWORTH both contain reasonable descriptions of the second offender whom the officers believe to be JAY. The statement of PC VALE includes details of how the officer recognized JAY, as he had interviewed him for some 20 minutes five months prior to the robbery taking place and had seen him about the town on numerous occasions.

E

EXERCISE 5.20

Code 'D' specifies circumstances when an identification procedure must be held. What are those circumstances?

Wherever a witness has

_____

_____

_____

or

wherever there is a witness available who

_____

_____

_____

_____

_____

and the suspect

_____

_____

Code 'D' states that an identification procedure need not be held in all circumstances. What are those circumstances?

_____

_____

_____

_____

_____

Should an identification procedure be held for JAY?

Yes / No

Why?

_____

_____

_____

_____

_____

Explanation 5.20

Code 'D' 3.12 states that an identification procedure must be held

i. wherever a witness has identified a suspect or purported to have identified him/her prior to any identification procedure; or

ii. wherever there is a witness available, who expresses an ability to identify the suspect, or where there is a reasonable chance of the witness being able to do so, and they have not been given the opportunity to identify the suspect in any identification procedures; *and* the suspect disputes being the person the witness claims to have seen.

An identification procedure shall be held unless it is not practicable or it would serve no useful purpose in proving or disproving whether the suspect was involved in the offence.

Remember that an identification procedure may also be held if the officer in charge of the investigation considers it would be useful.

An identification procedure should be held for JAY as he disputes his involvement in the offence and there are witnesses available who fall into both of the above categories.

See *Investigators' Manual*, para 1.9.2.3

MCQ 5.14   Which of the below statements is correct with regard to the initial selection of an identification process?

A   TI RIDDALL should offer a video identification to JAY.

B   JAY should be allowed to choose between a video identification and an identification parade.

C   JAY and Miss BAKER are not allowed to make representations regarding the identification procedure.

D   An identification parade should be offered to JAY.

Your answer	

The officers follow the Codes of Practice and prepare a notice explaining the identification process (as per *Code 'D' 3.17*), and this is served on JAY. JAY is re-interviewed and answers all questions with the response of 'no comment.' Several minutes into this interview, one of the tapes in the tape machine snaps. As a result, the content of the interview to the point where the tape snapped, is lost in its entirety.

?   Has this ever happened to you? What action did you take? If this happened in your next interview, what would you do?

E

EXERCISE 5.21

Code 'E' Note 4H deals with this situation.

What should be done with the tapes?

_____

_____

When the interview resumes, should it start where it left off or should it begin again?

_____

_____

Explanation 5.21

The tapes should be sealed in the suspect's presence and the interview should begin again.

TI RIDDALL follows procedure and the interview continues. JAY answers all questions with a *'no comment'* response. During the course of the interview, TI RIDDALL asks a question concerning the identification evidence of PC VALE. JAY responds to this question by saying, 'I might have known he'd be involved. That dickhead's been harassing me for ages and this is a stitch-up. He keeps stopping me for no reason and I want to make an official complaint about it.'

?   During one of your interviews, has a suspect ever made any type of complaint? What action was taken to deal with the complaint? Did this affect the interview in any way?

E

EXERCISE 5.22

TI RIDDALL decides to continue the interview. Is this the correct decision?

Yes / No

Why / Why not?

_____

_____

What should TI RIDDALL tell JAY regarding his complaint?

_____

_____

What should TI RIDDALL do at the conclusion of the interview?

_____

_____

If JAY's complaint concerned a provision of the Codes of Practice, would this alter the way in which the complaint would be dealt with? If so, how?

_____

_____

_____

_____

_____

Explanation 5.22

If a complaint is made about a matter not concerning Code 'C' or Code 'E', then the decision to continue the interview is at the discretion of the interviewing officer. As TI RIDDALL has decided to continue the interview, he should inform JAY that the complaint will be brought to the custody officer's attention at the conclusion of the interview. When the interview is concluded TI RIDDALL must, as soon as practicable, inform the custody officer about the existence and nature of the complaint.

Code 'E' Note 4F.

If the complaint related to a provision of the Codes then TI RIDDALL should record the complaint in the interview and inform the custody officer. The custody officer must, as soon as practicable, make a report to an officer of inspector rank or above who is not connected with the investigation.

Code 'C' 12.9 and 9.2.

The interview is concluded and the tape recorder is switched off. TI RIDDALL seals the master tape with a master tape label and both he and DC STYLES sign the label. JAY is asked to sign the label and does so, but when Miss BAKER is asked to sign the label she refuses.

MCQ 5.15   What should TI RIDDALL do?

A Make a note of the fact that Miss BAKER refused to sign the master tape label in his pocket book.

B Call an officer of at least inspector rank into the interview room to sign the master tape label.

C Pass the master tape label to DC STYLES (the senior officer present) to note the fact that Miss BAKER refused to sign the label.

D Call PS FAGAN (the custody officer) into the interview room and get him to sign the master tape label.

Your answer	

TI RIDDALL complies with the Code of Practice and JAY is returned to his cell via the custody officer. The officers discuss the case and decide that the interview phase (at this point) is complete.

The officers now consider obtaining fingerprints, photographs, and DNA samples from BOYD and JAY.

You will have taken fingerprints, photographs, and DNA from suspects on numerous occasions. How was this achieved? Have you ever experienced difficulty in obtaining them? Why? Were they obtained nevertheless?

EXERCISE 5.23

Examine the below statements and decide whether they are true or false.

1. A person's fingerprints may only be taken in connection with the investigation of an offence if they consent.

    True / False

2. If a suspect consents to fingerprints being taken from them, then the consent must be in writing.

    True / False

3. Consent is not required if a person is detained at a police station having been arrested for a recordable offence.

    True / False

4. The only time consent is not required to obtain fingerprints is when a suspect has been charged with an offence.

   True / False

5. Reasonable force may be used to obtain a person's fingerprints without their consent.

   True / False

6. An officer may only photograph a detainee with their consent.

   True / False

7. An officer may use reasonable force to take a detainee's photograph without their consent.

   True / False

8. Custody area video systems cannot be used to obtain an image of a detainee.

   True / False

9. An officer may use reasonable force to remove a baseball cap from a detainee's head if the detainee refuses to remove it.

   True / False

10. A swab taken from the mouth of a detainee is an intimate sample.

    True / False

11. Reasonable force may be used, if necessary, to take a non-intimate sample.

    True / False

Explanation 5.23

1. False—Consent is required unless the conditions in *Code 'D' 4.3* apply.

2. True—Where consent is given it must be in writing—*Code 'D' 4.2*.

3. True—Section 61 of the Police and Criminal Evidence Act 1984 provides a power to take fingerprints without consent—*Code 'D' 4.3*.

4. False—Fingerprints can be obtained without consent in these circumstances, but there are several other reasons why consent is not required—*Code 'D' 4.2*.

5. True—*Code 'D' 4.6*.

6. False—Photographs may be obtained without the detainee's consent if that consent is withheld or it is not practicable to obtain their consent—*Code 'D' 5.12(b)*.

7. True—*Code 'D' 5.14*.

8. False—A photograph may be obtained without the person's consent by making a copy of an image of them, taken at any time on a camera system installed anywhere in the police station—*Code 'D' 5.15*.

9. True—*Code 'D' 5.14*.

10. False—*Code 'D' 6.1(b)*.

11. True—*Code 'D' 6.7*.

Fingerprints, photographs, and DNA samples are obtained from BOYD and JAY and the relevant documentation completed.

Conclusion

In this case study, the location of the offence and the names of the participants are imaginary; the issues that have been raised from it are not. Although it is unlikely that in the investigation of one offence you would face every difficulty or problem that TI RIDDALL and DC STYLES faced when dealing with BOYD and JAY, you will nevertheless have first-hand experience of many of the dilemmas examined in the case study. In your future role as a detective these experiences will be broadened and amplified. You will also realise that these areas provide examiners with an abundance of material from which you can be tested. As a consequence you will appreciate how important it is, both as a practitioner and as a student, to possess a good knowledge and understanding of Codes 'C', 'D', and 'E' of the Codes of Practice.

6 | Special Warnings

Aim

The aim of this section is to provide you with an understanding of special warnings.

Objectives

At the end of this section you should be able to:

1. Explain why a special warning can be given (under ss 36 and 37 of the Criminal Justice and Public Order Act 1994).
2. Explain when a special warning should be given.
3. Explain who should give a special warning.
4. Explain what should be included in a special warning.
5. Apply your knowledge to multiple-choice questions.

Introduction

A special warning permits a court to draw adverse inferences in certain circumstances. Understanding why a special warning should be given, when it should be given, who should give it, and how it should be given will not only assist you in your preparation for the National Investigator's Examination, but should also provide you with useful practical information should the need to give a special warning during the course of an interview arise.

Multiple-choice Questions

Begin this section of the Workbook by answering the below multiple-choice questions. Mark your answer in the 'First Attempt' box. Then read and complete the exercises in the 'Special Warnings' section. Once you are satisfied that your knowledge is of a good standard, return to these questions and mark your answer in the 'Second Attempt' box. The answers to these questions can be found in the 'Answers Section' at the rear of the Workbook.

MCQ 6.1 DOOLEY breaks into a house and steals an antique gold necklace. The police are alerted to the burglary and PC COOK chases DOOLEY from the house into an alleyway. DOOLEY throws the stolen necklace onto the ground just before PC COOK detains him. PC COOK recovers the necklace. DOOLEY is interviewed by DC NEVIN and remains silent when questioned about the necklace.

Can DOOLEY be given a special warning under s 36 of the Criminal Justice and Public Order Act 1994 regarding the necklace?

A No, because the necklace was not found on DOOLEY's person.

B Yes, because it was found in a place in which he was at the time of his arrest.

C No, because it was not found in or on his clothing or footwear.

D Yes, but only if PC COOK gives DOOLEY the special warning.

First Attempt	
Second Attempt	

MCQ 6.2 A warehouse in DC HACKWORTH's area is totally destroyed by an arson attack. DC HACKWORTH has evidence that SINGH, who has previous convictions for arson, is responsible for the offence. DC HACKWORTH arrests him at his home address and brings him into the custody block. SINGH declines the services of a solicitor. PC FELLOWS overhears DC HACKWORTH relating the circumstances of the arrest and speaks to the officer. He tells DC HACKWORTH that he saw SINGH outside the warehouse two days before the arson attack. During his interview, SINGH answers 'no comment' to all the questions that are put to him.

Could DC HACKWORTH give SINGH a special warning in these circumstances?

A Yes, SINGH has failed to account for his presence near the scene of the crime.

B No, special warnings do not apply to 'no comment' interviews.

C Yes, but only if SINGH has a solicitor present in the interview.

D No, SINGH was not found at the crime scene, at or about the time of the offence.

First Attempt	
Second Attempt	

MCQ 6.3 PRIEST has been arrested in connection with an offence of rape and is being interviewed by DCs ROWLEY and SKILLEN. The officers decide to give PRIEST a special warning under s 36 of the Criminal Justice and Public Order Act 1994.

Which of the below is correct with regard to the delivery of the special warning?

A PRIEST does not need to be told what offence is being investigated.

B PRIEST does not need to be told what fact he is being asked to account for.

C PRIEST does not need to be told that a record is being made of the interview and that it may be given in evidence at any subsequent trial.

D PRIEST does not need to be cautioned at the conclusion of the special warning.

First Attempt	
Second Attempt	

Why Can a Special Warning be Given?

Section 36 of the Criminal Justice and Public Order Act 1994

E

EXERCISE 6.1

Examine the below scenario and answer the related questions.

HARDING is the victim of a serious sexual assault. In her statement she describes the person who attacked her as having a distinctive tattoo on his arm. She describes the tattoo as a rose with the words 'Mary Jane' written underneath it. Following a medical examination, samples of the offender's hair and semen are recovered from HARDING. HARDING also states that she had scratched her attacker on the right-hand side of his face. Several days later, COOPER is arrested in connection with the offence. A forensic examination confirms that the hair and semen samples recovered from HARDING match COOPER's DNA profile. COOPER has the tattoo on his right arm as described above and also has scratches on the right-hand side of his face.

During his interview, COOPER refuses to answer any questions.

Which of the above 'facts' may COOPER be special warned for and why?

Which of the above 'facts' would not be subject of a special warning and why?

Explanation 6.1

There are a number of reasons why a special warning can be given under s 36 of the Act. The reasons are in two parts: the 'physical' and the 'interview' parts. Both parts must be present for a special warning to apply.

The 'physical' part

Does the interviewing officer have any 'physical' evidence? If it helps you to remember, the mnemonic is **PC FOPSOMM.**

Where a person is arrested by a constable and there is on his/her

P	Person or
C	Clothing or
F	Footwear or
O	Otherwise in his possession or
P	Place at time of arrest a
S	Substance
O	Object
M	Mark
M	Mark on an object

If PC FOPSOMM is present, the interviewing officer must then ask himself/herself, do I believe the presence of PC FOPSOMM may be attributable to the suspect having taken part in the offence?

If the answer to this question is 'Yes', then the interviewing officer must examine the second part.

The 'interview' part

Has the suspect failed or refused to account for the presence of PC FOPSOMM?

If the answer is 'Yes', then a special warning can be given.

In this scenario, there are several 'facts' for which you may have considered COOPER could be subject to a special warning. These should have included COOPER's distinctive tattoo, the hair and semen recovered from HARDING, and the scratches to the right-hand side of COOPER's face.

Let's take these 'facts' one at a time and subject them to the above reasoning.

COOPER's distinctive tattoo

The tattoo could be classed as a mark on COOPER's person. However, the presence of the tattoo on COOPER's arm is not due to him having committed the offence. It was on COOPER's arm before the offence was committed, i.e. the reason why COOPER has the tattoo is not because he committed the offence. Therefore, the tattoo cannot be the subject of a special warning.

The hair and semen that matches COOPER's DNA

These items were not found on COOPER's person, clothing, footwear, otherwise in COOPER's possession, or at a place in which COOPER is at the time of his arrest. Therefore, the hair and semen (although excellent evidence) cannot be subject to a special warning.

The scratches on the right-hand side of COOPER's face

The scratches could be classed as a mark on COOPER's person. If the interviewing officer believes that the presence of the scratches is due to COOPER having committed the offence, then the 'physical' part is satisfied. As COOPER has refused to answer any questions during the course of the interview (a failure or refusal to account), then the 'interview' part is satisfied. Therefore, COOPER could be given a special warning in relation to the scratches.

Section 37 of the Criminal Justice and Public Order Act 1994

E

EXERCISE 6.2

Examine the below scenario and answer the related questions.

At 2.00 am this morning an automatic alarm was activated at St Andrew's Junior School. PC KERR arrived at the scene and saw a youth jump from a window of the school and run off. The youth was chased by PC KERR, but was lost in the dark. PC HARRIS (a dog handler) attended and searched the school grounds. PC HARRIS's dog tracked the youth to a store shed in the grounds of the school. A 2.10 am, the dog handler arrested the youth (TAYLOR) for the burglary. TAYLOR was searched and a screwdriver was found in his coat pocket. £100.00 cash was stolen from the school, but this has not been found anywhere. At 10.00 am this morning, DC EVERTON interviews TAYLOR. TAYLOR refuses to give an explanation for his presence in the store shed, but states that he found the screwdriver in the school grounds. DC EVERTON thinks that TAYLOR is lying about the screwdriver.

Which of the above 'facts' may TAYLOR be special warned for and why?

Which of the above 'facts' would not be subject of a special warning and why?

Explanation 6.2

As with s 36, the reasons for giving a special warning under s 37 can be split into the 'physical' and the 'interview' parts and, again, both parts must be present for a special warning to apply.

The 'physical' part

The important fact to remember here is that the 'arresting' officer and the 'finding' officer *must* be the same person.

The interviewing officer must ask himself/herself: was the arrested person found at a place at or about the time the offence was committed?

If the answer is 'Yes', then the interviewing officer must then ask himself/herself: do I believe that the presence of the suspect at that place and time may be attributable to the suspect having taken part in the offence?

If the answer to this question is 'Yes', then the interviewing officer must examine the second part.

The 'interview' part

Has the suspect failed or refused to account for their presence at that time and place?

If the answer is 'Yes', then a special warning can be given.

In this scenario, there are three 'facts' for which you may have considered TAYLOR could be subject to a special warning. These should have included TAYLOR's presence when he jumped out of the school window and his presence in the store shed (both under s 37), and the screwdriver found in his coat pocket (under s 36).

As with the first scenario, we will take these 'facts' one at a time and subject them to the above reasoning.

TAYLOR's presence when he jumped out of the school window

PC KERR 'found' TAYLOR at this point, but lost him and did not arrest him. The 'arresting' and 'finding' officer must be the same person and, as this is not the case, TAYLOR cannot be given a special warning for his presence at this location. If PC KERR had arrested TAYLOR outside the school window, then a special warning would be applicable if TAYLOR refused to account for his presence at the school.

TAYLOR's presence in the store shed

PC HARRIS 'found' TAYLOR in the store shed and arrested him. The 'arresting' officer and the 'finding' officer are one and the same. If DC EVERTON believes that TAYLOR's presence in the store shed is attributable to his participation in the offence, the 'physical' part is satisfied. TAYLOR has refused to account for his presence in the store shed, satisfying the 'interview' part. Therefore, a special warning could be given for this fact.

The screwdriver found in TAYLOR's coat pocket

The screwdriver is an object in TAYLOR's possession (PC FOPSOMM). If DC EVERTON believes that the presence of the screwdriver is attributable to TAYLOR having taken part in the offence, then the 'physical' part is satisfied. However, the 'interview' part is not satisfied. Regardless of DC EVERTON's beliefs, TAYLOR has given an account of why the screwdriver is in his possession. Therefore, a special warning is not applicable.

Try using the flowchart on the following page to assist you to work out if a special warning is applicable.

When Should a Special Warning be Given?

E

EXERCISE 6.3

Read the below scenarios and follow the instructions you are given.

GIBSON seriously assaults MILES using a knuckleduster. PC CALCUTT arrests GIBSON a short distance away from the scene of the offence and finds a knuckleduster in GIBSON's pocket. PC CALCUTT cautions GIBSON, who remains silent. PC CALCUTT escorts GIBSON to his police station and custody block, where the circumstances of the arrest are related to the custody officer. GIBSON states that he does not require a solicitor. GIBSON is later interviewed by DC ROBERTS. As DC ROBERTS is explaining the interview procedure, GIBSON interrupts her and states, 'I'm not answering any questions no matter what you say.' DC ROBERTS continues the interview procedure and cautions GIBSON. During the interview, GIBSON does answer some of DC ROBERTS's questions, but remains silent when asked any questions relating to the knuckleduster.

At what point(s) could GIBSON be special warned in relation to the knuckleduster?

Explanation 6.3

A special warning can only be given after caution. Although there is nothing in principle preventing a special warning being given by PC CALCUTT at the scene of the arrest, you should remember that requests for information under ss 36 and 37 are a form of questioning and should take place at a police station. In interview, the suspect has to be given an opportunity to answer questions about the 'fact' the interviewer wishes them to account for, because you cannot fail or refuse to answer questions about something you have not been asked about. Therefore, GIBSON's interruption of DC ROBERTS would not mean he should receive a special warning at that stage. GIBSON should be specially warned about the knuckleduster in interview after he has been given the opportunity to answer questions and has failed or refused to answer those questions.

The fact that GIBSON does not have a solicitor present does not make any difference to the situation, as he has been given the opportunity to consult one. If this opportunity has not been given to the suspect, then no adverse inferences can be drawn from the suspect's failure or refusal to account for the object etc.

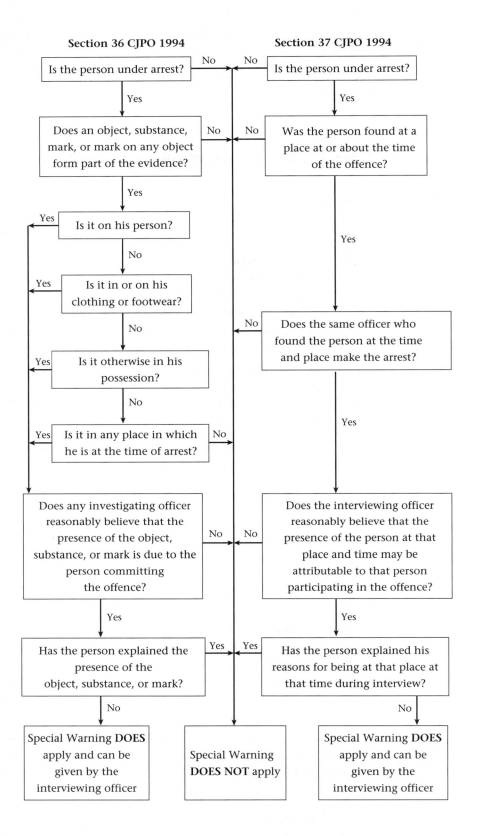

Section 36 CJPO 1994   **Section 37 CJPO 1994**

Is the person under arrest? — No → No ← Is the person under arrest?

Yes ↓   Yes ↓

Does an object, substance, mark, or mark on any object form part of the evidence? — No → No ← Was the person found at a place at or about the time of the offence?

Yes ↓   Yes ↓

Yes ← Is it on his person?

No ↓

Yes ← Is it in or on his clothing or footwear?

No ↓

Yes ← Is it otherwise in his possession?   No ← Does the same officer who found the person at the time and place make the arrest?

No ↓   Yes ↓

Yes ← Is it in any place in which he is at the time of arrest? — No →

Does any investigating officer reasonably believe that the presence of the object, substance, or mark is due to the person committing the offence? — No → No ← Does the interviewing officer reasonably believe that the presence of the person at that place and time may be attributable to that person participating in the offence?

Yes ↓   Yes ↓

Has the person explained the presence of the object, substance, or mark? — Yes → Yes ← Has the person explained his reasons for being at that place at that time during interview?

No ↓   No ↓

Special Warning **DOES** apply and can be given by the interviewing officer

Special Warning **DOES NOT** apply

Special Warning **DOES** apply and can be given by the interviewing officer

Who Should Give a Special Warning?

There are a number of myths with regard to who should give a special warning to the suspect. These include that the special warning must be given by the officer who finds the object, mark, etc. or by the officer who found the suspect at a place at or about the time of the offence. Quite simply, the interviewing officer gives the special warning.

What Should be Included in a Special Warning?

> **EXERCISE 6.4**
>
> There are five points that must be covered when an interviewing officer gives a special warning to a suspect. What are they?
>
> 1. _____
>
> _____
>
> 2. _____
>
> _____
>
> 3. _____
>
> _____
>
> 4. _____
>
> _____
>
> 5. _____
>
> _____

Explanation 6.4

PACE Code 'C' (para 10.11) provides that the interviewing officer *must* tell the suspect in *ordinary* language

- what offence is being investigated,
- what 'fact' he/she is asking the suspect to account for,
- that he/she believes the 'fact' may be due to the suspect's taking part in the commission of the offence,
- that a proper inference may be drawn if the suspect fails or refuses to account for the 'fact' about which he/she is being questioned, and
- that the interview is being recorded.

In relation to ss 36 and 37, the accused cannot be convicted solely on an inference drawn from a failure or refusal to respond. The court must first be satisfied that there is sufficient other evidence to establish a prima facie case to answer (s 38(3)).

E

EXERCISE 6.5

Using Example 6.2, write down below the special warning you would give to TAYLOR.

1. _____

_____

_____

2. _____

_____

_____

3. _____

_____

_____

4. _____

_____

_____

5. _____

_____

_____

Explanation 6.5

The special warning you have written should be similar to the below:

1. 'I am investigating a burglary for which you are under arrest, in which St Andrew's school was broken into and £100.00 cash was stolen.

2. You were arrested at 2.10 am this morning by PC HARRIS, who found you in the store shed contained within the grounds of the school.

3. I believe that you were in that store shed because you had just broken into the school.

4. I am going to ask you to explain why you were there and I must warn you that a court may draw their own conclusions if, from now on, you fail or refuse to account for why you were there.

5. I must remind you that this interview is being recorded.'

See *Investigators' Manual*, para 1.8.7

Try the same with the COOPER example in Exercise 6.1.

Conclusion

Now that you have finished this section of the Workbook, you should have a good understanding of special warnings. The correct application of the law relating to this subject will assist you in the National Investigator's Examination and will also ensure that you can carry out a professional interview, allowing a court the opportunity to draw an inference from a suspect's failure or refusal to account for a given fact.

Now that you have finished the Workbook section on 'Special Warnings', you should attempt the 'Recall Questions' before re-reading the relevant section in the Manual and making your second attempt at the multiple-choice questions. The answers to these questions are printed in the 'Answers Section' at the rear of the Workbook.

Recall Questions

Try and answer the questions below. Do not allow yourself to continue until you have answered the questions to your satisfaction.

- Why could you give a special warning under s 36 of CJPO 1994 (can you remember the mnemonic)?

- Why could you give a special warning under s 37 of CJPO 1994?

- When should you give a special warning?

- Who should give the special warning?

- What are the five points a suspect must be told when you give a special warning?

7 | Administration of Justice

Aim

The aim of this section is for you to comprehend the legislation relating to certain offences against the administration of justice.

Objectives

At the end of this section you should be able to:

1. Outline the offence of perjury in judicial proceedings.
2. Give practical examples of the offence of perverting the course of justice.
3. Outline the offence of intimidation of witnesses (s 51 of the Criminal Justice and Public Order Act 1994).
4. Identify when an offence of assisting an offender has been committed.
5. Apply your knowledge to multiple-choice questions.

Introduction

This section deals with offences against the administration of justice and public interest. Although not everyday occurrences, they are part of your syllabus and so you should have a rudimentary grasp of the fundamental points regarding these offences.

Multiple-choice Questions

> Begin this section of the Workbook by answering the below multiple-choice questions. Mark your answer in the 'First Attempt' box. Then read and complete the exercises in the 'Administration of Justice' section. Once you are satisfied that your knowledge is of a good standard, return to these questions and mark your answer in the 'Second Attempt' box. The answers to these questions can be found in the 'Answers Section' at the rear of the Workbook.

MCQ 7.1   MIRGA has been lawfully sworn as an interpreter at a court. During the course of the court proceedings he wilfully changes the words used by the defendant, making it sound as though the defendant is confessing to the offence.

Considering the offence of perjury in judicial proceedings (s 1 of the Perjury Act 1911), which of the below is correct?

A   Corroboration would be required to prove the offence of perjury.

B   MIRGA commits the offence, but only because he is interpreting for a court.

C   The offence cannot be committed by MIRGA, as he is an interpreter and not a witness.

D   MIRGA commits the offence that is punishable with life imprisonment.

First Attempt	
Second Attempt	

MCQ 7.2   JONES is arrested for burglary and is placed in a police cell while officers go to his house to carry out a search. During the search of JONES's house, a stolen mobile phone is found. JONES is later interviewed and during the interview he is questioned about the mobile phone. At this point JONES realizes that the person responsible for the theft of the mobile phone must have been his son. As his son has never been in trouble with the police before and is taking his exams, JONES confesses to stealing the mobile phone when interviewed.

Has JONES committed an offence of perverting the course of justice (contrary to common law)?

A   Yes, but he can only be charged with the offence with the consent of the DPP.

B   No, because he has not destroyed or concealed evidence of a crime.

C   Yes, but only because his confession would be classed as a positive act.

D   No, because JONES's activities do not involve the intimidation of witnesses or jurors.

First Attempt	
Second Attempt	

MCQ 7.3   KALE is in a bar when he has an argument with GRAINGER. KALE hits GRAINGER in the face, causing GRAINGER to lose a tooth. GRAINGER contacts the police and KALE is arrested, charged, and bailed for the offence of assault. KALE goes back to the bar and tells MOSS (a barmaid) that unless GRAINGER retracts his complaint, he will smash the windows of the bar the following week.

Has KALE committed an offence of witness intimidation (contrary to s 51 of the Criminal Justice and Public Order Act 1994)?

A   Yes, the offence is made out in these circumstances.

B   No, because the threat was made to MOSS instead of GRAINGER.

C   Yes, but only because the original offence was an assault.

D   No, because the threat is made otherwise than in the presence of GRAINGER.

First Attempt	
Second Attempt	

MCQ 7.4 BARKER commits an offence of assisting an offender (contrary to s 4 of the Criminal Law Act 1967). The original offence was a burglary of a dwelling (punishable with 14 years' imprisonment).

As a consequence, what is the maximum sentence that could be imposed on BARKER?
A Five years' imprisonment.
B Seven years' imprisonment.
C Nine years' imprisonment.
D 14 years' imprisonment.

First Attempt	
Second Attempt	

MCQ 7.5 DC NEWMAN has arrested GRIFFIN for an offence of burglary. She believes that BISHOP may have assisted GRIFFIN and has consequently committed an offence of assisting an offender (s 4 of the Criminal Law Act 1967). DC NEWMAN asks DS ENVER for some advice regarding this offence.

Which of the below statements is correct?
A The relevant offence committed by GRIFFIN must be one that carries more than five years' imprisonment for this offence to be committed.
B BISHOP can commit the offence before GRIFFIN is convicted of committing the burglary.
C BISHOP could attempt to commit this offence.
D The offence requires the consent of the Attorney General before a prosecution is brought.

First Attempt	
Second Attempt	

MCQ 7.6 PALTRY has her purse stolen. The purse was worth £ 10.00 and contained £ 50.00 in cash and several personal items with a combined value of £ 30.00. PALTRY is annoyed by the theft and makes enquiries into who was responsible for the offence. She finds out that JAMES took her purse. PALTRY confronts JAMES who confesses to the theft. JAMES states that he is truly sorry for what he did and that to make up for the loss PALTRY suffered he would like to compensate her loss by giving her £ 90.00 in cash. PALTRY agrees and accepts the money offered by JAMES.

Considering the offence of concealing relevant offences (contrary to s 5 of the Criminal Law Act 1967), which of the below statements is correct?
A PALTRY has committed the offence but the permission of the Attorney General is required before a prosecution could take place.
B PALTRY has not committed the offence in this situation because concealing relevant offences is only applicable to offences to offences with a maximum sentence of ten years' imprisonment.
C PALTRY has committed the offence but the consent of the DPP would be required before a prosecution can be brought.

D PALTRY has not committed the offence as she has only accepted reasonable compensation for the loss caused by the theft.

First Attempt	
Second Attempt	

Perjury (s 1 of the Perjury Act 1911)

E

EXERCISE 7.1

Write down your answers to the following questions about the offence of perjury.

Who can commit the offence of perjury?

Where can perjury be committed?

What must be done by the defendant?

How do you prove an offence of perjury?

What is the sentence for perjury?

Explanation 7.1

Your answers should have included the following details:

A lawfully sworn witness or interpreter can commit the offence.

The offence can be committed in *judicial proceedings*. This means proceedings before a court, a tribunal, or a person hearing evidence on oath (e.g. a magistrate).

The defendant must *wilfully* make a material statement that they know is *false* or they did not *believe to be true*.

The offence requires corroboration as to the falsity of the defendant's statement. You could use a transcript of the proceedings or call witnesses who were present.

Perjury is punishable with seven years' imprisonment.

See *Investigators' Manual*, para 1.14.1

Perverting the Course of Justice (Common Law)

It is an offence at common law to do an act tending and *intending* to pervert the course of justice.

The offence is punishable by life imprisonment.

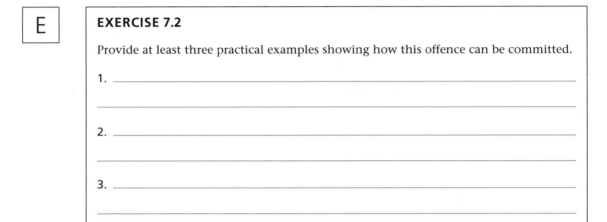

EXERCISE 7.2

Provide at least three practical examples showing how this offence can be committed.

1. _____

_____

2. _____

_____

3. _____

_____

Explanation 7.2

You may have provided the following practical examples:

Cases where evidence is deliberately destroyed, concealed, or falsified, intimidating witnesses or jurors, admitting to a crime to enable the true offender to avoid prosecution, abusing your authority as a police officer to excuse someone of a criminal charge, making a false allegation of an offence, or giving another person's details when being reported for an offence.

Remember that the offence requires some *positive* conduct by the defendant.

See *Investigators' Manual*, para 1.14.2

Intimidation of Witnesses (s 51 of the Criminal Justice and Public Order Act 1994)

EXERCISE 7.3

Write down your answers to the following questions about the offence of intimidation of witnesses.

1. There are two ways this offence can be committed. What are they?

   _____

   _____

   _____

2. Under s 51(1), who is 'the victim'?

   _____

   _____

   _____

3. Under s 51(2), who is 'the victim'?

   _____

   _____

   _____

4. What kind of harm to the victim is talked about?

   _____

   _____

5. Does the victim have to be present when the act or threat is made?

   _____

6. Can the act or threat be done or made to a person other than the victim?

   _____

Explanation 7.3

Your answers should have included the following:

1. By the offender doing an act, which does or is intended to intimidate or harm another person.

2. A person *assisting* in an investigation or *is* a witness or potential witness or a juror or potential juror (present tense offence).

3. A person who *has assisted* in an investigation into an offence or *has given* evidence in proceedings for an offence or *has acted* as a juror or concurred in a verdict (past tense offence).

4. The harm can be *physical* (to a person or their property) or *financial*.

5. No, the victim does not have to be present.

6. No, the threat can be made via a third party.

It is important to remember that the defendant must *know or believe* (not suspect) that the victim is or has assisted in an investigation, etc.

There are other offences relating to intimidation and harming of witnesses, and you should refer to the *Investigators' Manual* for more information regarding these offences.

See *Investigators' Manual*, para 1.14.3.1

Assisting Offenders

> **EXERCISE 7.4**
>
> Read the below circumstances and answer the questions posed, giving reasons for your answers.
>
> PARKER and ROSE share a flat. PARKER burgles a neighbour's flat and steals £1000.00 during the burglary. PARKER tells ROSE about the burglary and says that she is going on holiday and will return in a week. The neighbour reports the burglary to the police and DC ALI is assigned to investigate the offence. During his enquiries into the burglary, he learns that PARKER is responsible for the offence. DC ALI makes further enquiries regarding PARKER and finds that she is also wanted for a s 20 assault. He discovers PARKER's home address and attends it with a view to arresting her for both offences. When DC ALI arrives at the flat, he speaks to ROSE.
>
> 1. DC ALI asks ROSE if PARKER lives at the flat. ROSE replies, 'I don't have to tell you anything.'
>
>   Is ROSE assisting an offender at this stage?
>
>   Why / Why not?
>
>   _____
>
>   _____
>
> 2. DC ALI tells ROSE he is investigating a wounding (the s 20 assault) and he believes PARKER is responsible for the offence. ROSE knows nothing about the wounding, but from this point on she intends to stop the police arresting PARKER. She says, 'As far as I'm aware, PARKER hasn't done anything like that.'
>
>   Is ROSE assisting an offender at this stage?
>
>   Why / Why not?
>
>   _____
>
>   _____
>
>   _____
>
> 3. If ROSE responded by saying, 'PARKER's never lived here, I've never heard of her, you'd better try elsewhere.'

Would this change the situation?

Why / Why not?

_____

_____

_____

4. DC ALI tells ROSE that PARKER is also wanted for the burglary where the £1000.00 was stolen. ROSE replies, 'PARKER doesn't live here anymore, she moved out last week and I don't know where she went.'

   Is ROSE assisting an offender at this stage?

   Why / Why not?

   _____

   _____

   _____

5. DC ALI does not believe ROSE and considers arresting ROSE for the offence of attempting to assist an offender.

   Can this offence be attempted?

   _____

Explanation 7.4

At point 1, ROSE does not commit the offence. This is because there has to be some *positive* conduct by ROSE: doing or saying nothing is not positive conduct.

At point 2, ROSE would not have committed the offence. This is because no act has been carried out to impede PARKER's apprehension; this is merely a denial by ROSE.

At point 3, the offence would be committed. The fact that DC ALI has told ROSE he is investigating a wounding is immaterial. ROSE is aware that PARKER has committed a relevant offence (the theft) and she intends to impede PARKER's arrest.

At point 4, the offence is committed. ROSE is providing misleading information (the act), intending to impede PARKER's apprehension.

This offence cannot be attempted (point 5).

See *Investigators' Manual*, para 1.14.5

Conclusion

At this point you should be able to demonstrate your comprehension of some of the offences relating to the administration of justice.

Now that you have finished this Workbook section, you should attempt the 'Recall Questions' before re-reading the relevant section in the Manual and making your second attempt at the multiple-choice questions. The answers to these questions are printed in the 'Answers Section' at the rear of the Workbook.

Recall Questions

Try and answer the questions below. Do not allow yourself to continue until you have answered the questions to your satisfaction.

- Who can commit an offence of perjury?

- What are 'judicial proceedings'?

- Give five examples of how an offence of perverting the course of justice could be committed?

- Who is protected by s 51 of the Criminal Justice and Public Order Act 1994?

- How can a threat be made to a witness?

- What must the defendant intend in order to commit an offence of assisting an offender?

PART TWO

Property Offences

8 Theft

Aim

The aim of this section is to provide you with an understanding of the offence of theft.

Objectives

At the end of this section you should be able to:

1. Define the offence of theft contrary to s 1 of the Theft Act 1968.
2. Identify the different sections of the offence of theft.
3. Explain what is meant by the term 'dishonesty'.
4. Outline the ruling in *R v Ghosh* [1982] QB 1053.
5. State the meaning of ss 3, 4, 5, and 6 of the Theft Act 1968.
6. Demonstrate your knowledge by completing the exercises in this section.
7. Apply your knowledge to multiple-choice questions.

Introduction

Brushing up on your knowledge of the offence of theft is a crucial part of your revision. The offence can be the subject of questions in its own right, but you must not forget that theft has major links to a number of other offences such as robbery and burglary. Before you study any offence where theft forms part of the definition you must ensure that you have a good understanding of the basic material; this is what this section of the Workbook sets out to achieve.

Multiple-choice Questions

Begin this section of the Workbook by answering the below multiple-choice questions. Mark your answer in the 'First Attempt' box. Then read and complete the exercises in the 'Theft' section. Once you are satisfied that your knowledge is of a good standard, return to these questions and mark your answer in the 'Second Attempt' box. The answers to these questions can be found in the 'Answers Section' at the rear of the Workbook.

MCQ 8.1   The Theft Act 1968 sets out a number of circumstances where a person will not be treated as dishonest and one circumstance where a person may be dishonest.

In which of the below circumstances may the person have acted 'dishonestly' for the purposes of theft?

A ATKINSON takes £50.00 from GIBSON's wallet in the honest belief that he has the right in law to do so in settlement of a debt.

B KEYTE finds a diamond ring worth £1,000.00 and decides to keep it, as he believes he could never find the owner even though the owner could have been traced by making some simple enquiries.

C HILL urgently needs £100.00 to pay for repairs to his car and takes this amount from his employer's petty cash believing that his employer would consent if he knew of the appropriation and its circumstances.

D RAND is selling DVDs at a car boot sale. STOWE offers him £10.00 for a DVD, which RAND refuses. STOWE throws down a £10.00 note and takes a DVD.

First Attempt	
Second Attempt	

MCQ 8.2   WISEDALE is a member of a casino. She becomes involved in an argument with a croupier over the rules of roulette. As a result, the croupier removes WISEDALE's £100.00 stake. Had the bet stood, WISEDALE would have won £1,000.00. On her way out and feeling aggrieved, WISEDALE removes a picture (worth £1,000.00) from the wall of the casino. WISEDALE honestly believes that she has a legal right to the picture to replace her winnings.

Taking account of s 2 of the Theft Act 1968, which of the below statements is correct?

A WISEDALE's actions would be considered dishonest, as gambling debts are not legally enforceable.

B A belief in a legal right to the property is immaterial; WISEDALE has acted dishonestly and therefore commits theft.

C Although gambling debts are not legally enforceable, WISEDALE is not dishonest because she believes she has a right in law to take the property.

D WISEDALE's belief must be both honest and reasonable, and as this is not the case she would be viewed as dishonest.

First Attempt	
Second Attempt	

MCQ 8.3   ILINGWORTH is on trial for an offence of theft. The jury are considering her actions during the offence and in particular, they are considering whether or not she was dishonest. The circumstances of the case mean that s 2 of the Theft Act 1968 (dishonesty) does not assist the jury and as a result, the jury are given a direction to consider ILINGWORTH's actions in light of the case of *R v Ghosh* [1982] QB 1053.

What is that direction?

A   Whether, according to the ordinary standards of reasonable and honest people, what was done was dishonest and if it was whether ILINGWORTH herself must have realized what was done was dishonest by those standards.

B   Whether, according to the standards of honest people, what ILINGWORTH had done was wrong.

C   Whether according to ILINGWORTH's personal beliefs and standards, what was done was dishonest.

D   Whether, according to the standards of the reasonable man, what was done was dishonest.

First Attempt	
Second Attempt	

MCQ 8.4   SMITH buys a second-hand car from LAUDER for £25,000.00. This is a reasonable price for the car at current market values. SMITH is later stopped by the police who discover that the car is stolen and originally belonged to GOODALL. When SMITH is informed, she refuses to hand the car back to GOODALL.

Would SMITH attract liability for theft?

A   Yes, SMITH assumes the rights of the owner even though she has come by the property innocently.

B   No, SMITH has purchased the car in good faith and for a reasonable price.

C   Yes, when SMITH is informed of the circumstances and does not return the car she commits theft.

D   No, SMITH was not the original thief and the same property cannot be appropriated on more than one occasion.

First Attempt	
Second Attempt	

MCQ 8.5   WONG is a tenant, renting a three-bedroom detached house and accompanying gardens. WONG decides to buy a house but, before leaving the rented accommodation and whilst still a tenant, she decides that she will dig up an established rhododendron bush (including the roots) from the garden of the rented house. WONG takes the rhododendron bush to her new house and plants it in her garden.

Has WONG committed an offence of theft?

A   Yes, even though WONG is in possession of the land under a tenancy, the rhododendron bush forms part of the land to be used with it and as such is classed as 'property'.

B   No, there are no circumstances where a person can steal land or things forming part of land and severed from it.

C   Yes, although WONG is the lawful tenant, the rhododendron bush does not belong to her and her actions would amount to theft.

D   No, WONG is the legal tenant of the property and is in lawful possession of the rhododendron bush.

First Attempt	
Second Attempt	

MCQ 8.6   DELACY is a solicitor dealing primarily with mortgages. He is provided with £180,000.00 by BOOTH to buy a house. DELACY's business is in financial difficulties and so DELACY transfers BOOTH's mortgage money to his company account rather than holding the funds for the mortgage. DELACY knows that his actions are, at least, unethical.

Taking account of s 5 of the Theft Act 1968, which of the below statements is correct?

A   DELACY is under a legal obligation to deal with the money in a particular way. He has breached this obligation and has therefore committed theft.

B   Ownership of the money has been transferred to DELACY's firm. Therefore, if DELACY has possession/control of the money, he cannot commit theft.

C   When BOOTH transfers the money to DELACY, he revokes any proprietary interest in the money. This would be a contractual issue between BOOTH and DELACY.

D   The property belongs to both parties. BOOTH would have to prove that DELACY did not intend to repay the money to prove theft.

First Attempt	
Second Attempt	

MCQ 8.7   DC HENDLEY is speaking to NEWALL, who is the victim of an alleged robbery. NEWALL states that BUSH approached him, pushed him over, and demanded that NEWALL hand over his iPod or he would be assaulted. When NEWALL refused, BUSH took NEWALL's iPod headphones intending to steal them but then, stood on them, (rendering them useless), and then returned them to NEWALL. BUSH ran off empty-handed.

Considering the 'intention to permanently deprive' for the purposes of theft, which of the below statements is correct?

A   BUSH must totally destroy the headphones before he would permanently deprive NEWALL of them.

B   By rendering the headphones useless, BUSH has treated the headphones as his own and permanently deprives NEWALL of them.

C   BUSH has not disposed of the headphones and does not 'permanently deprive' in these circumstances.

D   BUSH has not actually permanently deprived NEWALL of anything and as such there is no theft and therefore no robbery.

First Attempt	
Second Attempt	

MCQ 8.8   Section 4 of the Theft Act 1968 defines the term' property'.

Which of the following is correct in respect of that definition?

A   Land could not be stolen under any circumstances.

B   A tamed wild creature would not be classed as 'property'.

C A cheque could not be stolen.

D A human body would not be classed as property.

First Attempt	
Second Attempt	

Theft

Theft is probably one of the first criminal law definitions any police officer learns 'off by heart'. You *must* be able to define the offence before progressing any further.

E

EXERCISE 8.1

What is the full definition of the offence of theft contrary to s 1 of the Theft Act 1968?

A person is guilty of theft if he
↓
_____
↓
_____
↓
_____
↓
_____
↓
_____

Explanation 8.1

Your answer should look something like this:

A person is guilty of theft if he
↓
dishonestly
↓
appropriates
↓
property
↓
belonging to another
↓
with the intention of permanently depriving the other of it

See *Investigators' Manual*, para 2.1.1

Identifying the Sections of the Offence of Theft

For a trainee investigator, defining the offence of theft should be relatively straightforward. However, it is not uncommon for questions to be posed that ask about the details of the specific sections of the offence. These questions will ask you about a *section* of the Theft Act 1968 rather than tell you *what* the section is. As a consequence you need to be able to identify the different sections of the offence.

> **EXERCISE 8.2**
>
> Answer the below questions and write your answer in the space provided.
>
> **What does s 4 of the Theft Act 1968 relate to?**
>
> _____
>
> **What does s 6 of the Theft Act 1968 relate to?**
>
> _____

Explanation 8.2

When a question is phrased in this fashion it becomes harder to answer, but you should be able to do so nevertheless. If you can remember the definition of theft then remembering what a section relates to should cause you little difficulty. This is because the way in which police officers often learn to remember definitions is to break them down into lines (as we have done above). Once you break the offence into lines then the sections of the offence simply follow in the same order as the lines.

Section 1 of the Theft Act 1968 is the *whole definition*. You then simply place numbers 2, 3, and so on next to each line of your definition, as demonstrated below.

	Section
A person is guilty of theft if he	
dishonestly	2
appropriates	3
property	4
belonging to another	5
with the intention of permanently depriving the other of it	6

You should now be able to identify what each relevant section relates to.

Dishonesty (s 2)

> **EXERCISE 8.3**
>
> Examine the below comments and decide whether they are 'true' or 'false'.
>
> 1. If a person cannot be shown to have acted 'dishonestly', he/she is not guilty of theft.
>
> True / False

2. The decision as to whether or not a defendant was in fact dishonest is one for the jury or magistrates.

   True / False

3. There is a statutory definition of 'dishonesty'.

   True / False

Explanation 8.3

Comments 1 and 2 are true; comment 3 is false.

Without 'dishonesty' there can be no theft. Although this part of the offence is important there is no actual definition of what dishonesty is; rather, there is a 'negative' definition set out in s 2(1) of the Act telling you when a defendant will *not* be dishonest.

See *Investigators' Manual,* para 2.1.2

E

EXERCISE 8.4

In the below examples state whether the defendant is dishonest or not and give a short reason for your answer.

1. ORPWOOD is owed £100.00 by his employer. Without the permission of his employer but believing he has a legal right to do so, ORPWOOD takes £100.00 from his employer's petty cash box.

   Is ORPWOOD dishonest?

   _____

   Why / Why not?

   _____

   _____

   _____

2. GAFFNEY is a cinema manager who needs £30.00 to repair his car. He takes £30.00 as an advance on his salary from the cinema till. He knows that he does not have a legal right to do so, but believes that the cinema owner would consent if he knew about the circumstances.

   Is GAFFNEY dishonest?

   _____

   Why / Why not?

   _____

   _____

   _____

   _____

3. ROBERTS finds a football season ticket with HUBER's details printed in it. ROBERTS keeps and uses the season ticket even though he knows he could easily find HUBER, by taking reasonable steps.

Is ROBERTS dishonest?

_____

Why / Why not?

_____

_____

_____

_____

4. BRUNTON finds a football season ticket with TAYLOR's details printed in it. Although BRUNTON realizes that he could easily find TAYLOR and return the ticket to him, he keeps it because he believes that he has a legal right to do so.

Is BRUNTON dishonest?

_____

Why / Why not?

_____

_____

_____

_____

5. ALLEN is a shoplifter who is arrested for theft. He has £20.00 in his pocket and states that he is willing to pay for the goods he has taken.

Is ALLEN dishonest?

_____

Why / Why not?

_____

_____

_____

_____

Explanation 8.4

If you have read the *Investigators' Manual* you may have decided that examples 1, 2, and 4 will not be dishonest. This is because of the effect of s 2 of the Theft Act 1968, i.e. the defendant honestly believed they could act in a certain way.

Remember a defendant will not be dishonest if *they honestly believe in the* **LAW**:

L   Legal right

A   Appropriated with consent

W   Will not find owner

Example 3 will be dishonest because ROBERTS can easily find HUBER. Example 5 *may be* dishonest under s 2(2).

R v Ghosh [1982] QB 1053

Sometimes, s 2 of the Theft Act 1968 will not be applicable and the jury or magistrates will have to take direction from the above-stated case.

The jury or magistrates will have to ask

i.   whether, according to the ordinary standards of reasonable and honest people, what was done was 'dishonest'; *and*, if it was,

ii.   whether 'the defendant himself must have realized that what was done was dishonest' *by those standards.*

As this is an important case, the first part of the direction needs to be remembered. You might want to try and remember it this way.

G

H

O   Ordinary

S   Standards

R *v*   Reasonable

H   Honest

See *Investigators' Manual*, para 2.1.3

State the Meaning of ss 3, 4, 5, and 6 of the Theft Act 1968

You should now examine the other sections of the Act beginning with s 3, 'appropriation'.

Appropriation

EXERCISE 8.5

Using only one sentence, describe what the term 'appropriation' means to you.

Explanation 8.5

You may have said something like 'an assumption by a person of the rights of an owner' and this would follow the spirit of s 3 of the Theft Act 1968. However, the meaning of the term has been modified by a number of stated cases. In order to test your knowledge, attempt the below exercises regarding appropriation.

E

EXERCISE 8.6

In each of the below examples, state whether there has been an 'appropriation' and give your reason(s) for your decision.

1. REINER is a tourist who gives his wallet (full of unfamiliar English currency) to a taxi driver to remove the correct fare. The taxi driver helps himself to more than the amount owed.

   Is this an appropriation by the taxi driver?

   _____

   Does it matter that REINER handed the wallet over with consent? Why / Why not?

   _____

   _____

   _____

2. VALE swaps a number of price labels on goods displayed for sale in a shop.

   Is this an appropriation by VALE?

   _____

   Would it matter that VALE has no intention actually to steal the goods? Why / Why not?

   _____

   _____

   _____

3. HUNT is given an absolute gift of a valuable picture by KELSO, who retains no proprietary interest in the picture.

   Is this an appropriation by HUNT?

   _____

   Could this become a criminal matter? Why / Why not?

   _____

   _____

   _____

4. CHAPPLE buys an iPod from HEATH for £100.00. The iPod is stolen but CHAPPLE does not know this.

Is this an appropriation by CHAPPLE?

_____

Would CHAPPLE be liable for theft at this stage? Why / Why not?

_____

_____

_____

CHAPPLE finds out that the iPod is stolen but refuses to give it back.

Would CHAPPLE be liable for theft at this stage? Why / Why not?

_____

_____

_____

Explanation 8.6

For examples 1, 2, and 3, case law has illustrated that:

Consent is irrelevant to the issue of appropriation, whether or not the owner consented to that appropriation (example 1). In this case there has been an appropriation by the taxi driver (see _Lawrence v Metropolitan Police Commissioner_ [1972] AC 626).

Swapping price labels amounts to appropriation (example 2). This is so regardless of any future intention (see _DPP v Gomez_ [1993] AC 442).

Providing an absolute gift in which no proprietary interest is held can amount to appropriation (example 3). Whether this becomes a criminal matter would depend on the circumstances of the case (see _R v Hinks_ [2000] 3 WLR 1590).

In example 4, s 3(2) of the Theft Act 1968 provides that although an appropriation has taken place, CHAPPLE will not, without more evidence, attract liability for an offence of theft.

See _Investigators' Manual_, para 2.1.4

Property

EXERCISE 8.7

Examine the below statements and decide whether they are true or false.

1. There are no circumstances under which land can be stolen.

   True / False

2. The term 'property' does not include money.

   True / False

3. Intangible property cannot be stolen.

   True / False

4. The term 'property' includes human bodies.

   True / False

5. Electricity is not property for the purposes of the Theft Act 1968.

   True / False

Explanation 8.7

If you examine the *Investigators' Manual* you will see that comments 1, 2, 3, and 4 are all false. Comment 5 is true.

See *Investigators' Manual*, para 2.1.5

The definition of the term 'property' is somewhat lengthy. Rather than trying to remember what property is, try to remember what property *is not*.

Broadly speaking property is not:

W Wild plants (unless the whole plant is taken for sale or reward (s 4(3))) or wild animals (unless the animal is in the process of being reduced into captivity (s 4(4))).

H Human corpse (note that products of the body, such as urine, can be stolen and bodies can be stolen if some skill has been exercised on them).

I Information (*Oxford v Moss* (1979) 68 Cr App R 183).

L Land (although land can be stolen by (a) trustees etc. (b) someone not in possession of the land can appropriate anything severed from the land, and (c) a tenant can appropriate any fixture (s 4(2)).

E Electricity (*Low v Blease* (1975) 119 SJ 695).

Belonging to another

E

EXERCISE 8.8

Consider the below scenario and decide who the property is appropriated from, giving your reason(s).

CARROW owns a plant hire business, hiring various tools to customers from a small industrial unit.

1. LINT enters the unit and takes a chainsaw from a display.

   Who does LINT appropriate from and why?

   _____

   _____

2. CARROW hires a wallpaper stripper to BRENT, who takes it to his home. LINT takes the wallpaper stripper from BRENT.

Who does LINT appropriate from and why?

_____

_____

_____

3. CARROW hires a cement mixer to FAY. FAY takes the cement mixer to PARK's house. PARK is using the cement mixer and leaves it unattended for several minutes. During this time, LINT takes the cement mixer.

    Who does LINT appropriate from and why?

    _____

    _____

    _____

4. CARROW hires a generator to RICE. RICE takes the generator home and leaves it outside his house. CARROW passes RICE's house and, seeing the generator, he decides to take it to compel RICE to pay for it. RICE tells CARROW the generator has gone and CARROW demands a replacement generator from RICE.

    Does CARROW appropriate property belonging to another? Why / Why not?

    _____

    _____

    _____

Explanation 8.8

Under s 5 of the Theft Act 1968, property will 'belong to another' if that person has possession or control of it or has a proprietary right or interest in it.

At point 1, LINT appropriates from CARROW who is the owner of the property.

At point 2, LINT appropriates from both CARROW and BRENT.

CARROW hires the wallpaper stripper to BRENT and therefore retains ownership of it; however, BRENT has possession of it.

At point 3, LINT appropriates from CARROW, FAY, and PARK. CARROW remains the owner of the cement mixer, FAY has control of it, and PARK has possession of it.

At point 4, CARROW appropriates property from RICE (even though he is the actual owner of the generator). This is because you can steal your own property in some circumstances (see _R v Turner_ [1971] 1 WLR 901).

See _Investigators' Manual_, para 2.1.7

Intention of permanently depriving

E

EXERCISE 8.9

Write down what the intention to permanently deprive means to you.

_____

_____

_____

Explanation 8.9

This part of the definition is often expressed using terms like, 'an intention to treat property as if it is your own' or 'ignoring others' rights regarding their own property', and terms similar to these are contained in the section.

Remember there is no need to prove that the victim _is_ actually permanently deprived of the property in question for the offence to be complete, but it must be shown that this was the _intention_ of the defendant at the time he/she took the property. In many circumstances this intention will be plain, but s 6 of the Theft Act 1968 gives you further direction as to when this intention can be inferred from the conduct of the defendant.

E

EXERCISE 8.10

Consider the below scenarios and explain if there is an intention to permanently deprive, giving your reason(s) why / why not?

1. BLACK takes a valuable painting belonging to DUFF. BLACK asks for £500.00 to be paid to a charity and then he will return the painting.

   Is there an intention here? Why / Why not?

   _____

   _____

   _____

2. COTTON borrows HILL's rugby season ticket for one game but then retains it, causing HILL to miss the remaining four games of the season.

   Is there an intention here? Why / Why not?

   _____

   _____

   _____

3. HURD is unemployed and pawns his mother's engagement ring for £1,000.00 in order to obtain money for cigarettes and beer.

> Is there an intention here? Why / Why not?
>
> _____
>
> _____
>
> _____

Explanation 8.10

In all of the scenarios there is an intention to permanently deprive by virtue of s 6 of the Theft Act 1968.

Holding property 'to ransom' qualifies as an intention to treat the property as one's own to dispose of, regardless of the other's rights (scenario 1). The same can be said for scenario 2, as the borrowing becomes the equivalent of an outright taking. Both are covered under s 6(1) of the Act.

Scenario 3 would also illustrate an intention to permanently deprive but under s 6(2) of the Act. Here, there is a likelihood that HURD will be unable to meet the conditions under which he parted with the property, i.e. there is little chance that HURD will ever have the money to obtain the ring from the pawnbrokers.

See *Investigators' Manual*, para 2.1.10

Conclusion

> You should now have a good understanding of the offence of theft and its constituent parts. If you do not understand theft then you will find it difficult to understand other offences where theft is a component part, and consequently you may answer a question incorrectly.

Now that you have finished the Workbook section on 'Theft', you should attempt the 'Recall Questions' before re-reading the relevant section in the Manual and making your second attempt at the multiple-choice questions. The answers to these questions are printed in the 'Answers Section' at the rear of the Workbook.

Recall Questions

Try and answer the questions below. Do not allow yourself to continue until you have answered the questions to your satisfaction.

- What is the full definition of theft (s 1 of the Theft Act 1968)?
- What are the three circumstances (under s 2 of the Act) when a defendant *will not* be dishonest?
- What *is not* property?
- What does s 5 of the Act relate to?

- What is the ruling in *R v Ghosh*?

- When can someone steal 'land or things forming part of the land and severed from it by him/her'?

- What does the term 'belonging to another' mean?

9 | Burglary and Aggravated Burglary

Aim

The aim of this section is to provide you with knowledge of the offences of burglary and aggravated burglary.

Objectives

At the end of this section you should be able to:

1. Define the offences of burglary contrary to ss 9(1)(a) and 9(1)(b) of the Theft Act 1968.
2. Identify when a defendant has 'entered' a building.
3. State what a 'building or part of a building' means.
4. Identify when a defendant becomes a 'trespasser'.
5. List the differences between the offences of burglary in ss 9(1)(a) and 9(1)(b).
6. Define the offence of aggravated burglary contrary to s 10.
7. Demonstrate your knowledge by completing the exercises in this section.
8. Apply your knowledge to multiple-choice questions.

Introduction

There is a strong chance that multiple-choice questions on the offences of burglary and aggravated burglary will form part of your National Investigators' Examination. Therefore, your revision and understanding of this area of law are vitally important if you are to be successful.

In this section of the Workbook you will examine these offences in some depth. This will involve breaking the offences down into their component parts in order to provide you with the necessary comprehension you require. Some of these component parts are common between all the offences relating to burglary.

You may believe that your working knowledge of this subject is good as, after all, burglary is considered by many police officers to be a 'bread and butter' offence. Whatever your ability in relation to this subject is, it is advisable to make sure that you do actually understand the law and can apply it to multiple-choice questions. You can be sure that your personal experiences of burglary as a police officer will not be enough.

Multiple-choice Questions

Begin this section of the Workbook by answering the below multiple-choice questions. Mark your answer in the 'First Attempt' box. Then read and complete the exercises in the 'Burglary' section. Once you are satisfied that your knowledge is of a good standard, return to these questions and mark your answer in the 'Second Attempt' box. The answers to these questions can be found in the 'Answers Section' at the rear of the Workbook.

MCQ 9.1   DISKIN breaks into a house owned by GLENN intending to steal anything he can find of value. DISKIN's neighbour witnesses GLENN breaking into the house and calls the police. DISKIN is arrested in the lounge of GLENN's house and is later charged with an offence of burglary.

If DISKIN were to be found guilty of this offence, what is the maximum sentence of imprisonment a court could impose on him?

A   Five years' imprisonment.

B   Seven years' imprisonment.

C   Ten years' imprisonment.

D   14 years' imprisonment.

First Attempt	
Second Attempt	

MCQ 9.2   MACKEY is a drugs dealer who is having problems with PAGE, another drugs dealer. MACKEY decides to teach PAGE a lesson and breaks into PAGE's house with the intention of stealing some of PAGE's property. PAGE's wife interrupts MACKEY as he is in the process of stealing some money. MACKEY punches her in the face, breaking one of her teeth. MACKEY is later arrested for burglary.

Which of the below statements is correct?

A   As MACKEY used violence in a dwelling the offence is triable on indictment.

B   MACKEY cannot be tried on indictment for this offence, as the 'ulterior offence' he committed is triable either way.

C   This offence is triable either way.

D   An offence of burglary cannot be tried on indictment in any circumstances.

First Attempt	
Second Attempt	

MCQ 9.3   REDGRAVE believes that he has been unfairly dismissed from his job as a garage mechanic. He plans to break into his ex-employer's garage and turn on all the electrical machines over the company's two-week Christmas break, thereby causing the company's electric bill to be

extremely expensive. REDGRAVE breaks into the garage and turns on all the machines. As he is doing this he loses his temper and smashes several car windscreens in the garage. He then decides to hide one of the cars being repaired in the garage and drives off in a car, abandoning it 10 miles away.

At what point, if at all, does REDGRAVE first commit an offence of burglary?

A When he initially breaks into the garage.
B When he smashes the car windscreens in the garage.
C When he drives the car away from the garage.
D No offence of burglary is committed in these circumstances.

First Attempt	
Second Attempt	

MCQ 9.4 For the offence of burglary to be complete, it must be shown that the defendant *'entered'* a building or part of a building.

Which of the below statements is correct with regard to the law relating to such entry?

A The test for entry into a building or part of a building requires the entry to be 'effective and substantial'.
B Entry need only be shown to have been 'effective'.
C A defendant must get his/her whole body into a building to qualify as an entry.
D If a person uses an object as an extension of himself/herself, this would not constitute an entry.

First Attempt	
Second Attempt	

MCQ 9.5 HILDRED is going on holiday for two weeks and asks her friend, BURTOFT, to look after her house while she is away. HILDRED tells BURTOFT she is free to use the whole of her house at any time while she is away. BURTOFT goes to the house one day to do some household chores and while cleaning an upstairs bedroom she finds £100.00 cash. BURTOFT decides to steal the money. She then decides to look around the bedroom for anything else of value and finds and steals an antique watch. BURTOFT then sees a loft hatch in the bedroom and decides she will search the loft for anything to steal. BURTOFT enters the loft but finds nothing of value.

Which of the below statements is true?

A BURTOFT commits a burglary contrary to s 9(1)(b) when she steals the £100.00 cash from the bedroom.
B BURTOFT commits a burglary contrary to s 9(1)(b) when she steals the antique watch from the bedroom.
C BURTOFT commits a burglary contrary to s 9(1)(a) when she enters the loft.
D BURTOFT never commits burglary because at no point is she a trespasser.

First Attempt	
Second Attempt	

MCQ 9.6   Under s 9(1)(a) of the Theft Act 1968, a burglary can only be committed when a person intends to commit a 'trigger' offence mentioned in s 9(2) of the Act.

Which of the following statements is correct regarding those 'trigger' offences?

A   FLYNN breaks into a house intending to cause criminal damage; this would not be a s 9(1)(a) burglary.

B   KINZETT breaks into a house intending to steal; this would not be a s 9(1)(a) burglary.

C   PARKER breaks into a house intending to rape the female occupier; this would not be a s 9(1)(a) burglary.

D   SIMS breaks into a house intending to cause grievous bodily harm; this would not be a s 9(1)(a) burglary.

First Attempt	
Second Attempt	

MCQ 9.7   For the offence of burglary to be complete it must be shown that the defendant entered a *'building or part of a building'*.

Which of the below statements is correct with regard to the law relating to buildings?

A   A tent used as a dwelling can be a building for the purposes of burglary.

B   An unfinished house can never be a building for the purposes of burglary.

C   An industrial freezer can be a building for the purposes of burglary.

D   A houseboat can never be a building for the purposes of burglary.

First Attempt	
Second Attempt	

MCQ 9.8   WARREN and OAK decide to break into and steal from a house owned by HOLLAND. They think HOLLAND may be inside the house when they break in so they take several lengths of rope with them to tie up HOLLAND. The two get to HOLLAND's house with WARREN carrying the rope. OAK has a screwdriver with him that he uses to force a window. OAK has sharpened the end of the screwdriver to use it against HOLLAND if the need arises; WARREN does not know of OAK's intentions regarding the screwdriver. When both men enter the house it becomes apparent that HOLLAND is not at home.

Considering the offence of aggravated burglary (contrary to s 10 of the Theft Act 1968) only, which of the below is true?

A   Neither WARREN nor OAK would commit the offence because HOLLAND is not in the house.

B   WARREN and OAK commit the offence, but WARREN only commits it in relation to the rope.

C   WARREN and OAK commit the offence in relation to both the rope and the sharpened screwdriver.

D   WARREN and OAK commit the offence, but only OAK commits it in relation to the sharpened screwdriver.

First Attempt	
Second Attempt	

MCQ 9.9   COOPER plans to burgle a jeweller's shop. The shop is located in an area patrolled by security guards and has a CCTV camera placed inside it. COOPER takes a black bin liner with him to place over and incapacitate the CCTV camera. COOPER approaches the shop and sees there is a security guard standing outside. COOPER picks up a stone and hits the guard on the head, fracturing the guard's skull. He throws the stone away and then breaks into the shop, puts the bag over the CCTV camera and steals jewellery. As he is stealing from the shop, another security guard interrupts him. COOPER puts his hand in his pocket and, pointing his fingers at the guard, tells the guard he has a gun and to stay back or he will be shot. COOPER then quickly picks up several necklaces to complete his haul before escaping.

At what stage, if at all, does COOPER commit the offence of aggravated burglary?

A When he causes grievous bodily harm to the first security guard.

B When he incapacitates the camera with the black bin liner.

C When he steals the necklaces.

D COOPER does not commit the offence in these circumstances.

First Attempt	
Second Attempt	

MCQ 9.10   COHEN shares a house with his friend, DALBY. COHEN intends to break into a neighbour's house to steal. To disguise himself he picks up and wears a hooded coat belonging to DALBY. Unknown to COHEN, there is a flick-knife in the pocket of the coat. COHEN breaks into the neighbour's house by forcing the front door, but as he is stealing some jewellery he is caught and arrested.

Does COHEN commit aggravated burglary?

A No, as COHEN did not know the knife is in the pocket of the coat.

B Yes, the fact that COHEN did not know the flick-knife was in the coat pocket is irrelevant.

C No, COHEN had no intention of using the knife.

D Yes, the fact that COHEN entered the building with the knife means the offence is complete.

First Attempt	
Second Attempt	

MCQ 9.11   FRANCIS is annoyed by his next-door neighbour's constant late parties and loud music. One night, with a party in full swing, FRANCIS decides that enough is enough and arming himself with a knuckleduster he goes to his neighbour's front door. FRANCIS intends to do nothing more than demand that his neighbour turn the music down. He stands outside the house and noisily demands entry, swinging his fist with the knuckleduster on it. His

neighbour answers the door and, reckless as to whether he is a trespasser or not, FRAN-CIS drops the knuckleduster and pushes past his neighbour telling all the partygoers to go home. Once inside the house FRANCIS steals a CD player from his neighbour to stop the party.

What offence does FRANCIS commit?

A FRANCIS commits burglary (contrary to s 9(1)(a) of the Theft Act 1968).

B FRANCIS commits aggravated burglary (contrary to s 10 of the Theft Act 1968).

C FRANCIS commits theft (contrary to s 1 of the Theft Act 1968).

D FRANCIS commits burglary (contrary to s 9(1)(b) of the Theft Act 1968).

First Attempt	
Second Attempt	

Burglary, s 9(1)(a)

There are hundreds of offence definitions contained within the *Investigators' Manual*. To set yourself the task of being able to memorize and recall every single one of them 'word perfect' may be difficult to say the least. However, because the offence of burglary is a relatively common occurrence it is highly likely that in order to answer questions on the subject correctly this is one of the offence definitions that you will need to know word for word.

EXERCISE 9.1

What is the full definition of the offence of burglary contrary to s 9(1)(a) of the Theft Act 1968? (Include the offences that the defendant must intend to commit under s 9(2) of the Act.)

A person is guilty of burglary if

↓

_____

↓

_____

↓

_____

↓

_____

↓

_____

↓

_____

Explanation 9.1

Although it is unlikely that you will ever see a question in your exam that asks you purely for the definition, it is critical that you are able to recall it; you may encounter difficulties in answering burglary questions if you cannot do so.

Your answer should look something like this:

A person is guilty of burglary if

he enters

any building or part of a building

as a trespasser

with intent to

steal anything in the building or part of the building

inflict on any person therein any grievous bodily harm

or do unlawful damage to the building or anything therein

Did you get the definition right? If not, return to the *Investigators' Manual* and make sure you know the definition off by heart before proceeding.

See *Investigators' Manual*, para 2.2.1

Now that you can define the basic definition of burglary under s 9(1)(a), you should examine each part of the offence in turn. Questions on offences such as burglary will often concentrate on the individual elements of the offence in order to test your knowledge and understanding of the subject.

Entry

EXERCISE 9.2

Consider the below scenarios and decide whether an 'entry' (for the purposes of burglary) has been made by the defendant.

1. CRAVEN and HAMILTON are walking past a house when CRAVEN pushes HAMILTON. HAMILTON falls over and through an open door leading into the hall of the house.

Entry / No Entry

2. BURSELL intends to steal and leans through a kitchen window in order to grab hold of a purse on a kitchen work surface. BURSELL's legs remain outside the building when he leans through the window.

Entry / No Entry

3. HICKSON puts his hand through a porch letterbox and steals some letters lying on the floor of the porch.

Entry / No Entry

4. McKAY pushes a fishing rod through a window to try and hook a wallet from the pocket of a coat hanging on a coat hook.

Entry / No Entry

Explanation 9.2

The test for whether an entry has been made is to ask if it was 'effective' (*R v Brown* [1985] Crim LR 212).

In example 1 there has been no 'entry' by HAMILTON. This is because his actions are involuntary, i.e. CRAVEN pushed him and he accidentally fell into the house. As entry is part of the *actus reus* of burglary and the *actus reus* of an offence must be voluntary, there can be no entry in these circumstances.

Examples 2 and 3, although slightly different as to the extent that the defendant's body crosses the threshold of the building, would both qualify as an 'entry'. In *R v Brown* (above) the defendant had leant through a shop window so that the upper half of his body was inside it (as with BURSELL in example 2).

The degree that a defendant's body enters may only need to be slight (as in example 3). In this example it is only HICKSON's hand that enters the porch, but this would still be an entry as it allows him to steal letters; in other words, it is 'effective'.

Example 4 also constitutes 'entry'. A defendant can use any object as an extension of themselves (such as McKAY using the fishing rod).

See *Investigators' Manual*, para 2.2.1

Building

The first question you must ask when looking at this part of the definition is 'What is a building?'

E

EXERCISE 9.3

Examine the below comments and decide whether they are 'true' or 'false'.

1. A burglary can only be committed if the building is a dwelling.

   True / False

2. An unfinished house can be a building.

   True / False

3. A tent can be a building.

   True / False

4. An industrial freezer can be a building.

   True / False

5. An inhabited houseboat is not a building.

   True / False

6. An abandoned caravan is a building.

   True / False

Explanation 9.3

Comments 1, 3, 5, and 6 are all false. Comments 2 and 4 are true. Your Manual details some of the cases that led to the above decisions.

Part of a Building

The second question you must ask is, 'What is part of a building?'

E

EXERCISE 9.4

How can you tell a person has moved from one part of a building into another? (Write your answer below.)

_____

_____

_____

Explanation 9.4

You are probably aware that just because someone legally enters one part of a building, it does not necessarily mean that they can then legitimately access all areas/rooms of that building. As such, your answer may have said that a person would have to walk through a doorway or enter a separate room, but what if there is no 'physical' separation like a door or barrier? This does not mean that a person has not entered a separate part of a building. A good example of this concept is the case of *R v Walkington* [1979] 1 WLR 1169, where it was held that a person entered an entirely separate part of a building when they moved from a shop floor to an area behind a moveable three-sided counter. Think of this as 'crossing a line in the sand'. If the defendant moves over the line, for example by walking into an area marked by a warning sign that says 'Private' or 'Staff only', then by crossing the line they have moved from one part of a building into another.

See *Investigators' Manual*, para 2.2.2

Trespasser

You should now consider whether or not the defendant is a 'trespasser' when he/she enters the building.

E

EXERCISE 9.5

In the below examples state whether the defendant is a trespasser or not and give a short reason for your answer.

1. MAYNE intends to steal and approaches a house belonging to STEELE. MAYNE smashes a front window and climbs into the living room. MAYNE knows that he does not have permission to enter the house.

   Is MAYNE a trespasser?

   _____

   Why / Why not?

   _____

   _____

   _____

   _____

2. STARK is wandering around a large shop. He sees a sign on a wall indicating that an area in front of him is open to staff only. STARK thinks that he may not be allowed into the area but goes in anyway.

   Is STARK a trespasser?

   _____

   Why / Why not?

   _____

   _____

_____

_____

3. YALE visits his friend, JINKS. JINKS allows YALE into his house and they sit in the lounge. JINKS then leaves the room and, while he is out, YALE steals some money from a shelf above the fireplace in the lounge.

Is YALE a trespasser?

_____

Why / Why not?

_____

_____

_____

_____

4. BRACE asks TALBOT to look after her house while she goes on holiday for a week. BRACE gives TALBOT the keys to her house and tells TALBOT she can use the house while she is away. TALBOT decides to steal BRACE's DVD player while she is away and enters with that intent.

Is TALBOT a trespasser?

_____

Why / Why not?

_____

_____

_____

_____

Explanation 9.5

The 'state of mind' required for the defendant to be a trespasser is knowledge that they do not have express or implied permission to enter, or subjective recklessness as to that fact.

This should not cause too many problems when faced with the obvious circumstances such as example 1, where MAYNE is a trespasser because he knows that he does not have permission to enter the house.

Example 2 deals with the subjective recklessness side of trespass. STARK is a trespasser because he realizes that he should not go in to the area but does so anyway.

In example 3, YALE is not a trespasser. There are two reasons for this:

i.   YALE never entered the house as a trespasser, i.e. JINKS invited him into his house, but more importantly and in addition to this fact,

ii.   YALE never had any of the criminal intentions required for burglary when he entered JINKS's house (see the explanation for example 4 for the difference when this intent is present).

The fact that YALE later steals from the lounge does not make him a trespasser.

What about example 4? Although BRACE has given TALBOT permission to enter her house, TALBOT is still a trespasser. This is because BRACE has given TALBOT a 'conditional permission' to use the house and TALBOT has exceeded that permission. Ask yourself the question, 'Would BRACE have expected TALBOT to enter her house and steal?' The answer must be 'No'. Therefore TALBOT's intention to steal makes her a trespasser from the moment she enters the house. Compare this with example 3. The subtle but important difference is the intention of the defendant when entering a building or part of a building. There have been a number of cases dealing with this issue, but perhaps the best way of remembering this information is to recall a comment made by Lord Justice Scrutton, who said, 'When you invite a person into your house to use the staircase you do not invite him to slide down the banister.'

See *Investigators' Manual*, para 2.2.1

To Steal, to Inflict Grievous Bodily Harm, and to Cause Damage

To steal (as per s 1 of the Theft Act 1968), to commit grievous bodily harm (as per s 18 of the Offences Against the Person Act 1861) and to commit criminal damage (as per s 1(1) of the Criminal Damage Act 1971).

Remember that it is only an intention to commit one of these three 'trigger' offences that will constitute an offence of burglary under s 9(1)(a).

As a consequence you must also consider any possible defences to those offences, particularly 'steal' and 'damage'. For example, if a defendant enters a building as a trespasser with the intent to steal, but believes he/she has a right in law to take the property, there will be no burglary.

This is because

i.   the defendant intends to appropriate property, but
ii.   does so in the belief that he has a right in law to deprive the other person of it, therefore,
iii. there is no dishonesty and, consequently,
iv.   there is no theft, and
v.   if the theft (steal) element is missing, there can be no burglary.

See *Investigators' Manual*, para 2.2.3

Burglary, s 9(1)(b)

E

EXERCISE 9.6

What is the full definition of the offence of burglary contrary to s 9(1)(b) of the Theft Act 1968?

A person is guilty of burglary if

↓

_____

↓

_____

↓

_____

↓

_____

↓

_____

Explanation 9.6

Your answer should look something like this:

A person is guilty of burglary if
↓
having entered
↓
any building or part of a building
↓
as a trespasser
↓
he steals or attempts to steal anything in the building or that part of it
↓
or inflicts or attempts to inflict on any person therein any grievous bodily harm

Just like burglary under s 9(1)(a), this is a definition you should know 'word for word'.

E

EXERCISE 9.7

What are the differences between the offences of burglary under ss 9(1)(a) and 9(1)(b)?

_____

_____

_____

_____

_____

_____

_____

Explanation 9.7

Your answer may have included:

i.   s 9(1)(a) relates to *enter*, whereas 9(1)(b) relates to *having entered*.
ii.   s 9(1)(a) has *three* 'trigger' offences; 9(1)(b) has *two*.
iii. The offence of *damage* is *excluded* from the s 9(1)(b) definition.
iv.   s 9(1)(b) *includes attempts* to commit the two 'trigger' offences.

The law relating to 'entry', 'building or part of a building', and 'trespasser' has already been discussed and the basic principles remain the same for the offence under s 9(1)(b).

E

EXERCISE 9.8

In this exercise you will begin to use your knowledge of both burglary offences. Look at the below diagram. Our potential defendant, KHAN, is signified by a ☉ mark. Underneath the diagram you are given a set of circumstances and questions. Answer these questions as you progress through the exercise.

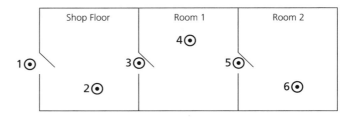

1. At point 1, KHAN is standing outside a shop. The shop has several rooms behind it but they are all part of the same building. He decides to go inside the shop and browse through the goods on display.

    Is KHAN a trespasser at this stage?

    _____

2. At point 2, KHAN is browsing through some DVDs and decides to steal them.

    Does this decision make KHAN a trespasser? (Give your reason(s).)

    _____

    _____

    _____

    If it does, does he commit burglary and under which section of the Act?

    _____

3. At point 2 again, KHAN *actually places* several DVDs into his coat pocket.

   Does this action make KHAN a trespasser? (Give your reason(s).)

   _____

   _____

   _____

   If it does, does he commit burglary and under which section of the Act?

   _____

4. KHAN sees a door marked 'Private—no customers allowed beyond this door'. He takes no notice of the sign and decides to go through it to have a look around out of curiosity. This takes place at point 3.

   As KHAN enters the door at point 3, is he a trespasser? (Give your reason(s).)

   _____

   _____

   _____

   If he is, does he commit burglary and under what section of the Act?

   _____

5. At point 4, KHAN is looking round the room when he sees a glass vase; KHAN smashes the vase out of spite.

   Does KHAN commit burglary and, if so, under what section of the Act?

   _____

6. After smashing the vase at point 4, KHAN decides to steal anything he can.

   Does this intention make KHAN guilty of burglary? (Give your reason(s).)

   _____

   _____

   _____

   If it does, under what section of the Act is it committed?

   _____

7. KHAN can see nothing of value in Room 1 and so decides he will steal anything he can find of value in Room 2. KHAN goes through the door into Room 2 (point 5).

   Does KHAN commit burglary and, if so, under what section of the Act?

   _____

> 8. At point 6, KHAN is searching for something to steal when GROVE, a shop assistant, interrupts him. KHAN pushes her to the floor and kicks her so hard that the force of the kick breaks her arm.
>
> Does KHAN commit burglary and, if so, under what section of the Act? (Give your reason(s).)
>
> _____
>
> _____
>
> _____

Explanation 9.8

1. Point 1. KHAN is not a trespasser, as he has not illegally entered any premises.

2. Point 2. KHAN has entered the shop as a legitimate customer but then decides to steal. This intention *does not* make KHAN a trespasser. **When a person enters a building or part of a building they must be a trespasser at the point of entry or they are not a trespasser at all.** Any subsequent criminal activity will not change the status of the person. At this point KHAN is not a trespasser and commits no offence of burglary.

3. Point 2. The above reasoning also applies when KHAN actually steals the DVDs. He is not a trespasser and does not commit burglary. At this stage, KHAN commits theft.

4. Point 3. KHAN is now a trespasser. The door is clearly marked and he is moving from one part of a building to another. However, because he has no criminal intent at this stage he does not commit burglary.

5. Point 4. Inside this room KHAN is a trespasser. However, once inside the room he can only become a burglar by committing one of the two 'trigger' offences under s 9(1)(b), i.e. theft or GBH. As KHAN commits criminal damage he is not a burglar at this stage.

6. Point 4. The only time a burglary under s 9(1)(a) can be committed is *at the actual entry point* to a building or part of a building, *not after entry*. KHAN has not committed a burglary at this stage.

7. Point 5. At this point KHAN becomes a burglar under s 9(1)(a). He is entering a part of a building as a trespasser with the intention to steal.

8. Point 6. KHAN commits another burglary at this point but this time under s 9(1)(b). Having entered the room as a trespasser he inflicts GBH on the shop assistant.

See *Investigators' Manual*, para 2.2.5

Aggravated Burglary

Before you study the offence of aggravated burglary, make sure that you understand the basic offences of burglary. If you do not, you will find it difficult to tell when an aggravated burglary has been committed.

E

EXERCISE 9.9

What is the full definition of the offence of aggravated burglary contrary to s 10 of the Theft Act 1968?

A person is guilty of aggravated burglary if
↓
_____
↓
_____
↓
_____
↓
_____
↓
_____
↓
_____
↓
_____

Explanation 9.9

Your answer should look something like this:

A person is guilty of aggravated burglary if
↓
he commits any burglary
↓
and at the time
↓
has with him
↓
any firearm
↓
imitation firearm
↓
weapon of offence
↓
or any explosive

The most common way of remembering the articles needed for the burglary to become aggravated is **WIFE.**

W	Weapon of offence
I	Imitation firearm
F	Firearm
E	Explosive

The definitions of firearm, imitation firearm, weapon of offence, and explosive are contained within your Manual.

The important parts of this definition are 'has with him' and 'at the time'. These elements will be considered in the next exercise.

See *Investigators' Manual*, para 2.3

E

EXERCISE 9.10

In this exercise you will use your knowledge of both burglary offences and your knowledge of aggravated burglary. Look at the below diagram. Our potential defendant, HALL, is signified by a ⊙ mark. Underneath the diagram you are given a set of circumstances and questions.

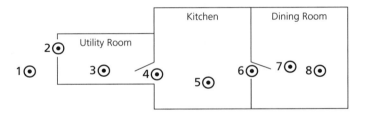

1. At point 1, HALL is standing outside a house. He intends to break in and steal from the house. HALL has a screwdriver in his possession in order to force a window into the utility room.

   At this stage, has HALL committed an offence in relation to burglary and, if so, what offence?

   _____

2. At point 2, HALL breaks into the house by forcing a window with the screwdriver.

   What type of burglary is this?

   _____

   Would it be aggravated in the circumstances? (Give your reason(s).)

   _____

   _____

   _____

3. At point 3, HALL is searching for something to steal when he hears a noise from the kitchen. He thinks it might be the occupier and quickly picks up an iron. He decides that he will use the iron to hit anybody who disturbs him.

   Is the iron a weapon of offence? (Give your reason(s).)

   _____

   _____

   _____

   Would this be an aggravated burglary? (Give your reason(s).)

   _____

   _____

   _____

4. HALL looks through the door into the kitchen and sees that a dog was making the noise. He puts the iron down and picks up several ties from a wash basket. He intends to steal from the kitchen, but wants to tie up the dog so that it does not cause him any problems during the burglary.

   Are the ties a weapon of offence? (Give your reason(s).)

   _____

   _____

   _____

5. At point 4, HALL enters the kitchen with the above intentions.

   Is this a burglary? (Give your reason(s).)

   _____

   _____

   If it is a burglary, is it aggravated? (Give your reason(s).)

   _____

   _____

   _____

6. At point 5, HALL has tied up the dog. He is now looking for something to steal when he hears a noise from the dining room. He sees an air pistol on the kitchen work surface and grabs hold of it to hurt anyone who gets in his way.

   Is the air pistol a firearm? (Give your reason(s).)

   _____

_____

_____

7. At point 6, and still in possession of the air pistol, HALL enters the dining room intending to steal.

What type of burglary is this?

_____

Is it aggravated? (Give your reason(s).)

_____

_____

_____

8. At point 7, PRIME (the occupier of the house) disturbs HALL. HALL takes out the screwdriver he used to force the window, and pointing it at PRIME he tells her to stay back or she will be stabbed.

Is the screwdriver a weapon of offence? (Give your reason(s).)

_____

_____

_____

Is this an aggravated burglary? (Give your reason(s).)

_____

_____

_____

9. At point 8, PRIME is backing away from HALL. Still pointing the screwdriver at PRIME, HALL grabs hold of some cash on the dining room table and then makes his escape.

What type of burglary is this?

_____

Is it aggravated? (Give your reason(s).)

_____

_____

_____

Explanation 9.10

1. Point 1. HALL has not committed an offence at this stage, but he has the required intent for an offence of burglary under s 9(1)(a).

2. Point 2. This is a burglary contrary to s 9(1)(a) but it is not aggravated. Although HALL has a screwdriver in his possession, the screwdriver is to facilitate entry and would not qualify as a weapon of offence.

3. Point 3. The iron is a weapon of offence. Although it is an innocent enough object in itself, HALL's intentions to use it to cause injury instantaneously change it from a household item into a weapon of offence. Absolutely anything at all, even the most innocuous of items, can immediately become a weapon of offence because of this intended use.

   At this point there is no aggravated burglary. This is because HALL has already entered the utility room and, once inside the room, he can only commit a burglary contrary to s 9(1)(b). Remember that aggravated burglary requires the **WIFE** to be with the defendant when the burglary takes place, so unless HALL actually steals, causes GBH, or attempts either, there is no offence under s 10 of the Act.

4. Point 3. The ties are not weapons of offence. This is because HALL intends to use them to incapacitate a dog and not a *person*.

5. Point 4. This is a burglary contrary to s 9(1)(a). HALL enters part of a building as a trespasser with the intention of stealing. It is not aggravated because the ties are not weapons of offence.

6. Point 5. The air pistol is a firearm by virtue of s 10(1)(a) of the Act.

7. Point 6. Once again, HALL commits a burglary contrary to s 9(1)(a). It is an aggravated burglary because *at the time of entry* he had a firearm with him.

8. Point 7. As explained above, the screwdriver changes from an instrument to force entry into an offensive weapon the moment HALL threatens PRIME with it. However, at this stage no aggravated burglary is committed because HALL only threatens PRIME; this threat would not qualify as an attempt to cause GBH.

9. Point 8. As soon as HALL steals he commits a burglary contrary to s 9(1)(b). As he *has with him* a weapon of offence (the screwdriver) when he commits the offence, this becomes an aggravated burglary.

See *Investigators' Manual*, para 2.3

Conclusion

Now that you have finished this section of the Workbook you should appreciate that although burglary may seem to be a simple offence, this is not always the case. Remember that each part of the definition of the offence must be proved in order for the offence to be complete. You should supplement the knowledge gained from this section and exercises with the continued examination of the law in the *Investigators' Manual*.

Now that you have finished this section, you should attempt the 'Recall Questions' before re-reading the relevant section in the Manual and making your second attempt at the multiple-choice questions. The answers to these questions are printed in the 'Answers Section' at the rear of the Workbook.

Recall Questions

Try and answer the questions below. Do not allow yourself to continue until you have answered the questions to your satisfaction.

- What two sections of the Theft Act 1968 define burglary?

- What section of the Theft Act 1968 defines aggravated burglary?

- What is the sentence for an offence of aggravated burglary?

- What is the sentence for an offence of burglary committed in a dwelling?

- What is the sentence for an offence of burglary committed in a shop?

- What are the three 'trigger' offences for the purposes of burglary under s 9(1)(a)?

- What are the 'trigger' offences for the purposes of burglary under s 9(1)(b)?

- State the full definition of the offence of aggravated burglary contrary to s 10.

- What does the term 'enter' mean?

- Define the full offence of burglary contrary to s 9(1)(b).

- What is a 'weapon of offence' for the purposes of aggravated burglary?

- Define the full offence of burglary contrary to s 9(1)(a).

- What is a 'firearm' for the purposes of aggravated burglary?

- Give different examples of a 'building'.

- What does the term 'trespasser' mean?

10 | Robbery and Blackmail

Aim

The aim of this section is for you to be able to identify when offences of robbery and blackmail may have been committed.

Objectives

At the end of this section you should be able to:

1. Define the offence of robbery contrary to s 8 of the Theft Act 1968.
2. Explain the law with regard to the use of force in a robbery offence.
3. Identify who can be the subject of force in a robbery offence.
4. Identify when a robbery can be committed.
5. Define the offence of blackmail contrary to s 21 of the Theft Act 1968.
6. Explain the meaning of the term 'gain and loss'.
7. Distinguish between the offence of robbery and the offence of blackmail.
8. Apply your knowledge to multiple-choice questions.

Introduction

Although you are more likely to have dealt with an offence of robbery than an offence of blackmail, it makes sense to deal with both offences at the same time. As you work through this section you will see that there are distinct similarities between the two offences and it is important that you are able to identify which offence you are dealing with.

Multiple-choice Questions

Begin this section of the Workbook by answering the below multiple-choice questions. Mark your answer in the 'First Attempt' box. Then read and complete the exercises in the 'Robbery and Blackmail' section. Once you are satisfied that your knowledge is of a good standard, return to these questions and mark your answer in the 'Second Attempt' box. The answers to these questions can be found in the 'Answers Section' at the rear of the Workbook.

MCQ 10.1   FISHER is expecting a parcel through the post. He is driving along the street where he lives when he sees the postman entering the street. FISHER stops his car, gets out and approaches the postman. FISHER asks the postman if there is a parcel for him and gives his name and address. The postman checks in his van, picks up a parcel addressed to FISHER at his address and says that there is. FISHER asks for it and the postman refuses, saying that he has to deliver it to the address stated upon it. Honestly believing he has a right in law to the parcel, FISHER demands the parcel and threatens to assault the postman, who again refuses to hand it over. FISHER then steps forward and punches the postman who drops the parcel to the pavement. FISHER picks the parcel up and walks to his car.

At what stage, if at all, does FISHER commit the offence of robbery?

A   When he demands the parcel and threatens to assault the postman.

B   When he punches the postman who drops the parcel to the pavement.

C   When FISHER picks the parcel up and walks to his car.

D   FISHER does not commit the offence in these circumstances.

First Attempt	
Second Attempt	

MCQ 10.2   BRANDON is shopping in a supermarket and is carrying a shopping basket containing her purse. DYTHAM approaches BRANDON from behind and wrenches the shopping basket out of her hand. DYTHAM runs away from BRANDON shouting, 'Don't call the police or I'll kick your head in!'

With regard to the offence of robbery, which of the below statements is correct?

A   The offence of robbery has not been committed because DYTHAM did not use force on BRANDON's person.

B   The indirect use of force against a person's property has been held to constitute an offence of robbery.

C   The offence has not been committed because there were no threats of violence made by DYTHAM at the time the property was stolen.

D   DYTHAM commits the offence of robbery but only when he threatens BRANDON with violence.

First Attempt	
Second Attempt	

MCQ 10.3   LEWIN approaches RIHAN who is sitting on a bench in a park. LEWIN says, 'Give me your wallet or I'll follow you to your house and beat you up'. RIHAN does not respond at all. LEWIN then says, 'Do you think I'm joking? Hand over your wallet or I'll beat you up right now!' RIHAN still does not respond. LEWIN produces a knife and waves it in front of RIHAN saying, 'Last chance before you get stabbed!' RIHAN does not respond. This is because RIHAN is deaf and blind and has not heard or seen any of LEWIN's threats.

When, if at all, does LEWIN commit an offence of attempted robbery?

A   When he threatens to follow RIHAN home and beat him up.

B   When he threatens to beat RIHAN up 'right now'.

C When he produces the knife and threatens to stab RIHAN.

D The offence is not committed in these circumstances.

First Attempt	
Second Attempt	

MCQ 10.4 TI FRAY has several reports on her desk. All the reports have been recorded as offences of robbery (contrary to s 8 of the Theft Act 1968). However, only one of the reports is actually an offence of robbery.

Which one of the following is actually an offence of robbery?

A ROSE was leaving work when an offender demanded her watch or he would beat her up when she left work the next day. ROSE handed over her watch.

B DREW was detained for robbery after he punched his employer and took £100.00 from his employer's pocket. DREW states that was legally entitled to the money as his employer had not paid him for a month.

C WARD (a tramp) intended to put GREY in fear of being then and there subjected to force and demanded GREY hand over her purse. GREY was not frightened or in fear but felt sorry for WARD and handed him her purse.

D PHIN (a pickpocket) was in the process of stealing a wallet from MONK while on a train when the train jolted and PHIN accidentally collided with MONK. In the process of the collision between the two, PHIN stole MONK's wallet.

First Attempt	
Second Attempt	

MCQ 10.5 GILPIN is a keen golfer and has entered a competition he believes he can win if he uses a high quality set of golf clubs. EGAN (GILPIN's friend) believes the same and approaches CORK (who works as a shop assistant in a golf shop) and asks if he can hire a set of clubs from the shop for GILPIN to use. CORK refuses. EGAN then tells CORK that he will tell CORK's employers that he has been stealing from the till if he does not allow him to use the clubs for free. CORK gives EGAN the clubs and after GILPIN wins the competition, EGAN returns them to COOK.

With regard to the offence of blackmail, which of the below statements is correct?

A EGAN does not commit the offence because 'gain' and 'loss' in blackmail only relate to money.

B The offence has not been committed because EGAN has made the demand with a view to gain for GILPIN.

C EGAN does not commit the offence because the 'gain' he has made is not permanent.

D In these circumstances, EGAN has committed the offence.

First Attempt	
Second Attempt	

MCQ 10.6   CHUNG and O'COUGHLAN work in the same office and are both up for promotion. There is only one promoted place available and CHUNG is determined to get it. CHUNG writes a letter to O'COUGHLAN stating that unless O'COUGHLAN pulls out of the promotion race, he will burn down O'COUGHLAN's house. CHUNG puts the letter into a postbox near his house but the letter gets lost in the post and O'COUGHLAN never sees it.

Is this an offence of blackmail (contrary to s 21 of the Theft Act 1968)?

A   No, because it is not possible to commit blackmail by sending the demand in the form of a letter.

B   Yes, but the permission of the DPP would be required to prosecute CHUNG.

C   No, because O'COUGHLAN never actually received the letter and does not know about CHUNG's demand.

D   Yes, and CHUNG could be sentenced to a maximum of 14 years' imprisonment for committing the offence.

First Attempt	
Second Attempt	

Robbery

As with so many other offences, you must know the definition of robbery before you move on to examine the offence in detail.

E

EXERCISE 10.1

What is the full definition of the offence of robbery contrary to s 8 of the Theft Act 1968?

A person is guilty of robbery if he

↓

_____

↓

_____

↓

_____

↓

_____

↓

_____

Explanation 10.1

Your answer should have included:

A person is guilty of robbery if he

↓

steals

↓

and immediately before or at the time of doing so

↓

and in order to do so

↓

he uses force on any person

↓

or puts or seeks to put any person in fear of being then and there subjected to force

Make sure you know this definition well before moving on to other parts of the robbery section.

Steals

If you have followed the Workbook in content order you will have completed the 'Theft' section at this stage. If you have not, then you should complete 'Theft' before you go any further. This is because the word 'steal' in the definition of robbery means 'theft' and therefore

if there is no theft then there can be no robbery.

As a consequence, if you do not understand theft then you cannot understand robbery. When you are considering whether there has been a robbery or not, you must first ask, 'Was there a theft?' You *must* consider *every* section of the theft definition when you ask that question.

EXERCISE 10.2

Answer the below scenarios and give a short reason for your answer. Remember to think theft!

1. BARKER believes his employer owes him £20.00 for petrol expenses. BARKER's employer refuses to give him the money so BARKER puts a knife to his employer's throat and demands the money. The employer hands over £20.00. BARKER honestly believes he has a right in law to the money and the demand is a proper way of reinforcing it.

   Is this a robbery?

   Yes / No

   Why / Why not?

---

2. SCOTT has wired his electricity supply to his neighbour's house. His neighbour discovers this and disconnects the wiring. SCOTT goes to his neighbour's house and once inside he puts a gun to his neighbour's head and tells him he will be shot if the electricity supply is not reconnected immediately. The neighbour reconnects the electricity supply.

   Is this a robbery?

   Yes / No

   Why / Why not?

   ---

3. NORTH is driving his car but is stationary at a set of traffic lights. HUGHES has been to a nightclub and needs to get home, but has no money for a taxi so he opens the driver's door of NORTH's car and tells NORTH to hand over the car or he will be stabbed. Fearing for his safety, NORTH jumps out of the car. HUGHES drives 5 miles to his home and abandons NORTH's car.

   Is this a robbery?

   Yes / No

   Why / Why not?

Explanation 10.2

If you were thinking 'theft' then you should have worked out that none of the above incidents would be classed as a robbery. This is because in each case there is no theft.

1. There is no dishonesty on BAKER's part because he honestly believes he has a right in law to deprive his employer of the £20.00 (see s 2(1)(a) of the Theft Act 1968).

2. There is no theft because electricity is not property for the purposes of the Theft Act 1968 (see s 4 of the Theft Act 1968).

3. There is no intention to permanently deprive and therefore no theft (see s 6 of the Theft Act 1968).

See *Investigators' Manual*, paras 2.1 to 2.1.10, and 2.4

Immediately before or at the time of doing so

EXERCISE 10.3

Think about this term and ask whether the below scenarios would fit it.

1. LIMM approaches DOWD in a street and says, 'I've been following you and I know where you live. Give me your watch or I'll be waiting for you outside your house to beat you up when you get home.'

   Is this a robbery?

   Yes / No

2. BURNS is in a shop and sees a cashier place a bag of coins near her till. BURNS grabs the bag of coins and runs out of the shop. The cashier chases BURNS into the street and shouts for help. PC HULL is near to the shop and tries to stop BURNS who punches PC HULL in the face.

   Is this a robbery?

   Yes / No

Explanation 10.3

Neither scenario would be a robbery.

1. This is a threat to use force *at a time in the future* and *at a place other than the scene*.

2. Violence has been used but this is *after* the theft.

In order to do so

EXERCISE 10.4

Consider this term when you examine the below scenario.

1. MASON is drinking at a pub with his girlfriend. FIRTH approaches MASON's girlfriend and asks her what she is doing hanging around with a loser like MASON. MASON punches FIRTH in the face and FIRTH falls to the floor. MASON kicks FIRTH a number of times while he is on the floor and FIRTH's wallet falls out of his jacket. MASON decides to steal the wallet.

   Is this a robbery?

   Yes / No

2. KING is a pickpocket. On a busy train he steals a wallet from inside PALIN's jacket. As KING is stealing the wallet he accidentally catches PALIN on the chin with the wallet.

Is this a robbery?

Yes / No

3. BREWIN sees ELLIOT steal £50.00 from a till of a pub. ELLIOT approaches BREWIN and says, 'If you tell anyone about what you just saw, I'll beat you to a pulp.'

Is this a robbery?

Yes / No

Explanation 10.4

None of the above scenarios would constitute a robbery.

1. This is not a robbery because the force was used for a reason *other than* to commit the theft. The whole point of the use or threatened use of force is to enable a theft to take place and nothing else.

2. The *accidental* application of force during a theft would not turn a theft into a robbery.

3. Once again, the threat of force is used for some other purpose than to commit theft, i.e. deterring a witness from revealing the theft.

He uses force on any person

EXERCISE 10.5

Examine the below statements and decide whether they are true or false.

1. RHONE was walking along a street holding a sports bag. WORLEY ran up behind him and pulled the bag from his hand and ran off. This is a robbery.

True / False

2. When force is used or threatened it must be towards the person from whom the theft is committed.

True / False

3. Pretending to use force on an accomplice in order to compel a third person to part with his/her property would not be a robbery.

True / False

4. WRIGHT is working behind the counter of a jeweller's shop. LIGHTFOOT walks into the shop and stands several feet away from WRIGHT, next to an expensive cut glass decanter. LIGHTFOOT shouts over to WRIGHT and says, 'Give me £100.00 or I'll smash the decanter.' This is a robbery.

True / False

Explanation 10.5

Comments 1 and 3 are true; comments 2 and 4 are false.

1. In *R v Clouden* [1987] Crim LR 56 it was held that force applied to a person's property is force applied to the person (see answer 4 for further detail). 'Force' is not defined, so whether a particular action amounts to force will be a question for the jury.

2. Force can be used or threatened on *any* person and not necessarily the person who is subject of the theft. For example, think about a security van (carrying cash belonging to a bank) being robbed. The van is stopped and an offender puts a shotgun to the head of the driver of the van. He shouts to a second security guard inside the 'vault' of the van to pass out the cash they are carrying or he will shoot the driver. The cash belongs to a bank but this does not matter. The guard inside the 'vault' is not being subjected to force or a threat of force, but the driver is and he is *any person*. This would be a robbery.

3. The use of force or a threat against an accomplice would not be classed as a robbery.

4. The force used must be on a person and not against property. This might seem contrary to point 1 above, but there is a difference between scenarios 1 and 4. In scenario 1 there is a direct physical connection between the sports bag and RHONE; this is not the case with WRIGHT.

Puts or seeks to put any person in fear of being then and there subjected to force

E

EXERCISE 10.6

Consider this term and decide whether there has been a robbery in the below scenarios, giving a short reason for your answer.

1. TELFER is walking along a street having just left a karate class. TELFER is an instructor and is highly qualified in martial arts. KOLADE approaches TELFER and points a knife at his chest, demanding his wallet. TELFER is not frightened at all and believes he could easily disarm KOLADE, but hands his wallet over to KOLADE as it has nothing of value in it.

   Is this a robbery?

   Yes / No

   Why / Why not?

   _____

   _____

   _____

2. JOYNER is in a pub when FIDDICK approaches her. FIDDICK says, 'My friend is behind you with a knife. Don't turn around or you'll be stabbed. Just hand over your bag and everything will be alright.' JOYNER believes the threat and hands her bag to FIDDICK. FIDDICK was lying to JOYNER, as there was no 'friend' standing behind her.

Is this a robbery?

Yes / No

Why / Why not?

_____

_____

_____

Does it matter what TELFER or JOYNER think or believe?

Yes / No

Why / Why not?

_____

_____

Explanation 10.6

There has been a robbery in both scenarios. This is because whether the victim is frightened or not, or whether the threats made are capable of being carried out or not, *does not matter*. What is important is the *intention* of the *offender*. If the offender actually puts or seeks to put the victim in fear of being then and there subjected to force, this part of the offence is complete.

See *Investigators' Manual*, para 2.4

Blackmail

As you worked through the offence of robbery you may well have seen where the connections to the offence of blackmail exist. For the moment we will concentrate on the offence of blackmail alone.

Complete Exercises 10.7, 10.8, and 10.9, before referring to their joint Explanation 10.9.

E

EXERCISE 10.7

Begin this part of the section by writing down what you know about the offence of blackmail.

_____

_____

_____

_____

_____

E

EXERCISE 10.8

Using the information you have written down, consider the below statements and decide whether they are true or false.

1. The offence of blackmail is all about the person making the demand actually gaining something; it has nothing to do with loss.

   True / False

2. An offence of blackmail can only be committed when the defendant makes a demand for his own benefit.

   True / False

3. There is no defence to making an unwarranted demand with menaces.

   True / False

E

EXERCISE 10.9

Using the information in the first exercise and your answers to the true/false statements, examine the below scenarios and state whether there has been an offence of blackmail or not. Give a short reason for your answer.

1. MUTCH is playing a gaming machine in a licensed club. He wins the jackpot of £250.00 that is still stored within the machine and has not yet been dispensed to him. BULL is watching this and walks up to MUTCH and tells him to walk away from the machine and not to collect the money. BULL tells MUTCH that if he does not agree then he will tell MUTCH's wife that he is having an affair with the barmaid. MUTCH is aware that BULL knows of his illicit affair and, in fear of his wife finding out, he walks away. BULL collects the winnings.

   Is an offence of blackmail committed?

   Yes / No

   Why / Why not?

   _____

   _____

   _____

   _____

2. DIXON buys a £1,000.00 television from a local electrical store owned by BUTLER. DIXON agrees to pay a monthly sum to settle the debt. There is no written agreement and there are no interest charges. DIXON falls behind with his payments and BUTLER visits him at his home. BUTLER tells DIXON that unless he

pays a substantial part of the money owed he will be barred from his shop, and he will take the matter to a small claims court and recover the money through bailiffs. BUTLER believes this is a reasonable demand in the circumstances and his threat is warranted.

Is an offence of blackmail committed?

Yes / No

Why / Why not?

_____

_____

_____

_____

Explanation 10.9

You will have probably remembered that the central element of the offence of blackmail is a 'demand with menaces', but there is more to the offence than that.

Let's break the offence down into two parts.

A person is guilty of blackmail if
↓
with a view to gain for himself or another
↓
or with intent to cause loss to another
↓
he makes an unwarranted demand with menaces

You can see from this part of the definition that statements 1 and 2 (in the true/false exercise above) are false. It also provides you with enough information to state that the first scenario (MUTCH) would constitute an offence of blackmail. This is because a demand with menaces has been made with a view to gain (on BULL's part) and an intention to cause loss (to MUTCH).

The next part of the offence is:

A demand with menaces is unwarranted unless the person making the demand does so
↓
in the belief that he has reasonable grounds for making the demand; and
↓
that the use of the menaces is a proper means of reinforcing the demand

This provides a defence and therefore statement 3 (in the true/false exercise above) is false. You will also see that in the second scenario (DIXON), the offence will not be made out. This is because the person making the demand does so believing he has reasonable grounds and the menaces are a proper means of reinforcing it.

Gain and loss

Section 34(2) of the Theft Act 1968 defines 'gain' and 'loss' for the purposes of blackmail.

> **E**
>
> **EXERCISE 10.10**
>
> Examine the below scenarios and decide whether there has been a 'gain' or 'loss' for the purposes of blackmail.
>
> 1. MILLS approaches NEAL and tells her that if she does not have sexual intercourse with him he will tell her husband that the two of them have been having an affair. This is not true, but NEAL is frightened of her husband and decides to have sexual intercourse with MILLS.
>
>   Gain?
>
>   Yes / No
>
>   Loss?
>
>   Yes / No
>
>   Why / Why not?
>
>   _____
>
>   _____
>
> 2. MACDONALD approaches JUKKA and tells her that unless she allows him to use her car for a day he will tell her employer she used to be a prostitute and get her fired.
>
>   Gain?
>
>   Yes / No
>
>   Loss?
>
>   Yes / No
>
>   Why / Why not?
>
>   _____
>
>   _____
>
> 3. HAYWOOD has borrowed a computer from DRAYCOTT. DRAYCOTT asks for the computer to be returned but, when asked, HAYWOOD tells DRAYCOTT that unless he lets him keep the computer he will spread rumours that DRAYCOTT is a paedophile. DRAYCOTT does not want his reputation to be damaged and allows HAYWOOD to keep the computer.
>
>   Gain?
>
>   Yes / No

Loss?

Yes / No

Why / Why not?

_____

_____

Explanation 10.10

1. There is no gain or loss in these circumstances. This is because the gain or loss in black-mail must be one of money or other property. Sexual favours would not fall into this category.

2. There is a gain for MACDONALD and a loss for JUKKA. A gain or loss can be temporary as well as permanent.

3. There is a gain for HAYWOOD and a loss for DRAYCOTT. This is because a 'gain' in-cludes a gain by keeping what one has (the computer) and a 'loss' includes a loss by not getting what one might get. This also applies to the MUTCH scenario above.

See *Investigators' Manual*, paras 2.5 to 2.5.1

Robbery, blackmail, or both?

EXERCISE 10.11

Go back to the beginning of the robbery part of this section and read every robbery scenario exercise, beginning at exercise 10.2, that begins with a capitalized name. Some of those scenarios will constitute offences of robbery only, some will be blackmail only, some will be both robbery and blackmail, and others will be neither. Compile a list of those surnames under the appropriate heading in the table below.

Robbery	Blackmail	Robbery and Blackmail	Neither

Explanation 10.11

Your finished list of surnames should look like the below table.

Robbery	Blackmail	Robbery and Blackmail	Neither
RHONE	SCOTT	TELFER	BARKER
	NORTH	JOYNER	BURNS
	LIMM		MASON
	BREWIN		KING
	WRIGHT		

Conclusion

Understanding the similarities and differences between robbery and blackmail is an important part of your revision and can only be accomplished by having a sound knowledge of both offences. Now that you have finished this section you should appreciate that blackmail is committed more often than you think. This is because an offence of robbery may also be an offence of blackmail, i.e. a robbery will often involve a demand with menaces. That said, it is far more likely that you would charge an offender with robbery, as not only may this be a more appropriate charge but also the offence carries a life imprisonment sentence as opposed to 14 years for blackmail.

Now that you have finished this section, you should attempt the 'Recall Questions' before re-reading the relevant section in the Manual and making your second attempt at the multiple-choice questions. The answers to these questions are printed in the 'Answers Section' at the rear of the Workbook.

Recall Questions

Try and answer the questions below. Do not allow yourself to continue until you have answered the questions to your satisfaction.

- What is the definition of robbery?

- What is the definition of blackmail?

- What is the defence in blackmail?

- Who can be subjected to force in a robbery?

- Can an accomplice in a robbery be subjected to force?

- Can you explain the meaning of the terms 'gain' and 'loss' in blackmail?

- What is the difference between the offences of robbery and blackmail?

Handling Stolen Goods

Aim

The aim of this section is to assist you to comprehend the law surrounding the offence of handling stolen goods.

Objectives

At the end of this section you should be able to:

1. Outline the offence of handling stolen goods contrary to s 22 of the Theft Act 1968.
2. Explain the term 'stolen goods' for the purposes of the offence of handling stolen goods.
3. Identify when guilty knowledge in cases of handling can be used in a trial under s 27 of the Theft Act 1968.
4. Apply your knowledge to multiple-choice questions.

Introduction

It has been said that without receivers, there would be no thieves (*R v Battams* (1979) 1 Cr App R 15). The symbiotic relationship between handler and thief is one reason why the offence of handling stolen goods is deemed to be a more serious offence than theft, with the maximum sentence for handling being set at 14 years as opposed to ten years for theft. When you are dealing with a suspect for an offence involving the theft of unrecovered property you will probably ask the suspect to tell you what he/she has done with that property. You will get a number of responses to this question and in some cases that could lead to an arrest for the offence of handling stolen goods. You may also come across the offence when you receive intelligence reports identifying premises where stolen goods are deposited or exchanged for cash. Therefore, the offence of handling stolen goods has practical as well as theoretical significance to you in your current role.

Multiple-choice Questions

Begin this section of the Workbook by answering the below multiple-choice questions. Mark your answer in the 'First Attempt' box. Then read and complete the exercises in the 'Handling Stolen Goods' section. Once you are satisfied that your knowledge is of a good standard, return to these questions and mark your answer in the 'Second Attempt' box. The answers to these questions can be found in the 'Answers Section' at the rear of the Workbook.

MCQ 11.1   HARDING offers to sell JONES a lawnmower for £30.00. JONES believes that this is a fair price to pay for the mower and buys it from HARDING in good faith. Several days later a 'Neighbourhood Watch' newsletter is delivered to JONES, which features an article on recent thefts from sheds in the area. The stolen items are all listed including serial numbers. JONES checks his lawnmower and finds it is stolen property. Instead of handing the mower to the police, he decides to get rid of it and approaches UXBRIDGE (a known 'handler') and asks him if he wants to buy the mower. UXBRIDGE offers him £20.00 and JONES accepts the money.

At what point, if at all, does JONES commit the offence of handling stolen goods (contrary to s 22 of the Theft Act 1968)?

A   When he pays HARDING £30.00 for the mower.

B   When he finds out the mower is stolen and does nothing about it.

C   When UXBRIDGE hands him the money.

D   The offence is not committed in these circumstances.

First Attempt	
Second Attempt	

MCQ 11.2   ELLIOT works on an offshore oil rig and decides to take a two-week holiday. He leaves the oil rig and is dropped off in Aberdeen (Scotland). He needs to get to his home in Manchester (England) and steals a car for that purpose. Stealing a car is an offence in Scotland. When ELLIOT arrives in Manchester he sells the car to SHEPHERD for £3,000.00 after telling SHEPHERD that he stole the car in Scotland. ELLIOT uses the £3,000.00 to buy a watch from WHITTAKER who does not know the origins of the money.

Which of the below statements correctly identifies the 'stolen goods' under s 24 of the Theft Act 1968 in this scenario?

A   None of the goods (the car, the £3,000.00, or the watch) would be classed as stolen goods at any time.

B   Only the car in the hands of ELLIOT and SHEPHERD would be classed as stolen goods.

C   The car, the £3,000.00, the watch in the hands of ELLIOT, and the car in the hands of SHEPHERD would be classed as stolen goods.

D   Only the car and the £3,000.00 in the hands of ELLIOT would be classed as stolen goods.

First Attempt	
Second Attempt	

MCQ 11.3 COWSER has been charged with an offence of handling stolen goods and has pleaded 'not guilty' to the charge. At his trial, the prosecution uses evidence admitted under s 27 of the Theft Act 1968 with regard to a two-year-old previous conviction COWSER has for an offence of theft.

What is the purpose of this evidence?

A To prove that he received, arranged, or assisted in the disposal of the stolen goods.

B To prove that he knew or believed the goods to be stolen.

C That COWSER is of 'bad character'.

D That COWSER is dishonest.

First Attempt	
Second Attempt	

MCQ 11.4 MARSH has just been charged with an offence of handling stolen goods (contrary to s 22 of the Theft Act 1968). The offence occurred yesterday. MARSH has a previous conviction for handling that was received four years ago and a conviction for theft received two years ago.

According to s 27 of the Theft Act 1968, which conviction, if any, could be used to prove MARSH knew or believed the goods from the current handling charge were stolen?

A Both of MARSH's previous convictions could be used for this purpose.

B Only the conviction for handling stolen goods.

C Only the conviction for theft.

D Neither conviction could be used.

First Attempt	
Second Attempt	

Handling Stolen Goods

> **EXERCISE 11.1**
>
> Examine the below scenario and then answer the associated questions. Give a short reason for your answer where you are asked.
>
> 1. FARRIN is a well-known handler of stolen goods. She receives a visit from one of her criminal associates, ISAACS, who has been a fruitful source of stolen goods in the past. ISAACS and FARRIN discuss the theft of a lorryload of cigarettes that ISAACS and his gang are going to steal that evening. After considerable haggling between the two, FARRIN agrees to pay ISAACS £5,000.00 when he delivers the cigarettes later on.
>
>   Does FARRIN commit the offence of handling stolen goods?
>
>   Yes / No

Why / Why not?

_____

_____

_____

2. MILLER owes PUGH £2,000.00 and has refused to pay the debt. PUGH is an accomplished burglar and breaks into an office owned by MILLER and takes a computer worth about £1,000.00 in settlement of the debt, because he believes he has a right in law to do so. PUGH takes the computer to his handler, SHARROD, and asks him if he wants to buy it. As it is PUGH who is offering the computer to him, SHARROD automatically presumes that it has been stolen during a burglary. SHARROD offers PUGH £100.00 and PUGH accepts the offer.

   Does SHARROD commit the offence of handling stolen goods?

   Yes / No

   Why / Why not?

   _____

   _____

   _____

3. Before you read the explanation of the above two scenarios, what can you remember about the offence of handling stolen goods?

   _____

   _____

   _____

   _____

   _____

   _____

Explanation 11.1

Let's begin this explanation with a look at the first few words of the definition of the offence of handling stolen goods:

A person handles stolen goods if

The first line of this definition is important. You can only handle *goods that have actually been stolen*. It is also a reminder that a thorough understanding of theft will assist you to comprehend other offences.

1. FARRIN does not commit the offence. There are no stolen goods to handle because the theft has yet to take place and you cannot handle goods that have yet to be stolen (you might have a conspiracy).

2. SHARROD does not commit the offence. PUGH has taken the goods in a belief that he has a legal right to and this affords him a defence under the Theft Act. Therefore, the goods are not stolen. It does not matter what SHARROD believes, the first part of the definition has not been satisfied (SHARROD may be guilty of an attempt).

EXERCISE 11.2

Answer the true or false questions below.

1. A person can only be guilty of handling stolen goods where they know or believe the goods are stolen at the time they do the act that constitutes handling.

   True / False

2. To be guilty of an offence of handling stolen goods the defendant must suspect that the goods are stolen.

   True / False

3. If you cannot prove that the defendant knew the goods were stolen, then it will be sufficient to prove that any reasonable person would have realised the goods were stolen.

   True / False

4. The *mens rea* required to prove handling is that the defendant knew or believed goods to be stolen.

   True / False

Explanation 11.2

The next lines of the definition of handling stolen goods are:

A person handles stolen goods if

(otherwise than in the course of stealing)

knowing or believing them to be stolen goods

he dishonestly receives the goods

or dishonestly undertakes or assists in their

retention, removal, disposal, or realization

by or for the benefit of another person

or if he arranges to do so

Comment 1 is true. If a person bought property in good faith and later found out that it was in fact stolen this would not make them guilty of handling.

Comment 2 is false. Mere suspicion, however strong, that the goods were stolen will not be enough.

Comment 3 is false. What you or I think about the circumstances in which a person obtains property does not matter. It is the mind of the defendant that is important (but there are special rules of evidence with regard to this offence).

Comment 4 is true.

See *Investigators' Manual*, paras 2.7 to 2.7.6

Stolen Goods

Section 24 of the Theft Act 1968 defines the term 'stolen goods' for the purpose of this offence. You have already seen the importance of ensuring that the goods are actually stolen, but now you must decide whether they fall within the terms of this part of the definition.

E

EXERCISE 11.3

Examine the below scenarios and decide whether the goods mentioned would be classed as stolen for the purposes of s 24 of the Act.

1. WHITE steals a diamond necklace from a jeweller's shop in Australia. The owner of the shop reports the theft to the Australian police, but WHITE manages to avoid capture for the offence and returns to his home in England. On his return to England, he takes the necklace to YEO and asks him if he wishes to buy it. YEO asks where the necklace came from and WHITE tells him how he obtained it.

   'Stolen goods'?

   Yes / No

   What is the key to deciding whether or not goods stolen in a place other than England and Wales are 'stolen goods' for the purposes of s 24?

   _____

   _____

   _____

2. LAPPER steals a laptop computer from JERRAM. LAPPER sells the laptop to his handler, GAGE, who knows that the laptop is stolen. GAGE sells the laptop to DOBSON, who has no idea that the laptop is stolen and pays GAGE a fair market price for the laptop.

   'Stolen goods' in the hands of LAPPER?

   Yes / No

   'Stolen goods' in the hands of GAGE?

   Yes / No

'Stolen goods' in the hands of DOBSON?

Yes / No

Explain your reasoning for each of the above decisions.

_____

_____

_____

_____

_____

_____

There are two occasions when 'stolen goods' will cease to be 'stolen'. What are they?

i. _____

_____

ii. _____

_____

3. TI O'BYRNE has arrested COOKE for an offence of burglary. When the officer and her colleagues searched COOKE's house, several items of property were recovered that did not belong to COOKE. In interview COOKE states that he bought them from a person he would not name, but admits that they are stolen property. TI O'BYRNE makes enquiries regarding the property and finds out the following:

   a. An antique gold watch (recovered from COOKE's living room table) was stolen in the course of a robbery.
   b. A flat-screen television (recovered in COOKE's bedroom) was stolen when a local electrical store was subject to an offence of fraud by false representation.
   c. A collection of rare coins (recovered in COOKE's kitchen) was taken from the owner who was blackmailed into parting with the coins.

   Deal with each item of property in turn. State whether the property would be 'stolen goods' and give a short reason why.

   a. _____

   _____

   b. _____

   _____

   c. _____

   _____

Explanation 11.3

1. The diamond necklace is 'stolen goods'. The rule is that if the goods are stolen outside England or Wales then they will be stolen goods if the stealing amounts to an offence *where* and *at the time* the goods were stolen.

2. The laptop is 'stolen goods' in the hands of all three people. Knowing or believing that the laptop is stolen is important when considering the offence of handling, but we are looking purely and simply at whether the property is 'stolen goods' and not at the offence as a whole. The laptop will remain 'stolen goods' until one of the following occurs:

   i. the goods are restored to the person from whom they were stolen or to other lawful possession or custody (e.g. the police); or

   ii. after that person and any other person claiming through him to have otherwise ceased as regards those goods to have any right to restitution in respect of the theft.

3. Goods are 'stolen goods' when they have been obtained as a consequence of an offence of theft, an offence of fraud (i.e. the general offence of fraud under s 1 of the Fraud Act 2006) or as a consequence of an offence of blackmail. All three items recovered from COOKE's house would fall within the definition.

This does not deal with the concept of 'stolen goods' in its entirety, as there is still the area under s 24(2)(a) and (b) to deal with. You will remember that these sections talk about goods that directly or indirectly represent the stolen goods in the hands of the thief or the handler.

E

EXERCISE 11.4

Look at the below unfolding scenario. As you examine the scenario, think about the term 'stolen goods'. A table follows the scenario and underneath the name of the person named you should state what 'stolen goods' they possess or possessed. A small section has been completed for you as an example.

1. BRAY steals a state-of-the-art computer from HART. BRAY takes the computer to TWEED who buys the computer from BRAY for £5,000.00, knowing that it has been stolen. Then,

2. BRAY contacts NIXON (a friend of his who is selling a Ford Fiesta car). BRAY boasts to NIXON about how he obtained the £5,000.00 and then offers NIXON the money in exchange for the Ford Fiesta he is selling. NIXON agrees. Then,

3. TWEED dismantles the computer. He sells half of the parts to RENSHAW for £3,000.00 and the other half to PRICE for £3,000.00. Neither RENSHAW nor PRICE knows or believes that the parts they have bought are stolen. Then,

4. NIXON uses the £5,000.00 paid for the car to buy a fitted kitchen for his house. Then,

5. TWEED uses the £6,000.00 he made from selling the computer parts to RENSHAW and PRICE to buy a Vauxhall Frontera 4 × 4 car. Then,

6. RENSHAW sells the computer parts he purchased from TWEED to POWELL for £4,000.00.

BRAY	TWEED	NIXON	RENSHAW	PRICE	POWELL
The computer The £5K from TWEED	The computer				

Explanation 11.4

Your table should have looked something like this:

BRAY	TWEED	NIXON	RENSHAW	PRICE	POWELL
The computer	The computer	The £5K from BRAY	The computer parts bought from TWEED	The computer parts bought from TWEED	The computer parts bought from RENSHAW
The £5K from TWEED	The £3K from RENSHAW	The fitted kitchen in his house			
The Ford Fiesta bought from NIXON	The £3K from PRICE				
	The Vauxhall Frontera 4 × 4				

1. The computer stolen from HART by BRAY is 'stolen goods' and remains so throughout the scenario, no matter who has possession of it or its parts and regardless of whether they knew or believed that it was stolen. This is because once goods become stolen they cannot be anything other than that unless they are returned to the owner, etc. (as per s 24(3) of the Act). Remember that just because someone has possession of stolen goods will not mean that they are a handler; the person *must know or believe* that the goods are stolen when they come into their possession. BRAY is paid £5K for the computer and this is 'stolen goods' because it represents the computer in the hands of the thief (BRAY).

2. BRAY then buys a car with the £5K. Now the car represents the computer in the hands of the thief (BRAY). The £5K paid to NIXON is 'stolen goods' because NIXON knows the origins of the money that now represents the stolen goods in the hands of the handler (NIXON).

3. As said above, the computer always remains stolen goods and that is the case for parts of the computer when it is dismantled. Thus the parts sold to RENSHAW and PRICE are 'stolen goods'. The £3K paid to TWEED by RENSHAW and the £3K paid to TWEED by PRICE are both 'stolen goods'. Both of these cash payments represent the stolen goods in the hands of the handler.

4. The fitted kitchen is 'stolen goods'; it represents the stolen goods in the hands of the handler (NIXON).

5. The Vauxhall Frontera is 'stolen goods'; it represents the stolen goods in the hands of the handler.

6. The computer parts sold to POWELL are 'stolen goods' as at 1. The £4K paid to RENSHAW by POWELL *is not* 'stolen goods'. Although the £4K represents the stolen goods it is not in the *hands of the thief or the handler*.

See *Investigators' Manual*, paras 2.7.1 to 2.7.2

Guilty Knowledge in Cases of Handling

Section 27 of the Theft Act 1968 allows the prosecution to admit evidence of the defendant's previous behaviour in support of the current charge.

E

EXERCISE 11.5

In the following examples state whether or not evidence of the defendant's previous behaviour would be admitted. ALL of the offences charged were committed in October 2008.

1. OPPITZ is charged with offences of theft and handling stolen goods. OPPITZ was convicted of handling in June 2005. Can OPPITZ's previous conviction for handling be admitted?

   Yes / No

   Why / Why not?

   _____

   _____

2. MATHAM is charged with handling stolen goods. In February 2008 he innocently bought a leather jacket that had been stolen in January 2008 and, although he was charged with handling the jacket, he was later acquitted of that offence. Can the fact that MATHAM had a stolen jacket in his possession in February 2008 be admitted?

   Yes / No

   Why / Why not?

   _____

   _____

---

3. GREATREX is charged with handling stolen goods. GREATREX was convicted of handling stolen goods in September 2002. Can this previous conviction be admitted?

Yes / No

Why / Why not?

_____

_____

Explanation 11.5

1. The previous conviction for handling cannot be used. This is because OPPITZ is charged with theft *and* handling. Section 27 can only be used when the charge against the defendant is one of *handling alone*.

2. MATHAM's previous conduct can be admitted. It does not matter whether MATHAM was innocent or not. MATHAM had, within 12 months of the offence charged, been in possession of stolen goods.

3. The previous conviction cannot be admitted. The conviction was received over five years prior to the offence charged.

Have a look at the illustration of the rule under s 27 of the Theft Act 1968 at the end of this section to assist your understanding.

See *Investigators' Manual*, para 2.7.7

Conclusion

The offence of handling stolen goods is probably one of the more difficult subjects that you will cover in the Property Offences section. Therefore, revision of this subject demands care and attention to detail. Remember that there are several key factors to consider, particularly whether the goods handled are stolen and the state of mind of the defendant at the time of the handling.

Now that you have finished this section, you should attempt the 'Recall Questions' before re-reading the relevant section in the Manual and making your second attempt at the multiple-choice questions. The answers to these questions are printed in the 'Answers Section' at the rear of the Workbook.

Recall Questions

Try and answer the below questions. Do not allow yourself to continue until you have answered the questions to your satisfaction.

- What is the definition of handling stolen goods?

- What is the *mens rea* required to prove an offence of handling stolen goods?

- What is the maximum sentence for an offence of handling stolen goods?

- The commission of which offences will make goods 'stolen goods'?

- When will 'stolen goods' cease to be 'stolen'?

- What are the relevant time periods relating to s 27 of the Theft Act?

- What types of misconduct can be admitted as evidence under s 27 of the Act?

Section 27 of the Theft Act 1968 Illustrated

Offence committed in: (EXAMPLE) **OCTOBER 2008**

Is the charge for **HANDLING ALONE?**

— YES → Involvement with stolen property from a theft occurring less than 12 months before this offence? **(OCTOBER 2007)** — YES (MATHAM) → Use s 27(3)(a)

— NO (OPPITZ) → **SECTION 27 OF THE THEFT ACT 1968 IS NOT APPLICABLE**

Conviction for theft or handling less than five years before this offence? **(OCTOBER 2003)** — YES → seven days' notice (in writing) given to the defendant? — YES → Use s 27(3)(b)

— NO → **SECTION 27 OF THE THEFT ACT 1968 IS NOT APPLICABLE**

— NO (GREATREX) → **SECTION 27 OF THE THEFT ACT 1968 IS NOT APPLICABLE**

12 | Criminal Damage

Aim

The aim of this section is to explain the law surrounding the offence of criminal damage and its associated offences.

Objectives

At the end of this section you should be able to:

1. Define the offence of simple damage contrary to s 1(1) of the Criminal Damage Act 1971.
2. Identify potential defences to the offence of criminal damage.
3. Give examples of when property has been damaged.
4. Outline the terms 'property' and 'belonging to another'.
5. Define the offence of aggravated damage contrary to s 1(2) of the Criminal Damage Act 1971.
6. State when an offence of threats to cause criminal damage contrary to s 2 of the Criminal Damage Act 1971 has been committed.
7. State when an offence of having articles with intent to destroy or damage property contrary to s 3 of the Criminal Damage Act 1971 has been committed.
8. Apply your knowledge to multiple-choice questions.

Introduction

It is reasonable to assume that you will have dealt with the offence of simple damage many times during your career. However, as you will remember from the theft section, this does not automatically mean you possess all of the relevant knowledge you require to answer criminal damage-related questions in your examination. Unlike theft, there is the more serious aggravated form of the offence to consider as well as preparatory offences. A thorough understanding of the simple offence will assist you to understand these associated crimes.

Multiple-choice Questions

Begin this section of the Workbook by answering the below multiple-choice questions. Mark your answer in the 'First Attempt' box. Then read and complete the exercises in the 'Criminal Damage' section. Once you are satisfied that your knowledge is of a good standard, return to these questions and mark your answer in the 'Second Attempt' box. The answers to these questions can be found in the 'Answers Section' at the rear of the Workbook.

MCQ 12.1   At 5.00 pm, ANSCOMBE finished work and decided to go for a drink with several work colleagues. ANSCOMBE meant to phone his wife and tell her what he was doing but as the evening passed by, he became drunk and forgot to call her. At 11.00 pm, his wife rang his mobile phone and told ANSCOMBE that she was locking him out of their house to teach him a lesson. At midnight, ANSCOMBE returned to his home and found that his front door was locked. Believing that he was outside his own house and was entitled to, ANSCOMBE forced and damaged the front door. As he opened the door he realized that it was in fact his next-door neighbour's house.

Has ANSCOMBE committed an offence under s 1 of the Criminal Damage Act 1971?

A   Yes, because he has damaged property belonging to another (although he may have a defence of lawful excuse).

B   No, because he believed that it was his property and he had a right to damage it.

C   Yes, because he was drunk he will be deemed to have acted recklessly.

D   No, as he did not actually intend to damage his neighbour's property.

First Attempt	
Second Attempt	

MCQ 12.2   The employees of 'Jukes and Sons' are on strike, but RATTLE (an employee of the company) has decided to keep working. TAYLOR (one of the strikers) is outraged by RATTLE's behaviour and visits RATTLE's house intending to intimidate him into joining the strike. TAYLOR has a revolver in his possession to accomplish this. TAYLOR speaks to RATTLE at his door but RATTLE ignores TAYLOR's threats, even when the revolver is produced, and he slams the door in TAYLOR's face. As TAYLOR walks away he sees RATTLE standing behind a window in his lounge. TAYLOR shoots at RATTLE intending to scare him with the bullet shot from the revolver. The bullet shatters the window but misses RATTLE, who remains unharmed.

Has TAYLOR committed an offence under s 1(2) of the Criminal Damage Act 1971 (aggravated damage)?

A   Yes, because had a reasonable bystander been present, they would have seen the possible risk to life.

B   No, as RATTLE was unharmed by the attack.

C   Yes, as TAYLOR intended to injure RATTLE and damage was caused as a consequence of his actions.

D   No, it was the bullet and not the damage to the window that endangered RATTLE's life.

First Attempt	
Second Attempt	

MCQ 12.3 HARRISON is dismissed from his job as a tool setter owing to an allegation of his being responsible for bullying his colleagues. He is so angry about his dismissal that he writes a letter to LINTON, the manager of the company, threatening to set fire to the factory sometime in the following week. HARRISON intends that LINTON will believe the threat and worry about it, even though he has no intention of carrying out the threat. LINTON reads the letter and believes the threat.

Has HARRISON committed an offence under s 2 of the Criminal Damage Act 1971?

A Yes, because he intended LINTON to believe that the threat would be carried out.

B No, as the threat was to set fire to the factory in the future.

C Yes, but only because LINTON believed the threat.

D No, as he had no intention of carrying out the threat.

First Attempt	
Second Attempt	

MCQ 12.4 ALINERI is a squatter and is standing outside the door of an unoccupied house he intends to squat in. ALINERI has a screwdriver in his coat pocket, and in the boot of his car (which is parked 10 metres away from the front door of the house) he has a crowbar. ALINERI intends to use both items to force the front door of the unoccupied house if the need arises.

Considering the offence under s 3 of the Criminal Damage Act 1971 only, which of the below statements is correct?

A ALINERI commits the offence, but only in relation to the screwdriver as this is the only item he has with him.

B ALINERI does not commit the offence because he only intends to use the items if the need arises.

C ALINERI commits the offence in relation to both the screwdriver and the crowbar.

D ALINERI does not commit the offence because he has not actually used either item to attempt to damage property belonging to another.

First Attempt	
Second Attempt	

MCQ 12.5 PCs GARRETT and MOLBY are dealing with TRENT who has been arrested for an offence of 'simple' criminal damage contrary to s 1(1) of the Criminal Damage Act 1971. TRENT smashed a large pane of glass at the front of a kebab shop causing damage amounting to £2,000.00. While the officers are waiting to interview TRENT a witness comes forward who states that he saw TRENT smash the window and heard him shout 'bloody foreigners' at the owners of the kebab shop as he did so. When the offence was committed there was nobody actually inside the kebab shop.

Which of the following comments is correct?

A This is criminal damage but is not racially aggravated as the words 'bloody foreigners' would not be enough to be classify this offence in that category.

B This is criminal damage but it is not racially aggravated as there was nobody in the kebab shop to hear the remark made by TRENT.

C This is racially aggravated criminal damage.

D This is criminal damage; there is no such offence as racially aggravated criminal damage.

First Attempt	
Second Attempt	

Simple Damage

E

EXERCISE 12.1

Begin this section by writing down the definition of criminal damage. If it helps, there are some similarities between the phrases used in the definition of this offence and the offence of theft, and there are clues where that information may assist you.

A person who
↓

_____
↓

_____
↓

(what is being damaged?) _____
↓

(whose is it?) _____
↓

_____
↓

_____

Explanation 12.1

Your definition should have included:

A person who
↓
without lawful excuse
↓
destroys or damages
↓
property
↓
belonging to another
↓
intending or being reckless
↓
as to whether any such property would be destroyed or damaged

You can see the similarities to the Theft Act 1968 in the above definition and indeed the two Acts were meant to have connections. However, the terms used do not mean exactly the same as those in the Theft Act 1968. In order to understand the terms you will examine each one briefly.

Lawful Excuse

E

EXERCISE 12.2

Examine the below scenario and consider the defence of 'permission' under s 5(2) of the Criminal Damage Act 1971. The storyline for the scenario is below. Read the storyline and then deal with the situation at 1. Then use the same storyline but deal with the situations at 2 and 3.

Storyline

It is 10.00 am and COOPER is asleep in bed having worked a nightshift. His next-door neighbour's house alarm activates and this wakes COOPER. The alarm rings continuously and COOPER cannot get back to sleep. This is not the first time that this has happened and COOPER is extremely annoyed about the situation.

1. COOPER has complained to his next-door neighbour (HUDSON) about the alarm activating in the past, but HUDSON has done nothing about it. Believing that he has a right in law to do so, COOPER goes outside and puts a ladder against HUDSON's house wall. He climbs the ladder and smashes the alarm box using a hammer.

   Do you think that COOPER would have a lawful excuse to commit this damage?

   Yes / No

   Why / Why not?

   _____

   _____

   _____

2. COOPER has complained to his next-door neighbour (HUDSON) about the alarm activating in the past. HUDSON has apologized and said he can understand COOPER's frustration and tells COOPER that he will get rid of the alarm. Believing that HUDSON would consent if he knew of the circumstances, COOPER goes outside and puts a ladder against HUDSON's house wall. He climbs the ladder and smashes the alarm box using a hammer.

   Do you think that COOPER would have a lawful excuse to commit this damage?

   Yes / No

   Why / Why not?

   _____

---

3. COOPER picks up his phone and rings his next-door neighbour (HUDSON) to complain. HUDSON's nephew (who is using his uncle's computer to write an essay) answers the phone. COOPER complains about the alarm and HUDSON's nephew replies that if he is so annoyed by it he should do something about it himself. COOPER thinks that he was talking to HUDSON rather than his nephew and, believing HUDSON has consented, he goes outside and puts a ladder against HUDSON's house wall. He climbs the ladder and smashes the alarm box using a hammer.

Do you think that COOPER would have a lawful excuse to commit this damage?

Yes / No

Why / Why not?

Explanation 12.2

There is a link to theft with this part of 'lawful excuse' insofar as if the defendant believes that he has the consent of the person entitled to give consent, committing damage is permissible (see s 2(1)(b) of the Theft Act 1968).

1. COOPER commits damage in this scenario and does not have a lawful excuse. Believing that you have a lawful right to damage property does not provide a defence under this section.

2. COOPER would have a lawful excuse in this scenario. This is because at the time of the damage he believes that HUDSON (the person entitled to consent) would consent if he knew of the circumstances of the damage.

3. COOPER would have a lawful excuse in this scenario. Although it is not actually HUDSON whom COOPER speaks to, he believes that the person entitled to consent to the damage (HUDSON) has given his consent.

EXERCISE 12.3

In the below exercises, consider the element of 'protection' under s 5(2) of the Criminal Damage Act 1971.

1. TRECARN is married to the deputy warden of a block of flats for the elderly. TRECARN is not happy about the state of the fire precautions in the block of flats and believes that if they are not improved, the elderly residents will be at risk and could be injured. TRECARN decides to call attention to this inadequacy by setting fire to some bedding. The police are called and TRECARN is arrested for arson.

Do you think TRECARN would have a lawful excuse to damage the property?

Yes / No

Why / Why not?

_____

_____

_____

2. Look at the above circumstances regarding TRECARN. This time TRECARN's motivation is not to protect the lives of the elderly residents, but to show that the block of flats could be seriously damaged by fire.

   Do you think TRECARN would have a lawful excuse to damage the property?

   Yes / No

   Why / Why not?

_____

_____

_____

Explanation 12.3

When you are considering the lawful excuse of protection you need to ask three questions:

   i.   Was the destruction or damage to property caused *in order to protect property*? If 'Yes' then,

   ii.   Was the property in *immediate* need of protection? If 'Yes' then,

   iii.   Were the means adopted *reasonable having regard to all the circumstances*?

1. In this scenario, TRECARN fails at the first question. The damage was caused in order to prevent harm to the elderly residents and not to protect property.

2. Even if the first question is answered 'Yes' as in this scenario, TRECARN fails at the second question, as the property was not in immediate need of protection. This scenario is similar to the case of *R v Hunt* (1978) 66 Cr App R 105.

See *Investigators' Manual*, paras 2.9.2 to 2.9.2.7

Destroys or Damages

The *Oxford English Dictionary* defines the word 'destroy' as to 'put out of existence by severe damage or attack'. There is no legal definition of the word and you should use your own common sense to tell you whether or not something has been destroyed.

The word 'damage' is, like the word 'destroy', undefined. However, case history has provided examples of when property will be 'damaged'.

EXERCISE 12.4

Look at the below statements and decide whether damage has been caused.

1. BLAKE uses a marker pen to write a biblical quotation on a concrete pillar outside the Houses of Parliament.

   Damage / Not Damage?

2. HARDMAN is a CND supporter and sprays human silhouettes on a pavement using water-soluble paint. The next rainfall will wash away the silhouettes.

   Damage / Not Damage?

3. Graffiti smeared in mud on a wall by ROE.

   Damage / Not Damage?

4. COX stuffs a blanket into a cell toilet and repeatedly flushes the toilet flooding the cell in the process.

   Damage / Not Damage?

Explanation 12.4

Examples 1 to 4 are all classed as damage. Generally, damage is something that can be perceived by the senses, i.e. you can see it. But this is a *general* rule. Please be aware that this is *not always the case* and remember that there does not necessarily have to be an economic cost to repair something for damage to be caused.

See *Investigators' Manual*, para 2.9.2.2

Property

This section is similar to the section on property for the offence of theft, but you should take care as there are some fundamental differences between the two definitions.

EXERCISE 12.5

Using the same statements from the theft (property) section of the Workbook, decide whether the below are true or false in respect of criminal damage.

1. There are no circumstances under which land can be damaged.

   True / False

2. The term 'property' does not include money.

   True / False

3. Intangible property cannot be damaged.

   True / False

4. The term 'property' includes human bodies.

   True / False

5. Electricity is not property for the purposes of the Criminal Damage Act 1971.

   True / False

Explanation 12.5

If you have read and understood this section in the *Investigators' Manual*, you will realize that statements 3, 4, and 5 are true and statements 1 and 2 are false.

1. Land cannot be stolen but it can be damaged.

2. Money can be stolen and damaged.

3. Intangible property can be stolen, but it *cannot* be damaged. To damage something, the property must be *tangible*, i.e. you can touch the property subjected to the damage.

4. You cannot steal a human body (unless it has been altered), but you can damage a human body.

5. You cannot steal or damage electricity. This goes back to point 3; electricity is *intangible*.

See *Investigators' Manual*, para 2.9.2.3

Belonging to Another

EXERCISE 12.6

Examine the below scenario and answer the questions that follow it.

Owing to escalating house prices, GRANT, DERBY, and FLOWERS decide to buy a house together to get on the property ladder. After a short while, DERBY moves out from the house because of an argument with FLOWERS. As FLOWERS and GRANT do not have enough money to buy DERBY out, they remain in the house. DERBY is living in a flat and is desperate for money and, one night when FLOWERS and GRANT are out of the house, he lets himself in with a door key. DERBY removes a fitted oven and hob from the kitchen, but in doing so damages the units and work surface.

Has DERBY committed criminal damage?

Yes / No

Why / Why not?

_____

_____

_____

Explanation 12.6

Having custody or control over something is a simple enough concept, but remember that you can damage property belonging to yourself *if* someone else has a proprietary right or interest in it. DERBY has bought the house with FLOWERS and GRANT and therefore the units and work surface belong to him. However, they also belong to FLOWERS and GRANT.

See *Investigators' Manual*, para 2.9.2.4

Aggravated Damage

E

EXERCISE 12.7

Read the below scenario and answer the questions relating to it. Although you will be able to use the information you have obtained from the simple damage section of the Workbook to help you answer the below questions, be mindful that there are significant differences between the two offences.

ROBEY owns a large firm but business is bad and, as the financial situation becomes worse, ROBEY speaks to one of his employees, SIDWELL. ROBEY tells SIDWELL that he will go bankrupt and have to close the business unless SIDWELL can help him out. ROBEY persuades SIDWELL to overload the first floor of the business premises so that the roof will give way. The plan is that the first floor and the items stored on it will fall to the ground floor and everything will be destroyed, causing millions of pounds worth of damage. ROBEY tells SIDWELL that some workers on the ground floor might die from the cave in, but it will look more like an accident if that is the case. Over a period of days SIDWELL places extremely heavy items on the first floor. However, the floor is stronger than SIDWELL believes and although a small part of the floor eventually gives way it only causes minor damage and nobody is hurt. The plan comes to light and SIDWELL is arrested. The police interview SIDWELL, who states that he has not committed criminal damage because he had a 'lawful excuse' to commit the damage: ROBEY asked him to do it (permission).

1. Would this defence be allowed?

   Yes / No

   Why / Why not?

   _____

   _____

2. Would the defence of 'protection' be allowed in response to a charge of aggravated damage?

   Yes / No

3. The actual damage caused by part of the roof caving in was minor. What effect will this have?

   _____

   _____

4. Does it make any difference that nobody was injured as a consequence of the damage?

Yes / No

Why / Why not?

_____

_____

_____

5. Imagine that SIDWELL was not involved and that the person responsible for the damage was ROBEY. What effect would this have and why?

_____

_____

_____

6. What effect would it have if the only person working in the factory was ROBEY, and therefore when the damage took place the only life endangered was his?

_____

_____

Explanation 12.7

There are several significant differences between the simple and aggravated forms of criminal damage. These should have been highlighted by your answers.

1. The defence of 'permission' under s 5(2)(a) of the Act would not be allowed. This is because the words 'without lawful excuse' in the offence of aggravated damage do not have the same effect as those in simple damage. An example of the type of 'lawful excuse' envisioned in aggravated damage might be where the defendant caused life-threatening damage, but this was in self-defence.

2. The defence of 'protection' under s 5(2)(b) would not be allowed for the same reason as in 1.

3. The fact that the actual damage caused was only minor has no bearing whatsoever on the offence.

4. The fact that nobody was injured makes no difference. When you examine aggravated circumstances surrounding criminal damage, the question is, 'What was the *potential* for life to be endangered?'

5. This would have no effect as in the aggravated form of criminal damage; the defendant can damage *his own* as well as another person's property.

6. This would affect the scenario. The offence is committed when the life of *another* is endangered. If the only life being threatened is the defendant's, then there is no aggravated offence.

One other important point to bear in mind is that it is *the damage* itself that must endanger life.

See *Investigators' Manual*, para 2.9.3

Threats to Destroy or Damage Property

E

EXERCISE 12.8

Read the below scenarios and answer the questions.

Scenario 1

BISHOP owns a house that is split into two bedsits. BISHOP occupies one bedsit and rents the other bedsit out to CARMICHAEL. Constant loud noise from CARMICHAEL's room has disturbed BISHOP's sleep. BISHOP knocks on CARMICHAEL's door and asks him to 'quieten down', but CARMICHAEL ignores the request. BISHOP pushes a note under CARMICHAEL's door that states, 'If you don't turn that music down, I will burn your flat down right now and take you with it!' BISHOP intends that CARMICHAEL believes the threat.

1. Has an offence contrary to s 2 (threats to destroy/damage property) been committed?

   Yes / No

   Why / Why not?

   _____

   _____

   _____

2. Would an offence be committed if the note said, 'The next time you wake me up with that loud music, I'll burn your flat down and take you with it!' (BISHOP intends that CARMICHAEL believes the threat.)

   Yes / No

   Why / Why not?

   _____

   _____

   _____

Scenario 2

Two friends, CASTLE and SPENCER, are standing in a public house having a drink. CASTLE has found out that SPENCER is having an affair with his wife and warns him to stay away from her. SPENCER just laughs and denies the affair. CASTLE gets upset and states to SPENCER that he is going to go outside to the car park to damage SPENCER's car, intending SPENCER to believe the threat. Unknown to CASTLE, SPENCER walked to the pub and had sold his car yesterday so the car cannot be damaged.

Has an offence contrary to s 2 (threats to destroy/damage property) been committed?

Yes / No

Why / Why not?

_____

_____

_____

Scenario 3

CLIFTON and ROBERTS are neighbours and have been having problems related to parking for years. CLIFTON regularly leaves his car parked across ROBERTS's driveway to cause him annoyance. CLIFTON parks his car across ROBERTS's drive when ROBERTS is expecting visitors. ROBERTS sees this and comes out and states to CLIFTON that if CLIFTON does not move his car he will tip paint stripper on it. CLIFTON does not believe the threat from ROBERTS.

Has an offence contrary to s 2 (threats to destroy/damage property) been committed?

Yes / No

Why / Why not?

_____

_____

_____

Explanation 12.8

Scenario 1

1. An offence has been committed by BISHOP. This is because BISHOP has made a threat, intending that CARMICHAEL would fear that it would be carried out, to destroy or damage his own property in a way which he knows is likely to endanger the life of CARMICHAEL.
   You will see in the following scenarios that the crux of this offence is the *intention* of the person making the threat. If they make it *intending the recipient to believe it*, then the offence is committed.

2. As above. It does not matter that the threat to cause the damage is one that may be carried out in the future.

Scenario 2

An offence has been committed. Once again, it is the intention of the defendant that is important. It does not matter that the commission of the damage threatened is impossible.

Scenario 3

An offence has been committed. It does not matter that the victim does not believe the threat.

See *Investigators' Manual*, para 2.9.5

Having Articles with Intent to Destroy or Damage Property

E

EXERCISE 12.9

Examine the following scenario and provide answers to the questions that follow it.

TUIBA and BRADBURN run a carpet fitting business together. The two have an argument over how their business should be operated, resulting in the partnership being dissolved. Both men form their own respective businesses fitting carpets, with TUIBA forming a new partnership with LAKER. One afternoon, TUIBA and LAKER are driving to a warehouse when they see BRADBURN's car parked outside a leisure centre. TUIBA decides that he will get revenge against BRADBURN by damaging BRADBURN's car. TUIBA has a knife that he uses for fitting carpets in his jacket pocket and he intends to use this to scratch the paintwork of BRADBURN's car. He also has a hammer in the boot of the car he is driving and intends to ask LAKER to use this to smash the windscreen of BRADBURN's car.

1. Does TUIBA commit the offence under s 3 of the Criminal Damage Act 1971?

   Yes / No

   Explain why / why not in relation to the knife and the hammer.

   _____

   _____

   _____

   _____

2. What is the 'Road Policing' connection to this offence?

   _____

3. Would this situation change if TUIBA had put a hammer in his car boot, intending to damage BRADBURN's car with it if he saw BRADBURN's car while he was driving around?

   Yes / No

   Justify your answer.

   _____

   _____

Explanation 12.9

1. TUIBA commits the offence. This is because the knife and hammer are in his *custody or control* and he *intends* to use (in the case of the knife) and cause (in the case of the hammer) them to damage BRADBURN's property.

2. '**Use** it or **cause** or **permit**.'

3. It would not change. This is another offence that is all about the *intention* of the defendant. A conditional intent, for example, to use an item if the need arose would be enough.

Remember that this is custody or control and not possession.

See Investigators' Manual, para 2.9.6

Conclusion

As you worked through this section of the Workbook, you will have been reminded that 'simple' offences do not necessarily live up to their names. You should possess a solid understanding of the four offences discussed and you should be able to identify when and which offences have been committed using your knowledge of the specific terms examined.

Now that you have finished this section, you should attempt the 'Recall Questions' before re-reading the relevant section in the Manual and making your second attempt at the multiple-choice questions. The answers to these questions are printed in the 'Answers Section' at the rear of the Workbook.

Recall Questions

Try and answer the questions below. Do not allow yourself to continue until you have answered the questions to your satisfaction.

- What is the definition of 'simple' damage?

- Explain the term 'property' for the purposes of criminal damage.

- Give four examples of damage.

- What are the two defences to damage under 'lawful excuse'?

- Explain both of them.

- What is the difference between 'simple' damage and 'aggravated' damage?

- What is the central element of the offences under ss 2 and 3 of the Act?

Assaults, Drugs, Firearms, and Defences

13 | Homicide

Aim

The aim of this section is to supply you with an insight into the offences of murder and manslaughter.

Objectives

At the end of this section you should be able to:

1. Define the offence of murder.
2. Outline the circumstances in which one of the 'special defences' to murder could be advanced.
3. Distinguish between offences of voluntary and involuntary manslaughter.
4. Describe the different types of manslaughter.

Introduction

Homicide is the most serious violent crime. Although it only accounts for a small percentage of all recorded violent crime it has a major impact on policing across the country and you will be aware of the requirements that investigating even the simplest of these offences makes of the police. As there is a strong chance that you may be involved in the investigation of one or more of these offences during your career it is essential that you know the law with regard to the offence you are investigating. Thankfully these offences are rare (in terms of crime statistics), but just because they are not as commonplace as offences of burglary or criminal damage does not mean they will not be questioned in your examination.

Multiple-choice Questions

Begin this section of the Workbook by answering the below multiple-choice questions. Mark your answer in the 'First Attempt' box. Then read and complete the exercises in the 'Homicide' section. Once you are satisfied that your knowledge is of a good standard, return to these questions and mark your answer in the 'Second Attempt' box. The answers to these questions can be found in the 'Answers Section' at the rear of the Workbook.

MCQ 13.1 Adrian MILLER lives with his wife Joan who is eight months' pregnant by Adrian. They have a volatile relationship and one night during an argument Adrian stabs Joan in her side with a kitchen knife. When Adrian stabbed Joan he intended to cause her grievous bodily harm; he accomplishes his aim but in the process he also injures the unborn foetus in Joan's womb. Joan is taken to hospital suffering from severe shock and a deep wound to her side. The shock causes her to go into labour and after 12 hours the baby is born. The baby has a separate existence from the mother (Joan) but dies six hours after being born as a result of the knife injury received whilst in the womb.

Which of the below statements is correct with regards to the criminal liability of Adrian MILLER?

A He is guilty of the murder of the baby, as he intended to commit grievous bodily harm to Joan and the baby died as a result of his actions.

B He is guilty of the manslaughter of the baby, as he did not intend to kill Joan when he attacked her, only cause her grievous bodily harm.

C He has no criminal liability for murder or manslaughter in these circumstances.

D He would be guilty of the murder of the baby, owing to the doctrine of transferred malice.

First Attempt	
Second Attempt	

MCQ 13.2 PLANT is attacked and seriously injured by HARPER. Four years after the attack, PLANT dies as a direct consequence of the injuries she received during the attack.

If a person dies more than three years after receiving their injury, whose consent is required before bringing a prosecution?

A The consent of the Director of Public Prosecutions is required.

B The consent of the Home Secretary is required.

C The consent of either the Attorney General or Solicitor General is required.

D The consent of the European Court of Justice is required.

First Attempt	
Second Attempt	

MCQ 13.3 Andrew and Diane TAYLOR (husband and wife) are going through a bad time in their relationship because Diane keeps accusing Andrew of having an affair. Her accusations are unfounded. Andrew is working hard trying to set up a new business and one night he arrives home late, having just won a large contract. Diane accuses him of arriving late because he was meeting his lover. This accusation is the 'last straw' for Andrew and, suddenly losing all self-control, he picks up a nearby stainless steel rolling pin and hits Diane across the head with it, intending to kill her. Although Diane's injuries are substantial she survives the attack.

Which of the below statements is correct?

A Andrew TAYLOR would be guilty of the attempted murder of his wife as his intention was to kill her.

B Andrew TAYLOR would be guilty of the attempted murder of his wife, but could use the defence of provocation.

C Andrew TAYLOR would be guilty of the attempted murder of his wife, but in the circumstances he could raise the defence of provocation and this would reduce the offence to one of a s 18 wounding.

D Andrew TAYLOR would be guilty of the attempted murder of his wife, but could use the defence of provocation with the permission of the Director of Public Prosecutions.

First Attempt	
Second Attempt	

MCQ 13.4 CLARKE and SUMPTER are chatting in CLARKE's house. They are very good friends and they are not drunk. CLARKE goes upstairs and brings down his father's army pistol to show to SUMPTER. He points the gun at SUMPTER who is not at all scared by this action, as CLARKE is his friend. When CLARKE points the gun at SUMPTER he has no intention to cause him to apprehend the immediate and unlawful use of violence; he is not even reckless to the fact. CLARKE pulls the trigger believing that it will not fire, but there is a 'live' round in the chamber and the gun goes off, killing SUMPTER.

Considering the offence of manslaughter by unlawful act only (and that the only possible unlawful act in these circumstances is one of assault), which of the below statements is correct?

A CLARKE is guilty of manslaughter by unlawful act and could be sentenced to life imprisonment for this offence.

B CLARKE is guilty of manslaughter by unlawful act because he had no intention to kill SUMPTER or to cause him grievous bodily harm.

C CLARKE is guilty of manslaughter by unlawful act for which there is a mandatory 10-year prison sentence.

D CLARKE is not guilty of the offence because he does not have the required *mens rea* for an offence of assault.

First Attempt	
Second Attempt	

MCQ 13.5 The Corporate Manslaughter and Corporate Homicide Act 2007 came into force on 6 April 2008 and deals with incidents where death results from an organizational failure.

Which of the following comments is correct with regard to this legislation?

A It would apply to a death in custody, such as a detained person dying in a custody block.

B The offence is punishable by a maximum sentence of ten years' imprisonment.

C Proceedings for the offence cannot be instituted without the permission of the Director of Public Prosecutions.

D There are no exceptions to the relevant duty of care obligation.

First Attempt	
Second Attempt	

Murder

E

> **EXERCISE 13.1**
>
> Write down anything that you can recall about the definition of murder under common law.
>
> _____
>
> _____
>
> _____
>
> _____

Explanation 13.1

Your answer should have included the following elements:

Murder is committed when a person

↓

unlawfully kills

↓

another human being

↓

under the Queen's Peace

↓

with malice aforethought

Case Study

Read the below case study. You will use the information presented to you to complete exercises in this section of the Workbook.

RAY is 26 years old and works on a fish counter in a large department store. His common-law wife, QUIRK, works at the same store on the checkout tills and is seven months pregnant. RAY is at work when he accidentally overhears two colleagues talking about QUIRK having an affair with HUGHES, who is RAY's supervisor. RAY had suspected that the two were having an affair for some time but had never had proof. Having heard this, he decides that QUIRK is carrying HUGHES's baby and not his. He listens to the conversation and hears that QUIRK and HUGHES had been seen kissing each other in a nearby pub called 'The Fox'. RAY decides that he will catch QUIRK and HUGHES at the pub, kill them both and in the process kill the unborn child.

The next day, RAY contacts a criminal associate and obtains a revolver to commit the crime.

Several days later, QUIRK tells RAY that she is going out for a drink with some friends and will not be back until the early hours of the morning. RAY pretends that he is not bothered but an hour after QUIRK has left, he loads the revolver and drives to 'The Fox' pub intending to kill QUIRK and HUGHES if he finds them together. RAY runs into the pub and sees QUIRK and HUGHES sitting together in a small alcove. He walks up to the couple and pointing the revolver at HUGHES says, 'I hope she was to die for because that's exactly what you're going to do!' RAY shoots HUGHES in the head, killing him instantly. He points the revolver at QUIRK's stomach and she tries to move away as RAY pulls the trigger. QUIRK is shot in her left side causing her serious injury but not, as RAY had planned, her death. RAY sits down at the table and shouts out, 'Call the police, I've done what I have to!' The police arrive and RAY is arrested.

QUIRK is rushed to hospital and although her injuries are serious, they are not life threatening. However, the trauma causes QUIRK to go into labour and although the baby is born alive it dies several hours later. The cause of the death of the baby is directly connected to RAY's attack on QUIRK.

A murder incident room is set up and DCs HEXTALL and FARRELL are seconded to the enquiry. This is the first time either officer has been part of a murder investigation and after the first briefing they are driving to see a possible witness. During the journey they discuss the offence and the circumstances of the incident.

E

EXERCISE 13.2

The officers make a number of comments during their conversation. Answer the below questions about those comments and provide reasons for your answers where appropriate.

1. DC HEXTALL says, 'If RAY is found guilty of this he'll definitely get life.'

   Is DC HEXTALL right?

   Yes / No

   Does a judge have any discretion regarding the sentence for an offence of murder?

   Yes / No

2. DC FARRELL says, 'Why did they bother saying ''unlawfully kills'', surely all killing is ''unlawful''?'

   What does the term 'unlawfully kills' actually mean?

Give an example of when killing someone might be 'lawful'.

3. DC HEXTALL says, 'He'll get done for the murder of HUGHES, the murder of the baby, and the attempted murder of QUIRK.'

   Is DC HEXTALL right?

   Yes / No

   What is the required *mens rea* for the offence of murder?

   What is the required *mens rea* for an offence of attempted murder?

4. At what point would QUIRK's baby become 'another human being'?

5. RAY did not shoot the baby; he shot QUIRK. Why could RAY be prosecuted for the murder of QUIRK's baby?

   Would this change if RAY attacked QUIRK intending to cause her grievous bodily harm?

   Yes / No

   Why / Why not?

6. DC FARRELL says, 'Yes, he'll get done for murder but only if we can prove that it was premeditated.'

   Does this offence require premeditation?

   Yes / No

Explanation 13.2

1. DC HEXTALL is right. The offence of murder is punishable with a life sentence. A judge has no option but to sentence a defendant to life imprisonment if found guilty as this is a mandatory sentence (the sentence for manslaughter is also life, except that a judge has discretion where sentencing is concerned).

2. The term 'unlawful killing' means causing the death of an individual without justification and includes situations where someone has failed to act after creating a situation of danger. An example of a 'lawful' killing could be when a police officer uses lethal force to protect life or when a person acts in self-defence.

3. DC HEXTALL is right. Remember that the *mens rea* for murder is the intention to kill *or* the intention to cause grievous bodily harm. This changes for the offence of attempted murder when the required *mens rea* will be an intention to kill *only*.

4. Trainee Investigators often worry about this point, but your Manual is clear and states that 'another human being' includes a baby who has been born alive and has an existence independent of its mother. If it helps, there is no need for the umbilical cord to have been cut, but the baby must have been totally expelled from the mother's womb.

5. If a person injures a baby (as RAY has done) while it is in the mother's womb and it subsequently dies from those injuries after being born, an appropriate charge may be murder. Circumstances would change if RAY attacked QUIRK intending to cause her grievous bodily harm. If the baby died as a consequence of such an attack it may support a charge of manslaughter.

6. Premeditation is *not required* for this offence.

See *Investigators' Manual*, paras 3.1.2 to 3.1.2.2

Special Defences

E

EXERCISE 13.3

There are three 'special defences' available to a charge of murder. What are they?

1. _____

2. _____

3. _____

Explanation 13.3

Your answer should have included:

1. Diminished responsibility.

2. Provocation.

3. Suicide pact.

There are a host of general defences to a criminal charge, such as insanity, intoxication, or mistake. What makes these defences *special* is the fact that they can only be used in defence to a charge of *murder* and *murder alone*. If one of these defences is used successfully it allows a conviction for *voluntary manslaughter* as opposed to murder.

What follows is an outline of these special defences using a two-question approach to consider the issue.

Diminished responsibility

Ask yourself these questions:

1. Was the defendant suffering from an abnormality of the mind?

2. Did it substantially impair his/her mental responsibility for his/her acts?

Provocation

Ask yourself these questions:

1. Was the defendant provoked by things said, done, or a combination of both?

2. Would a 'reasonable man' have suddenly lost self-control at the time of killing as a result of the provocation?

Suicide pact

Ask yourself these questions:

1. Was there a suicide pact (i.e. an agreement to kill each other)?

2. Did the defendant have the settled intention of dying at the time the killing took place?

EXERCISE 13.4

Let's return to DCs HEXTALL and FARRELL and the case study. Their conversation continues—answer the questions regarding their conversation.

DC HEXTALL says, 'Of course RAY will probably come up with some defence to get him off.'

Using the two-question approach, do you think that RAY could use one or more of the special defences in answer to:

A charge of murder with regard to HUGHES?

Yes / No

If 'Yes', what special defence and why, and if 'No', why not?

_____

_____

_____

A charge of murder with regard to QUIRK's baby?

Yes / No

If 'Yes', what special defence and why, and if 'No', why not?

_____

_____

_____

A charge of attempted murder with regard to QUIRK?

Yes / No

If 'Yes', what special defence and why, and if 'No', why not?

_____

_____

_____

Explanation 13.4

The special defence of a suicide pact is obviously not available, so you are left with diminished responsibility and provocation. At no stage in the case study has it been mentioned that RAY was suffering from an abnormality of the mind that substantially impaired his mental responsibility; therefore, that defence would not be available to any of the charges. Provocation may have caused you to think a little more about the circumstances. The murder of HUGHES and QUIRK's baby and the attempted murder of QUIRK were brought about by RAY's reaction to the news that QUIRK was having an affair with HUGHES. This could possibly form the basis for provocation as it answers the first question positively. However, RAY spent several days planning the attack (e.g. the purchase of the revolver), so that the attack could never be said to be a 'sudden' reaction to a set of circumstances and the defence would therefore fail. In addition, remember that the defences would *never* be available to the charge of attempted murder of QUIRK; she is not dead.

If we made some changes to the circumstances of the case study, provocation could be raised. For example, if HUGHES were standing near to RAY when RAY overheard the conversation about the affair and RAY, in a fit of rage, picked up a knife and stabbed HUGHES to death, the defence may be available because of the sudden loss of self-control.

It must be stressed that this is a basic approach to special defences and you should refer to your Manual for a full explanation.

See *Investigators' Manual*, paras 3.1.3 to 3.1.3.3

Manslaughter

At this stage of the Workbook you have examined murder and voluntary manslaughter. The final category in the Homicide section is *involuntary manslaughter*.

The critical difference between the offences of murder and voluntary manslaughter and the offence of involuntary manslaughter is that the later requires *no* mens rea *to kill or cause grievous bodily harm*.

E

EXERCISE 13.5

There are three categories of involuntary manslaughter examined in your Manual. What are they?

1. _____

2. _____

3. _____

Explanation 13.5

You may have mentioned:

1. Manslaughter by unlawful act.

2. Manslaughter by gross negligence.

3. Corporate manslaughter.

Manslaughter by unlawful act

E

EXERCISE 13.6

Examine the below scenarios and decide if the person concerned has committed an offence of manslaughter by unlawful act and provide a short reason for your answer.

1. PARKS has an argument with MOORE. The argument becomes heated and PARKS deliberately punches MOORE, intending to cause him a serious injury. MOORE falls over and hits his head on a kerbstone. MOORE receives serious head injuries and dies as a result.

   Would this constitute manslaughter by unlawful act?

   Why/Why not?

   _____

   _____

   _____

   _____

---

2. HUDSON is sacked from his job as a train driver. To get revenge against his employer he decides to cause damage to some signalling and safety equipment. As a direct consequence of his actions, a goods train is derailed and the driver of the train is killed.

   Would this constitute manslaughter by unlawful act?

   Why / Why not?

   _____

   _____

   _____

   _____

3. FISHER steals a warning sign indicating that a footbridge is weak and should not be used. ACFORD crosses the bridge, which collapses and ACFORD falls to her death.

   Would this constitute manslaughter by unlawful act?

   Why / Why not?

   _____

   _____

   _____

   _____

When you are considering whether this offence has been committed or not you must ask three questions:

1. Has an inherently unlawful act been committed?
   (Do not limit yourself to offences where physical harm is a natural consequence. Theft and criminal damage are inherently unlawful acts.)
2. Would the general public consider that the consequences of this act involve a risk of someone being harmed?
   (There must be a risk of harm and that risk is judged objectively. An objective judgement takes no account of what the individual who carried out the act thought; that is irrelevant. What is relevant is what a group of onlookers (the jury?) would think.)
3. Did the defendant have the required *mens rea* for the unlawful act?
   (All you are concerned with is if the defendant had the *mens rea* for the original unlawful act, nothing more.)

You might want to try and remember these questions in the below format:

R Risk of harm (objective)?

U Unlawful act (inherently)?

M *Mens rea* for the act?

In light of this information you should return to the above scenarios and ensure that your understanding of the subject is correct.

Explanation 13.6

In all three scenarios the offence has been committed. Putting the three questions to each scenario and using the acronym would lead you to the below:

1. (**R**) Risk of harm (objective)? Yes, it seems obvious that all the acts involve a risk of someone being harmed.

2. (**U**) Unlawful act (inherent)? Yes, assault/criminal damage/theft.

3. (**M**) *Mens rea* for the act? Yes, in all three cases.

Manslaughter by gross negligence

The title of this offence tells you a great deal about it. Where an individual has died due to the *gross negligence* of another, there may be criminal liability. A good example of this offence was *R v Adomako* [1995] 1 AC 171, where an anaesthetist had failed to notice (for six minutes) that a patient's oxygen supply had become disconnected from a ventilator during an operation. As a result, the patient suffered a cardiac arrest and died.

Corporate manslaughter

The ability of a company to commit an offence of manslaughter arises from the fact that companies have their own legal identity and can be prosecuted for offences. Historically, the problem in prosecuting companies for such offences was that it was extremely difficult to find the 'directing or controlling mind', particularly when prosecutions were attempted against large corporations, e.g. prosecutions arising from the *Herald of Free Enterprise* disaster (a prosecution against P & O Ferries) failed. However, on 6 April 2008 the Corporate Manslaughter and Corporate Homicide Act 2007 came into force. This effectively provides that where an organization has a 'duty of care' towards a person and the organization is responsible for the death of a person because a grossly negligent breach of the duty of care, the organization is criminally responsible. You should note that although the Act contains provisions relating to deaths in custody, these are unlikely to be enacted for at least three years. Punishment is by way of fine. As the Act is so new, there are no court decisions in respect of its implementation yet.

You might find it easier to remember the basic requirements of the offence by using the below acronym:

A	A duty of care was owed
B	Breached that duty
C	Criminal punishment is deserved because
D	Death was caused

See *Investigators' Manual*, paras 3.1.4 to 3.1.4.3

Conclusion

You should now possess a good knowledge of the offences of murder and manslaughter and you should be able to differentiate between the types of offences and liability that can possibly occur when an individual dies. If you are still unsure, you might want to examine the homicide flowchart that takes you through the offences.

Once you have examined the flowchart, you should attempt the 'Recall Questions' before re-reading the relevant section in the Manual and making your second attempt at the multiple-choice questions. The answers to these questions are printed in the 'Answers Section' at the rear of the Workbook.

Recall Questions

Try and answer the questions below. Do not allow yourself to continue until you have answered the questions to your satisfaction.

- What is the sentence for murder/manslaughter?
- What is the definition of the offence of murder under common law?
- What does 'the Queen's Peace' mean?
- What is the *mens rea* for murder and attempted murder?
- What happens if a victim of an attack dies more than three years after the attack?
- What are the 'special defences' relating to murder?
- What are the questions you must ask when considering those 'special defences'?
- What is the difference between voluntary and involuntary manslaughter?
- What are the three questions you should ask when considering an offence of manslaughter by unlawful act?
- What is the acronym for manslaughter by unlawful act?
- What is gross negligent manslaughter all about?
- What are the three questions you should ask when considering an offence of corporate manslaughter?
- What is the acronym for corporate manslaughter?

Homicide Flowchart

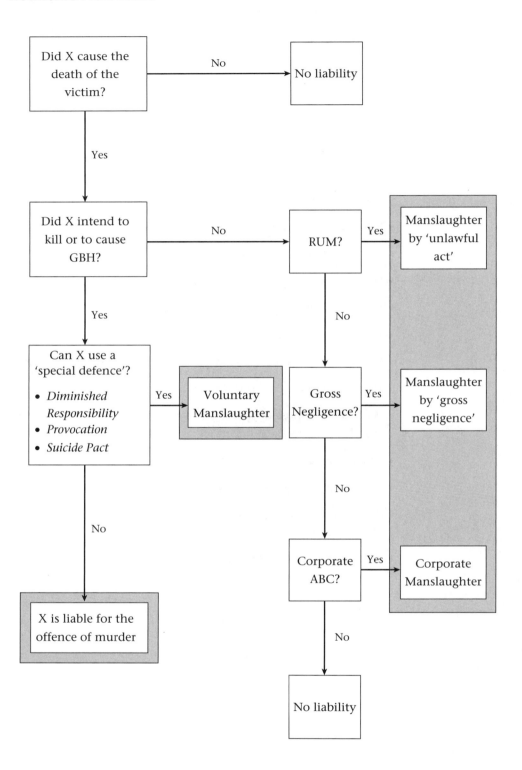

14 | Offences Against the Person

Aim

The aim of this section is to amplify your current knowledge surrounding offences of assault.

Objectives

At the end of this section you should be able to:

1. Define the term 'assault'.
2. Explain the terms within the definition of assault.
3. Identify when the defences of 'consent' and 'lawful chastisement' may be used.
4. Define the offences under ss 47, 20, and 18 of the Offences Against the Person Act 1861.
5. Give examples of the injuries that will amount to 'actual bodily harm' and 'grievous bodily harm'.
6. Interpret the terminology of the Offences Against the Person Act 1861.
7. Apply your knowledge to multiple-choice questions.

Introduction

Assaults will form a significant part of your workload as a detective and it is more or less inevitable that you will be involved in the investigation of offences recorded as s 47, 20, or 18 assaults (if you have not been involved in these investigations already). Therefore, it is necessary that you are familiar with the law surrounding these offences. Concentrating on and understanding the basic terminology of the offence of assault will achieve this. As you will discover, the language you feel familiar and secure with is not all it appears to be.

Multiple-choice Questions

Begin this section of the Workbook by answering the below multiple-choice questions. Mark your answer in the 'First Attempt' box. Then read and complete the exercises in the 'Offences Against the Person' section. Once you are satisfied that your knowledge is of a good standard, return to these questions and mark your answer in the 'Second Attempt' box. The answers to these questions can be found in the 'Answers Section' at the rear of the Workbook.

MCQ 14.1 ABBOTT and KENNA are next-door neighbours, but do not get on as they share a driveway and are always in dispute about car parking. One afternoon ABBOTT parks his car, leaving a small part of it on KENNA's side of the driveway. KENNA comes out of his house and begins a heated argument with ABBOTT about his parking. Another neighbour calls the police and PC RAYSON arrives to sort the incident out. While the officer is dealing with the two men they calm down. The neighbour who called the police attracts the attention of PC RAYSON and while the officer speaks to the neighbour, ABBOTT whispers in KENNA's ear, 'I've had enough of you, you tosser. You're lucky this copper's here because if he wasn't I'd chin you.'

Does ABBOTT commit an assault in these circumstances?

A No, an assault has not been committed because the words used by ABBOTT make this a hypothetical threat.

B Yes, this would be an assault as the words used imply that as soon as PC RAYSON has left the scene, KENNA will be assaulted.

C No, an assault has not been committed, as you cannot assault someone by the use of words alone.

D Yes, ABBOTT has committed an assault as he has intentionally caused KENNA to apprehend unlawful violence.

First Attempt	
Second Attempt	

MCQ 14.2 In certain circumstances a person can consent to the use of force on their person. Although the courts have accepted 'consent' as a feature that may mean an offence of assault has not been committed, they have been reluctant to accept this feature in a number of notable cases.

Considering the defence of, 'consent' regarding assaults, which of the below comments is correct?

A Injuries caused to SMITH in an off-the-ball incident in a football match would not constitute an assault.

B Injuries caused by ALDAY branding his initials on his wife's buttocks would not constitute an assault.

C Injuries caused to LEIGH in an unauthorized prizefight would not constitute an assault.

D Injuries caused to KING during sado-masochistic activity would not constitute an assault.

First Attempt	
Second Attempt	

MCQ 14.3   TI SAINT has been asked to help DC EALING deal with a number of assault cases. DC EAL-ING provides TI SAINT with several crime reports and associated papers that have all been categorized as s 47 assaults (actual bodily harm). TI SAINT examines the papers and realizes that one of the reports is actually a s 20 wounding.

Based on the injuries received by the victim, which report is it?

A   CARTER assaulted HAQUE outside a nightclub. The assault broke HAQUE's two front teeth.

B   McCONE was attacked during the course of a fight in a pub. The attack left McCONE with a minor fracture to his left wrist.

C   REDGATE was assaulted by NUNN at a family party. NUNN punched REDGATE in the jaw, causing a tooth to puncture REDGATE's cheek.

D   LANGTON was attacked by HINIS. The force of the attack caused LANGTON to have a temporary loss of sensory functions.

First Attempt	
Second Attempt	

MCQ 14.4   JOHAL is wanted for a number of burglaries and is spotted in a shopping precinct. PC HARRIS chases JOHAL through a shop and up some stairs. JOHAL climbs through a window and as PC HARRIS tries to grab him he slams the window shut, intending to escape. JOHAL realizes this may cause an injury to the officer. The window smashes against PC HARRIS's face, causing multiple cuts requiring 90 stitches and leaving the officer with a permanent visible disfigurement. JOHAL is caught and arrested several minutes later.

With regard to assaults under the Offences Against The Person Act 1861, what offence, if any, does JOHAL commit?

A   In these circumstances, JOHAL has 'inflicted' rather than 'caused' the injury and so the appropriate offence would be a s 20 wounding.

B   JOHAL commits a s 20 wounding, as there was no intent to wound.

C   JOHAL's actions would be viewed as 'accidental' and so he does not commit any offence relating to the Offences Against the Person Act 1861.

D   JOHAL's actions were malicious and carried out in order to resist arrest. This means that he commits a s 18 wounding.

First Attempt	
Second Attempt	

MCQ 14.5   MATONI is walking along the street holding her three-month-old child in her arms when she is approached by THEAKSTON who was, up until two weeks ago, living with MATONI. An argument develops between the two resulting in MATONI walking away from and past THEAKSTON. As MATONI passes THEAKSTON and has her back to him, THEAKSTON punches MATONI in the back of her head causing minor bruising and some swelling to MATONI's head. The force of the blow causes MATONI to drop her three-month-old child. The child falls to the pavement and receives a 'black eye' as a direct consequence of the fall.

What is THEAKSTON's liability in this matter?

A THEAKSTON is liable for a common battery (contrary to s 39 of the Criminal Justice Act 1988) against MATONI but there is no liability for the injury caused to the child.

B THEAKSTON is liable for a common battery against MATONI and a common battery against the child (both contrary to s 39 of the Criminal Justice Act 1988).

C THEAKSTON is liable for a common assault against MATONI (contrary to s 39 of the Criminal Justice Act 1988) and a s 47 assault (contrary to the Offences Against the Person Act 1861) against the child.

D THEAKSTON is liable for a s 47 assault (contrary to the Offences Against the Person Act 1861) against MATONI and the child.

First Attempt	
Second Attempt	

MCQ 14.6   TI HOVE is dealing with a public order incident where several people were arrested for affray. DUBLIN, one of the people arrested for affray, assaulted the police officer who arrested him in an effort to resist the arrest. RUNCORN, a member of the public, saw what was happening and attempted to assist the police officer who was restraining DUBLIN. As RUNCORN tried to help the officer, DUBLIN assaulted him as well.

Considering the offence of assault with intent to resist arrest (contrary to s 38 of the Offences Against the Person Act 1861), which of the following statements is correct?

A DUBLIN has committed the offence but only in respect of the police officer who arrested him for affray.

B DUBLIN has committed the offence in respect of both the police officer and also RUNCORN.

C DUBLIN would have a defence to the offence if he could show that he was innocent of the offence of affray.

D The offence has not been committed as DUBLIN was trying to resist his arrest and not trying to prevent the arrest of some other person.

First Attempt	
Second Attempt	

MCQ 14.7   WEST has an argument with SARTIN and CRAIG. During the argument SARTIN and CRAIG provoke WEST about the fact that he lost an arm in a car crash. WEST becomes very angry and shouts, 'You pair are the biggest idiots I've ever met and you don't deserve to live. In fact I'll sort that problem out. I've got a shotgun and I'll visit you both tomorrow and kill you, one arm or not!' WEST does not intend either SARTIN or CRAIG to believe the threat, he just wants to shut them up. SARTIN laughs at WEST as he does not believe the threat but CRAIG runs away as he does believe that WEST will kill him the following morning.

Considering the offence of threats to kill (contrary to s 16 of the Offences Against the Person Act 1861), which of the following statements is correct?

A WEST has not committed the offence in this situation.

B WEST has committed the offence but only in respect of CRAIG.

C WEST has committed the offence in respect of both SARTIN and CRAIG.

D WEST has committed the offence but would be able to use the defence of provocation.

First Attempt	
Second Attempt	

Assault

The term 'assault' is not defined in statute but in common law. Nevertheless, you will probably have a good idea of what the term means.

EXERCISE 14.1

Write down the essential elements of an 'assault' (you have been provided with pointers to assist you).

An assault is any act whereby the defendant

↓

(state of mind?) _____

↓

(does what?) _____

↓

(time?) _____

↓

(what do they fear?) _____

Explanation 14.1

This interpretation of the term 'assault' came from the case of *Fagan v Metropolitan Police Commissioner* [1969] 1 QB 439. The name may not be familiar to you but the facts probably will be, as you will have come across this case when you first joined the police. The brief facts are that a constable told Fagan to park his car near to a kerb. Fagan did so but unintentionally parked on the constable's foot. The constable is reported to have said, 'Get off, you are on my foot,' to which Fagan replied, 'Fuck you, you can wait,' and switched off the car ignition. Fagan was convicted of assaulting the constable and appealed. His appeal was dismissed in the speech of James J, who said:

> *'An assault is any act which intentionally—or possibly recklessly—causes another person to apprehend immediate and unlawful violence.'*

E

EXERCISE 14.2

The *mens rea* for the offence of assault is intention or recklessness. Answer the below questions with regard to these terms.

1. What do you think 'intention' means?

_____

_____

2. Recklessness in assaults must be 'subjective'. In your own words, explain what subjective recklessness means to you.

_____

_____

_____

_____

Explanation 14.2

1. There are a number of issues with regard to 'intent' that are discussed at greater length in the section on 'State of Mind and Criminal Conduct'. For the purposes of this question we will keep the answer simple: intent means that you *meant something to happen*.

2. Recklessness is also discussed in the 'State of Mind and Criminal Conduct' section. Subjective recklessness is all about *what the defendant thinks*. In assaults, the defendant will be subjectively reckless if he/she saw a risk that someone would be harmed, but went on to take that risk nevertheless.

See *Investigators' Manual*, paras 3.2.4 and 3.2.5

Cause to Apprehend

E

EXERCISE 14.3

Look at the following scenario and answer the associated questions.

1. EARL and ASH used to be business partners but fell out when the company they had formed went bankrupt. EARL blames ASH for the bankruptcy and wants to make ASH pay for the trouble he has caused. EARL buys an imitation revolver and waits outside ASH's house. ASH leaves his house and EARL approaches him. He points the imitation revolver at ASH and says, 'It's all your fault and now you're gonna pay for it by getting kneecapped!' It is EARL's intention to make ASH believe that he is going to be assaulted.

Based on these circumstances alone, do you have enough information to decide whether there has been an assault?

Yes / No

Why / Why not?

_____

_____

2. ASH looks at the imitation revolver, immediately realizes that it is a fake and believing that he is in no danger whatsoever says to EARL, 'You always were a dick weren't you? I know that's not real so piss off and leave me alone!' and walks away.

   How, if at all, will this affect the situation?

   _____

   _____

3. Let's change the situation slightly. When ASH sees the imitation revolver he believes that it is real and thinks that he is going to be kneecapped by EARL there and then.

   Does this change the situation?

   Yes / No

   Why / Why not?

   _____

   _____

   Does the fact that the revolver is an imitation and can never actually harm ASH make any difference?

   Yes / No

Explanation 14.3

1. You do not. This is because you need to know the state of mind of ASH as well as the state of mind of EARL. The victim must apprehend (believe) that they are going to be subjected to immediate and unlawful violence.

2. You now possess information on the state of mind of the victim but this will not be an assault. ASH does not fear immediate and unlawful violence.

3. This does change the situation because you have the victim's belief that they are about to be subjected to unlawful violence. The fact that the gun cannot fire bullets does not matter as EARL's desired intentions have come to fruition.

See _Investigators' Manual_, para 3.2.4

Immediate

This word always causes doubt in the minds of those examining the law surrounding assaults. What does 'immediate' actually mean?

EXERCISE 14.4

Answer the below questions relating to the concept of 'immediacy'. You can presume that in all the scenarios the state of mind required for offender and victim is present.

1. CARP is sitting in her house watching the television when she sees GARNET looking at her through her lounge window.

   This would satisfy the requirements of the term 'immediacy'.

   True / False

2. AMBROSE is working in his back garden, which backs on to a railway line. A train passes en route to a station two miles away from AMBROSE's house and JELPH (a passenger on the train) leans out of a window and shouts to AMBROSE, 'I'm coming for you!'

   This would satisfy the requirements for 'immediacy'.

   True / False

3. FOULTON and MERTON are on separate sides of a deep and raging river. There is no way to cross the river. FOULTON shouts to MERTON, 'I'm going to kick your head in!'

   This would not satisfy the requirements of the term 'immediacy'.

   True / False

4. CREW is standing outside HODSON's house. CREW phones HODSON using his mobile phone. When CREW answers the phone, HODSON says, 'I'll be round to your house in a minute or two to kick your head in!'

   This would not satisfy the requirements for 'immediacy'.

   True / False

Explanation 14.4

1. True (*Smith v Chief Superintendent, Woking Police Station* (1983) 76 Cr App R 234).

2. False.

3. True.

4. True (*R v Ireland* [1997] 4 All ER 225).

   Immediacy has been described as meaning 'imminent' (in *R v Ireland*) but not 'instantaneous' (*Horseferry Road Magistrates ex p Siadatan* [1991] 1 All ER 324). Hence the 'minute or two' time frame might be enough (as stated in *Ireland*). This is the only precise time frame referred to in your *Investigators' Manual* regarding assaults. Remember that the victim must fear *violence* immediately. In the circumstances at 2 and 3, violence *cannot* be feared immediately because of the circumstances.

See *Investigators' Manual*, para 3.2.4.2

Words, Gestures, and Conditional Threats

E

EXERCISE 14.5

Consider the use of words when completing the following exercises.

1. Write down an example of the use of words alone to commit an assault.

_____

_____

_____

2. Provide an example of the use of a gesture alone to commit an assault.

_____

_____

_____

3. An assault cannot be committed by the use of silence.

   True / False

4. You cannot commit an assault by sending someone a letter containing a threat of immediate unlawful violence.

   True / False

5. Explain what a 'conditional threat' is.

_____

_____

6. PARK is leaving his house for a weekend business trip. As he kisses his wife he says, 'If I hear one word about you sleeping around while I'm away, I'll beat you black and blue.'

   PARK does not commit an assault, as this is a conditional threat.

   True / False

7. BRISTOW is having an argument with his wife. BRISTOW puts a knife to his wife's throat and says, 'Shut it or I'll cut your throat!'

   BRISTOW does not commit an assault, as this is a conditional threat.

   True / False

Explanation 14.5

1. Words alone can constitute an assault and there is no requirement that they be offensive. 'I am going to kick your head in' will suffice.

2. The same applies for gestures. Dragging a finger across the throat or shaking a fist will be enough.

3. False (*R v Ireland* (above)). The defendant made a large number of phone calls to three women—on one occasion, 14 to one of them within an hour—and remained silent when the phone was answered.

4. False (*R v Constanza* [1997] 2 Cr App R 492). The victim, who had for some time been harassed by the defendant, received two letters from him, one on 4 June and one on 12 June, which she interpreted as clear threats. It was held that they amounted to an assault occasioning actual bodily harm.

5. You should have stated that a conditional threat negates an assault. For example, 'I'd beat you up if the police officer wasn't here' actually means, 'Because the police officer is here *I am not* going to beat you up.'

6. True, this is a good example of a conditional threat.

7. False. This might seem like a conditional threat that negates an assault, but it is not as it is an immediate threat that will be carried out if the demand is not met. If the wife does not shut up she will have her throat cut there and then—do this *now* or else this will happen *now*.

See *Investigators' Manual*, para 3.2.4.1

Battery

Like the offence of assault, 'battery' is an offence under common law. It is often associated with the offence of assault because where there is a battery there will often be an assault, although this is not an automatic result in all cases.

E

EXERCISE 14.6

Answer the below questions with regard to the offence of 'battery'.

1. What is a battery?

_____

_____

2. What degree of violence will constitute a battery?

_____

_____

3. Force can be applied directly but can it be applied indirectly?

Yes / No

---

4. If you replied 'Yes' then give an example of the indirect application of force constituting a battery. If you replied 'No' then justify your answer.

_____

_____

_____

Explanation 14.6

1. A battery consists of the *actual* infliction (intentionally or recklessly) of unlawful physical violence (*R v Rolfe* (1952) 36 Cr App R 4).

2. The slightest degree of contact will be enough as the merest touching without consent is a criminal offence (although there is an implied consent to touching that takes place in the course of everyday life).

3. Force *can* be applied *indirectly*.

4. Your Manual provides an example of a defendant punching a woman, causing her to drop and injure a child she was holding.

See *Investigators' Manual*, para 3.2.4

Unlawful

In certain circumstances, an assault/battery will not be committed because the action will be lawful. Your Manual concentrates on two significant defences to these offences: consent and lawful chastisement.

E

EXERCISE 14.7

Answer the following questions in relation to the defence of consent.

1. The courts are prepared to accept consent to injury as a defence in certain circumstances. Provide three examples.

    i. _____

    ii. _____

    iii. _____

2. In what circumstances might the courts limit the defence of consent? (Think about the degree of harm)

_____

_____

3. Based on your answers and your knowledge of the subject, state whether consent would provide a potential defence in the following circumstances:

   i.   KHAN injures LOWE during a properly conducted wrestling match.
        Defence / No defence

   ii. GABLE scores a goal in a football match. Three minutes later, DABNER jumps on and breaks GABLE's leg as revenge for scoring the goal. Neither of the men were near the ball when this occurred.
        Defence / No defence

   iii. FARR injures his wife (at her request) by branding his initials on her buttocks with a hot knife.
        Defence / No defence

   iv. CEDER and BLASÉ are members of a sado-masochistic group who injure each other (at each other's request) for their own gratification.
        Defence / No defence

4. HOLROYD (a male doctor) has served his local community as a GP for a number of years. BAKEWELL (a female patient) has just been examined by HOLROYD after discovering a lump in her breast. HOLROYD was suspended two weeks ago by the General Medical Council for neglect of a patient and has not informed anyone.

   Has an offence been committed against BAKEWELL?

   Yes / No

   Why / Why not?

   _____

   _____

   _____

5. CARD falsifies a set of formal dental qualifications and obtains a job as a dentist. He carries out a dental operation on PHILLIPS before his deception is discovered.

   Has an offence been committed against PHILLIPS?

   Yes / No

   Why / Why not?

   _____

   _____

   _____

Explanation 14.7

1. There are a number of examples of where consent may be allowed. These include injuries received during the course of a properly conducted sporting event, injuries received when receiving a tattoo, and injuries received as a consequence of a medical operation.

2. This was mentioned in *R v Brown* [1994] 1 AC 212. The courts stated that all assaults resulting in more than transient harm will be unlawful unless there is a good reason for allowing the plea of 'consent'.

3. The answers are as follows:
   i. Defence allowed—this is a properly conducted sporting event.
   ii. No defence as the activity falls outside the parameters of a properly conducted sporting event (*R v Barnes* [2004] EWCA Crim 3246).
   iii. Defence allowed—see *R v Wilson* [1997] QB 47.
   iv. No defence—see *R v Brown* [1994] 1 AC 212.

4. An offence has not been committed. This is because BAKEWELL has not been deceived as to the nature and quality of the act, nor the *identity* of HOLROYD (the fact that HOLROYD concealed his suspension does not affect his identity).

5. An offence has been committed, as CARD has no formal qualifications at all.

EXERCISE 14.8

Examine the below scenario and consider the defence of lawful chastisement when answering the questions.

WILLIAMSON is in favour of physical discipline as part of his Christian beliefs. He sends his son, Adam, to a local secondary school and tells the headmaster that he can impose corporal punishment on his son should he merit it.

1. The European Convention on Human Rights requires a State to have regard to the religious and philosophical convictions of parents. As a result, the headmaster could use corporal punishment on Adam.

   True / False

2. Corporal punishment has been outlawed in all British schools by the School Standards and Framework Act 1998.

   True / False

3. The headmaster of the school would be acting in *loco parentis* of Adam and may use corporal punishment if necessary.

   True / False

4. There are no circumstances where a teacher can use reasonable force to control the behaviour of a child.

   True / False

Explanation 14.8

1. False. Although this is a consideration it does not provide a licence to use corporal punishment.

2. True.

3. False. Corporal punishment has been outlawed.

4. False. Staff may use reasonable force in restraining violent and disruptive pupils (Education Act 1996).

See *Investigators' Manual*, paras 3.2.6 to 3.2.9

Section 47 Assault

You have examined 'assault' and 'battery' and these activities may well constitute an offence contrary to s 39 of the Criminal Justice Act 1988. However, the nature of the injury received by the victim may make the offence committed by the defendant a more serious one. A s 47 assault is an assault causing actual bodily harm. While the section does not provide a definition as such, 'bodily harm' has been held to be *any hurt or injury calculated to interfere with the health and comfort of the victim (R v Donovan* [1934] 2 KB 498). As the *mens rea* for this offence is exactly the same as for the offence of assault, the central issue is to decide whether the injury qualifies as ABH.

To assist you in defining what ABH actually is according to your *Investigators' Manual*, try remembering the mnemonic **PESTS**.

P   Psychiatric injury going beyond fear and stress

E   Extensive or multiple bruising

S   Sensory functions lost

T   Teeth lost or broken

S   Stitches and fractures

Cutting a person's hair or fingernails (without their consent) will also amount to an offence of s 47 assault.

See *Investigators' Manual*, para 3.2.19

Section 20 Wounding

The next level of assault is catered for under s 20 of the Offences Against the Person Act 1861. This legislation is probably the oldest you will come across in your study. The actual age of the legislation is not a problem on its own; the true problem lies in interpreting legislation that is approaching 150 years old.

EXERCISE 14.9

The definition of this offence has been supplied for you. Your task is to substitute the words and phrases highlighted in **bold** with their accepted legal meaning. If you cannot do this then substitute the words or phrases with a modern equivalent.

	Whosoever shall
s 20 OAPA 1861 =	Unlawfully and **maliciously**
Your translation =	_____
s 20 OAPA 1861 =	**wound**
Your translation =	_____
s 20 OAPA 1861 =	or **inflict**
Your translation =	_____
s 20 OAPA 1861 =	any **grievous bodily harm** upon any person
Your translation =	_____
s 20 OAPA 1861 =	**either with or without any weapon or instrument**
Your translation =	_____
	shall be guilty of an offence

Explanation 14.9

Maliciously does not mean some kind of evil intention or malice, it means 'subjective recklessness' as discussed earlier in this section. This is the state of mind required to commit the offence.

Wound means to break the continuity of the whole skin (seven layers).

Inflict means 'cause'.

Grievous bodily harm means serious or really serious harm. Examples of this are

- permanent disability or visible disfigurement;
- broken or displaced limbs or bones;
- injuries requiring blood transfusion or lengthy treatment; or
- infection of another with HIV.

Either with or without any weapon or instrument. So therefore:

- This offence can be committed with a weapon.
- This offence can be committed with an instrument.
- But you can also commit it without either of these.

In other words, you can commit this offence by any means, *so why bother with this line of the definition?*

A simple and modern version of this offence should read:

Whoever

↓

unlawfully and recklessly

↓

breaks the 7 layers of the skin

↓

or causes

↓

serious harm to anyone

↓

commits an offence

See *Investigators' Manual*, para 3.2.20

Essentially this offence is a reckless assault resulting in serious injury.

Section 18 Wounding

What would you say if you were told that a s 18 wounding *can* be committed recklessly?

Most police officers think of this offence as one where serious injury (as per the GBH in s 20) is caused to the victim, but the significant difference is the defendant *intended* to cause that injury. There is nothing wrong with this approach and it is a simple but effective way of understanding *part* of the offence.

The offence is committed as below:

Whosoever shall unlawfully and maliciously by any means whatsoever wound or cause any grievous bodily harm to any person with intent to do some grievous bodily harm to any person, or with intent to resist or prevent the lawful apprehension or detainer of any person, shall be guilty of a felony.

There are *two* offences here.

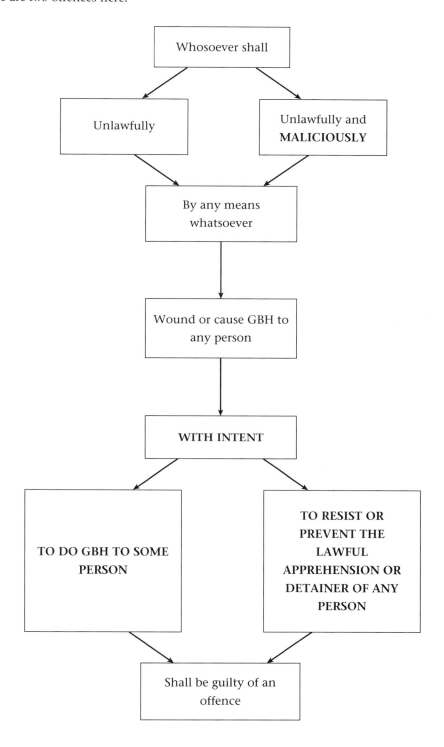

The first offence is committed when the offender wounds or causes GBH intending to do so. This is the s 18 you will be familiar with.

Now think about the translation of the s 20 offence and apply those principles to the other side of the offence.

Whosoever shall

unlawfully and **RECKLESSLY**

by any means whatsoever

wound or cause GBH

At this point the wounding or GBH is caused recklessly

with **INTENT**

TO RESIST OR PREVENT THE LAWFUL APPREHENSION OR DETAINER OF ANY PERSON

shall be guilty of an offence

The intention here is to resist arrest or prevent arrest, *NOT* to wound or cause GBH. For example, a police officer is chasing a suspect who picks up a wooden box and throws it at the officer intending to stop the officer from arresting him. The offender realizes that if the box strikes the officer it will hurt him, but he throws it anyway. The box hits the officer and breaks his arm. The s 18 offence is committed.

See *Investigators' Manual*, para 3.2.21

Conclusion

> Now that you have finished this section of the Workbook your viewpoint in relation to assault-related offences should have changed. You will realize that the basic offence forms the foundation for any understanding of the more serious offences associated with it. These offences require deciphering from their Victorian origins into the language of the twenty-first century.

You should now attempt the 'Recall Questions' before re-reading the relevant section in the Manual and making your second attempt at the multiple-choice questions. The answers to these questions are printed in the 'Answers Section' at the rear of the Workbook.

Recall Questions

Try and answer the questions below. Do not allow yourself to continue until you have answered the questions to your satisfaction.

- What is the definition of an assault according to *R v Fagan*?

- What is a battery?

- What does the term 'immediate' mean?

- Explain what is meant by a 'conditional threat'?

- When would consent be a valid defence to a charge of assault?

- List the injuries (according to CPS Charging Standards) that would constitute a s 47 assault?

- Provide a modern definition of the offence of s 20 wounding.

- Give four examples of injuries (according to CPS Charging Standards) that would constitute a s 47 assault.

15 | Child Abduction

Aim

The aim of this section is to help you understand the law relating to child abduction.

Objectives

At the end of this section you should be able to:

1. Outline the offence of child abduction (contrary to s 1 of the Child Abduction Act 1984).
2. Outline the offence of child abduction (contrary to s 2 of the Child Abduction Act 1984).
3. Identify when a defence to an offence under ss 1 and 2 of the Child Abduction Act 1984 may be available.
4. Apply your knowledge to multiple-choice questions.

Introduction

Offences relating to child abduction are covered in just over two pages of your *Investigators' Manual*. Nevertheless, these offences can easily be made the subject of questions within your examination. As such you will require an understanding of how and who can commit these offences, along with their related defences.

Multiple-choice Questions

Begin this section of the Workbook by answering the below multiple-choice questions. Mark your answer in the 'First Attempt' box. Then read and complete the exercises in the 'Child Abduction' section. Once you are satisfied that your knowledge is of a good standard, return to these questions and mark your answer in the 'Second Attempt' box. The answers to these questions can be found in the 'Answers Section' at the rear of the Workbook.

MCQ 15.1 COLETO has been divorced from his wife for several years. He is the father of three children by the relationship with his wife: Anthony (aged 16 years), Phillippa (aged 14 years) and Mark (aged 12 years). His wife has lawful custody of all three children. COLETO takes all three children on a trip to Italy for six weeks, even though he knows his wife does not consent to the trip.

Considering the offence under s 1 of the Child Abduction Act 1984 only, which of the below statements is correct?

A   COLETO commits an offence with regard to all three children.

B   COLETO commits an offence with regard to Phillippa and Mark.

C   COLETO commits an offence with regard to Mark only.

D   COLETO does not commit an offence because he is the father of the children.

First Attempt	
Second Attempt	

MCQ 15.2 James PERSHORE and Andrea YOUNG were common-law husband and wife for 12 years before they separated two months ago. Stuart PERSHORE is their 10-year-old child and his father and mother have an informal agreement that James PERSHORE has parental control of Stuart. James PERSHORE goes on a hiking holiday to Peru for a month, leaving Stuart in Andrea YOUNG's care. In the meantime, Andrea YOUNG wins a holiday for two to Spain. She does not attempt to contact James PERSHORE, as she believes in these circumstances he would consent to her taking Stuart to Spain for two weeks and consequently takes Stuart on the holiday.

With regard to the offence of child abduction (under s 1 of the Child Abduction Act 1984), which of the below comments is true?

A   Andrea YOUNG commits the offence and has no defence because Stuart PERSHORE has been taken out of the United Kingdom without the consent of James PERSHORE.

B   Andrea YOUNG does not commit the offence because she has taken Stuart PERSHORE out of the United Kingdom for less than a month.

C   Andrea YOUNG commits the offence because she has not taken all reasonable steps to communicate with James PERSHORE.

D   Andrea YOUNG commits the offence but would have a defence, as she believes James PERSHORE would consent in the circumstances.

First Attempt	
Second Attempt	

MCQ 15.3 LEE (who is 12 years old) is playing in a park with a group of friends (his parents are not present in the park). CURTIS (who is 18 years old) approaches LEE and asks him to help him search for his lost wallet (this is a lie as CURTIS's real motive is to sexually assault LEE). LEE agrees and looks behind several bushes in another part of the park along with CURTIS. LEE becomes bored and tells CURTIS he is going back to continue playing with his friends. CURTIS tries to persuade LEE to stay with him, but LEE pays no attention and walks off.

Has CURTIS committed an offence of child abduction under s 2 of the Child Abduction Act 1984 (person not connected with a child)?

A Yes, because CURTIS has removed LEE from his parents' lawful control.

B No, CURTIS has not used force or tried to physically restrain LEE.

C Yes, but only because CURTIS has an ulterior motive in mind.

D No, because LEE consented to accompany CURTIS.

First Attempt	
Second Attempt	

MCQ 15.4 Seven months ago PELL had a sexual relationship with DAY but then the two split up. Some time later, PELL discovers that DAY has a six-month-old daughter and, because PELL knows that DAY is a loner and very rarely has any relationships, he believes that the child is his. PELL is mistaken in this belief. Although PELL asks, DAY repeatedly refuses to let PELL near her child. One afternoon when DAY is pushing the child in a pram, PELL approaches mother and child and grabs hold of the child. PELL holds on to the child for several minutes before giving her back to DAY.

Considering the offence under s 2 of the Child Abduction Act 1984 only, which of the below statements is correct?

A In these circumstances PELL commits the offence, as he is not the father of the child.

B PELL commits an offence but would have a defence if he believes, on reasonable grounds, that he is the father of the child.

C The only defence is that at the time of the offence the defendant believes the child has attained the age of 16.

D PELL does not commit the offence because he did not remove the child from DAY's lawful control.

First Attempt	
Second Attempt	

Child Abduction (s 1: Person Connected with the Child)

E

EXERCISE 15.1

There are five points to prove in relation to this offence. You have been given the first but what are the rest? (Do not worry about the order of the points to prove.)

A person connected with a child is guilty of child abduction if

↓

_____

↓

_____

↓

_____

↓

_____

Explanation 15.1

Your answer should have included:

A person connected with a child is guilty of child abduction if

↓

he takes or sends

↓

a child under the age of 16

↓

out of the United Kingdom

↓

without the appropriate consent

'Connected' with a child

It is important to note that the only person capable of committing this offence is someone 'connected' with the child. Section 1(2) of the Act details those persons who fall into this category. Rather than attempt to remember this section think about the potential offender and ask, 'Does this person have a biological (e.g. a parent) or legal (e.g. a guardian) connection with the child?' If the answer is 'no' then they are not 'connected' to the child and cannot commit this offence.

Age

A common requirement of the offences under ss 1 and 2 of the Act is that the child victim of the offences *must be under 16*!

The UK

EXERCISE 15.2

MILTON and his daughter live in London. MILTON decides to take his 12-year-old daughter on a two-week holiday without the appropriate consent. Consider the below statements and decide whether they are true or false.

1. If MILTON took his daughter to Wales, the offence would be complete.

   True / False

2. If MILTON took his daughter to Scotland, the offence would be complete.

   True / False

3. If MILTON took his daughter to Northern Ireland, he would not commit the offence.

   True / False

4. If MILTON took his daughter to Eire (Southern Ireland), the offence would be complete.

True / False

Explanation 15.2

Although more geography than law, not knowing what countries the United Kingdom consists of could lead to difficulty in the examination. The United Kingdom consists of England, Wales, Scotland, and Northern Ireland. On that basis, comments 3 and 4 are true and comments 1 and 2 are false.

Appropriate consent

Appropriate consent is covered by s 1(3) of the Act. Ask the question, 'Who has a biological or legal connection with the child?' and compile a list of answers; think of this as a school register. Whoever appears on that register *must* have a 'tick' next to their name in a column entitled 'consent given'. If the 'consent given' column is not full then an offence has been committed as the consent of *each and every one* in that column is required.

See *investigators' Manual*, para 3.3.1

Defences to an Offence under s 1 of the Child Abduction Act 1984

E

EXERCISE 15.3

Consider the following statements and decide whether the named person would have a defence to a charge under s 1 of the Act. Give a short explanation for your answer.

1. SMITH has a residence order in force (in his favour) in respect of his eight-year-old child Rebecca. He takes Rebecca to Germany for six weeks without the consent of Rebecca's mother.

   Defence available?

   Why / Why not?

   _____

   _____

   _____

2. EMMS takes his six-year-old child to France for two weeks without the consent of the child's mother. EMMS mistakenly believes the child's mother has consented to the trip.

   Defence available?

   Why / Why not?

   _____

3. PRATT takes his two-year-old child to Spain for a week. This is against the wishes of the child's mother who has unreasonably refused to consent to the trip.

   Defence available?

   Why / Why not?

Explanation 15.3

In the first scenario no defence is available. SMITH has a residence order in his favour regarding his child and this satisfies the first part of the defence under s 1(4)(a). However, he has taken the child out of the UK for more than a month and, therefore, does not satisfy the requirement under the second part of this defence under s 1(4)(b). If he had taken the child to Germany for less than one month the defence would be available. The *only* occasion where the time period of *one month* is relevant to this offence is when this defence is raised.

In the second scenario a defence is available under s 1(5)(a). This is because EMMS has taken his child out of the UK in the belief that the child's mother consented to the trip.

In the third scenario a defence is available under s 1(5)(c) as, although PRATT has taken his child out of the UK without the appropriate consent, the mother of the child has unreasonably refused to consent to the trip.

There are several other occasions where a defence may be available. You should refer to the *Investigators' Manual* to ensure you have a full understanding of these defences.

See *Investigators' Manual*, para 3.3.2

Child Abduction (s 2: Person Not Connected with the Child)

E

EXERCISE 15.4

There are six points to prove in relation to this offence. You have been given the first but what are the rest? (Do not worry about the order of the points to prove.)

A person not connected with a child is guilty of child abduction if

↓

↓

```
                            ↓
    _____
                            ↓
    _____
                            ↓
    _____
```

Explanation 15.4

Your answer should have included:

A person not connected with a child is guilty of child abduction if

↓

without lawful authority or reasonable excuse

↓

he takes or detains

↓

a child under the age of 16

↓

so as to remove him from or keep him out of the lawful control of

↓

any person having or entitled to lawful control of the child

E

EXERCISE 15.5

Read the below circumstances and then answer the following questions. Give reasons for your answers where appropriate.

OAKES (a 30-year-old male) enters a child's play area in a park where he sees VATER (an eight-year-old child) playing on some swings. VATER's mother is talking to some friends nearby. OAKES approaches VATER and asks VATER to come and play on a roundabout 20 feet away. VATER consents and walks with OAKES towards the roundabout. VATER's mother sees OAKES walking with her child and asks him what he is doing. OAKES tells the mother to shut up or he will hit her. The mother fears for herself and her child and does nothing. OAKES has no criminal intentions with regard to VATER and talks with her for a few minutes before leaving the play area.

1. OAKES is not 'connected' to VATER.

   Why?

   _____

   _____

   _____

2. Does the fact that VATER's mother is nearby make any difference?

   Why / Why not?

3. VATER consented to walk to the roundabout with OAKES. Does this have any effect when considering an offence under s 2?

   Why / Why not?

4. Does the fact that OAKES has no ulterior criminal intention with regard to VATER make any difference?

   Why / Why not?

5. OAKES has not used any form of physical violence or a fraud to get VATER to accompany him to the roundabout. Does this prevent him committing an offence under s 2?

   Why / Why not?

Explanation 15.5

1. OAKES is not 'connected' to VATER because he has no *biological or legal connection* to the child. This offence is the 'stranger' abduction and can only be committed by a person to whom s 1 of the Act *does not apply,* i.e. a person other than a parent, a guardian, a person having custody of the child, etc.

2. It does not matter where VATER's mother is. What matters is that her *lawful control* of the child has been substituted by OAKES's control.

3. The consent of the victim is irrelevant; it is the consent of the person with lawful control that matters. In *R v A* (Child Abduction) [2000] Cr App R 418, the Court of Appeal held that the offence of taking a child may be disclosed notwithstanding that the child consents to the taking, the test being whether the accused caused the child to accompany him/her.

4. OAKES's lack of an ulterior criminal intent does not preclude an offence under this legislation (although you would have to consider whether he had lawful authority or a reasonable excuse). In *R v Mousir* [1987] Crim LR 561 it was said that the phrase 'so as to' in s 2(1)(a) of the Act is concerned with the objective consequences of the taking or detaining, and not with the accused's subjective motives.

5. Force or fraud of any kind does not form part of this offence and a lack of one or both of these factors will not prevent OAKES from committing the offence.

Removal of control/keep out of control

When you consider this part of the offence you should bear in mind the Court of Appeal's comments in *R v Leather* [1994] Cr App R 179.

- The court held that the concept of 'control' does not have any 'spatial' element, and it followed that the phrase 'so as to remove from the lawful control' did not impose a geographical element to the offence *(in other words, the child does not have to be physically moved by the actions of the defendant for the offence to be committed)*.
- The test to be applied is whether the child has been deflected by the action of the accused from doing that which he/she would have been doing with the consent of the person having lawful control of the child *(in other words, the authority of the person in 'lawful control' has been substituted by that of the offender and the child is now under his/her control)*.

See *Investigators' Manual*, para 3.3.3

Defences to an Offence under s 2 of the Child Abduction Act 1984

E

EXERCISE 15.6

There are three defences to an offence under s 2 of the Act. What are they? (You have been provided with the first part of this section.)

It shall be a defence for the defendant to prove (where the father and the mother of the child in question were not married to each other at the time of his birth)

1. _____

2. _____

   or

3. _____

   _____

Explanation 15.6

Research these defences by referring to your *Investigators' Manual*.

See *Investigators' Manual*, para 3.3.4

Conclusion

> You will have realized that these offences are not straightforward and demand concentration to understand, particularly when you have to consider the various defences available. This section should have assisted you in that task.

Now that you have finished this Workbook section, you should attempt the 'Recall Questions' before re-reading the relevant section in the Manual and making your second attempt at the multiple-choice questions. The answers to these questions are printed in the 'Answers Section' at the rear of the Workbook.

Recall Questions

Try and answer the questions below. Do not allow yourself to continue until you have answered the questions to your satisfaction.

- What is the relevant age of a child for offences under ss 1 and 2 of the Child Abduction Act 1984?
- What is the United Kingdom?
- You are explaining 'appropriate consent' to a colleague; what will you say?
- When is the time period of one month relevant?
- What are the defences to a charge under s 1 of the Child Abduction Act 1984?
- Who can commit an offence under s 2 of the Child Abduction Act 1984?
- What are the defences to a charge under s 2 of the Child Abduction Act 1984?
- What does the phrase 'so as to remove from lawful control' actually mean?

Flowchart for ss 1 and 2 of the Child Abduction Act 1984

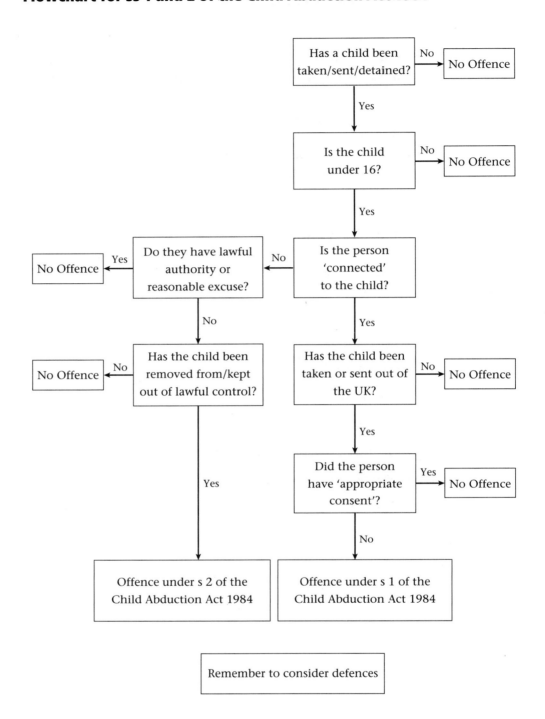

16 Public Order Offences and Racially and Religiously Aggravated Offences

Aim

The aim of this section is to provide you with an understanding of public order offences and the legislation in relation to racially and religiously aggravated offences.

Objectives

At the end of this section you should be able to:

1. Outline the offence of violent disorder contrary to s 2 of the Public Order Act 1986.
2. Outline the offence of affray contrary to s 3 of the Public Order Act 1986.
3. List the offences that can become racially or religiously aggravated under ss 28 to 32 of the Crime and Disorder Act 1998.
4. Identify the central elements of a racially aggravated offence.
5. Identify who is covered by s 28 of the Crime and Disorder Act 1998.
6. Apply your knowledge to multiple-choice questions.

Introduction

When the National Investigator's Examination began in March 2003, ss 1 to 5 of the Public Order Act 1986 were all examinable material. Although your syllabus has changed so that only violent disorder (s 2) and affray (s 3) are covered, you should not be fooled into thinking that these subjects are irrelevant to your revision. The law in relation to racially and religiously aggravated offences can be the subject of questions in its own right but perhaps more importantly it can form part of multiple-choice questions based on the offences that can be racially or religiously aggravated. You may understand the law in relation to the basic criminal offence being committed, but if you do not know whether it is racially or religiously aggravated then you will have difficulty answering the question correctly.

Multiple-choice Questions

> Begin this section of the Workbook by answering the below multiple-choice questions. Mark your answer in the 'First Attempt' box. Then read and complete the exercises in the Public Order Offences and Racially and Religiously Aggravated Offences section. Once you are satisfied that your knowledge is of a good standard, return to these questions and mark your answer in the 'Second Attempt' box. The answers to these questions can be found in the 'Answers Section' at the rear of the Workbook.

MCQ 16.1   BARKER, VENT, and OTTEY are involved in a heated argument with DRAPER who is the doorman of a private nightclub. The argument takes place inside the nightclub at a bar. During the argument, BARKER attacks DRAPER and injures him. While this is happening, VENT threatens to 'glass' DRAPER and OTTEY smashes a bar stool.

Who, if anyone, is guilty of an offence of violent disorder (contrary to s 2 of the Public Order Act 1986)?

A Only BARKER commits the offence.

B BARKER and VENT commit the offence.

C BARKER, VENT, and OTTEY commit the offence.

D No offence of violent disorder is committed in these circumstances.

First Attempt	
Second Attempt	

MCQ 16.2   JUKES, DOUGLAS, and FARLEY approach HAWKINS in a busy town centre street on Saturday afternoon. JUKES and DOUGLAS shout abuse at HAWKINS and then set about him, causing serious injuries to his face and body. FARLEY stands several feet away from the incident and does not say or do anything. The police arrive and JUKES, DOUGLAS, and FARLEY are all arrested. They are later charged, amongst other offences, with violent disorder (s 2 of the Public Order Act 1986). The case goes to Crown Court but, because of a lack of evidence against FARLEY, the charge of violent disorder against him is dropped.

What effect, if any, will this have on the charge of violent disorder against JUKES and DOUGLAS?

A The fact that there are now only two defendants makes no difference to the court case because there were three persons arrested for the offence in the first place.

B Unless it can be proved that there were others taking part in the disorder who were not charged, JUKES and DOUGLAS should be acquitted.

C Although FARLEY took no active part in the incident and has been acquitted, his presence at the scene would be enough for the charge against JUKES and DOUGLAS to be heard.

D Regardless of the number of people involved in the initial offence, if one defendant is acquitted then all the defendants charged with violent disorder would be acquitted.

First Attempt	
Second Attempt	

MCQ 16.3   SILVA has had a long standing dispute with his next-door neighbour, CROW, over parking outside their respective houses. One day, SILVA see CROW's car parked in an area he considers to be his parking space. He decides he has had enough and walks round to CROW's front door and shouts through CROW's letterbox 'You're a tosser CROW, why don't you step outside so I can kick your head in?' Getting no response from CROW, SILVA picks up a stone and throws it at CROW's car; the stone hits and dents the bonnet of the car. SILVA then picks up a spade lying in CROW's garden and waves it around his head shouting, 'C'mon CROW, I'm gonna wrap this spade around your head!' SILVA still receives no response; this is because there is nobody inside CROW's house to hear or see SILVA.

At what stage, if at all, does SILVA commit the offence of affray (contrary to s 3 of the Public Order Act 1986)?

A   When he initially threatens CROW by shouting through the letterbox.
B   When he picks up a stone and uses it to damage CROW's car.
C   When he picks up the spade and threatens CROW.
D   The offence of affray is not committed in these circumstances.

First Attempt	
Second Attempt	

MCQ 16.4   TI MADGE is investigating a number of incidents and is unsure as to whether they are racially aggravated (under s 28 of the Crime and Disorder Act 1998).

Which of the incidents the officer is investigating could be racially aggravated?

A   A s 20 wounding (grievous bodily harm, Offences Against the Person Act 1861).
B   An affray (contrary to s 3 of the Public Order Act 1986).
C   An aggravated criminal damage (contrary to s 1(2) of the Criminal Damage Act 1971).
D   A robbery (contrary to s 8 of the Theft Act 1968).

First Attempt	
Second Attempt	

MCQ 16.5   Racial or religiously aggravated offences can only be carried out against a person who is a member of a racial or religious group.

Which of the below comments is correct in respect of such racial or religious groups?

A   A Rastafarian could not be subject to a racially or religiously aggravated offence.
B   A Scottish person could not be subject to a racially or religiously aggravated offence.
C   A Muslim could not be subject to a racially or religiously aggravated offence.
D   A Traveller could not be subject to a racially or religiously aggravated offence.

First Attempt	
Second Attempt	

Violent Disorder

EXERCISE 16.1

What is the definition of the offence of violent disorder contrary to s 2 of the Public Order Act 1986? (there are some hints to help you)

Where

$\downarrow$

(how many?)

_____

$\downarrow$

(are what?)

_____

$\downarrow$

(do what?)

_____

$\downarrow$

(and what?)

_____

$\downarrow$

(would cause who to fear what?)

_____

_____

$\downarrow$

(who is guilty?)

_____

_____

Before you actually look at the definition try Exercise 16.2.

EXERCISE 16.2

Examine the below comments and decide whether they are 'true' or 'false'.

1. Violent disorder is punishable with a maximum sentence of ten years' imprisonment.

   True / False

2. Violent disorder requires three persons to be present for the offence to be committed.

   True / False

3. Violent disorder can be committed by a defendant who threatens unlawful violence.

   True / False

4. Violent disorder requires all the defendants charged with the offence to be using or threatening violence simultaneously.

   True / False

5. A person of reasonable firmness needs to be present at the scene for an offence of violent disorder to be committed.

   True / False

6. Violent disorder can be committed in private as well as in public.

   True / False

7. If there are only three defendants and one is acquitted, the other two must also be acquitted unless you can show there were others taking part who were not charged.

   True / False

8. 'Violence' for the purposes of violent disorder can include violent conduct towards property.

   True / False

Your answer should look something like this:

Explanation 16.1

Where

(*how many?*)

3 or more persons

(*are what?*)

who are present together

(*do what?*)

use or threaten unlawful violence

(*and what?*)

and the conduct of them (taken together) is such as

(*would cause who to fear what?*)

would cause a person of reasonable firmness present at the scene to fear
for his personal safety

(*who is guilty?*)

each of the persons using or threatening unlawful violence is guilty of violent disorder

Explanation 16.2

1. False. Violent disorder is punishable with a maximum of five years' imprisonment.

2. True. Three or more persons are required for the offence to be complete.

3. True. Violent disorder can be committed by a person who actually uses *or* threatens unlawful violence.

4. False. Section 2(2) of the Act states that it is immaterial whether or not the three or more use or threaten violence simultaneously.

5. False. Section 2(3) states that *no* person of reasonable firmness need actually be, or be likely to be, present at the scene.

6. True. Section 2(4) states that violent disorder may be committed in private as well as public places. In fact, any of the offences from ss 1 to 5 can be committed in private or public and, although ss 1, 4, and 5 are not on your syllabus, you might as well remember that fact should it come up in a relevant question in your examination.

7. True. So if you have three defendants charged with violent disorder and one is acquitted the others will be acquitted as well. If you can show there were other persons there (for example by showing CCTV of the incident that shows that there were others there, even if you do not know who they are, etc.) the charge could still be proved.

8. True (s 8 of the Act).

See *Investigators' Manual*, para 3.6.3

Affray

You can use your knowledge of the offence of violent disorder to assist you in Exercise 16.3 (there are some similarities in both definitions).

E

EXERCISE 16.3

What is the definition of the offence of affray contrary to s 3 of the Public Order Act 1986? (there are some hints to help you)

(who is guilty?) _____

↓

(if what?) _____

↓

(to whom?) _____

↓

(and what?) _____

↓

(would cause whom to fear what?) _____

_____

Explanation 16.3

Your answer should look something like this:

(*who is guilty?*)

A person is guilty of affray

↓

(*if what?*)

if he uses or threatens unlawful violence

↓

(*to whom?*)

towards another

↓

(*and what?*)

and his conduct is such as

↓

(*would cause whom to fear what?*)

would cause a person of reasonable firmness present at the scene
to fear for his personal safety

Were you able to use your prior knowledge of violent disorder to assist you? The below diagram may help.

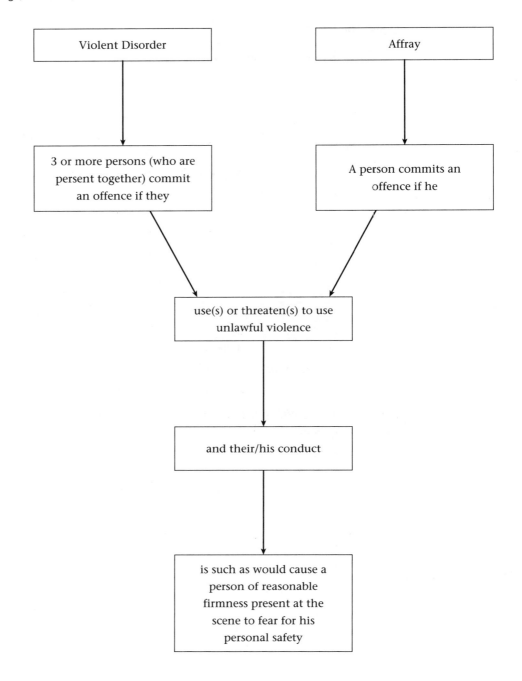

On the surface, affray appears to be a relatively straightforward offence but this is not necessarily the case.

E

EXERCISE 16.4

Examine the following circumstances and decide whether an affray has been committed; give a short explanation for your answer.

1. BARR and LEWIN are having an argument in the street. During the course of the argument BARR says, 'My patience is running out with you, one more word and I'm going to put you in intensive care for a month!'

Affray? Yes / No

Why / Why not

_____

_____

2. THOMPSON has never liked CORRE. THOMPSON is walking past a pub and sees CORRE's motorbike parked outside and CORRE standing nearby. THOMPSON approaches the motorbike and shouts to CORRE, 'Bikers are a menace to the road!' and kicks CORRE's motorbike, knocking it off its stand and onto the tarmac causing a large dent to the motorbike's petrol tank.

Affray? Yes / No

Why / Why not?

_____

_____

3. MARLOW is in a bad mood after his favourite football team have lost a cup final match. Carrying a baseball bat he walks out of his house and into the road outside and swinging the baseball bat he shouts, 'C'mon you bastards, I'll fight anyone and break their legs!' The street is completely deserted and nobody can hear MARLOW because the nearest building to his house is half a mile away.

Affray? Yes / No

Why / Why not?

_____

_____

There are three areas that you should be aware of where the subject of affray can become tricky to answer in multiple-choice questions.

Explanation 16.4

An affray _has not_ been committed in any of the above three scenarios.

1. Although words will probably play an important part in many affray offences, words alone cannot amount to an offence. Section 3(3) states that for the purposes of this section a threat cannot be made by the use of words alone. In other words they must be accompanied by some sort of action or gesture, e.g. the shaking of a fist.

2. Do not get caught out by this element of the offence. Violence for most public order offences includes violence towards property as well as violent conduct towards person; however, in affray **that is not the case**. Affray can only be committed by violent conduct towards persons.

3. This may sound somewhat strange as the legislation clearly states that a person of reasonable firmness need not be present at the scene for the offence to be committed. However, the House of Lords has ruled that the unlawful violence has to be towards a person(s) present at the scene, meaning that if there is no person present at the scene then there is no offence of affray.

So for an affray to be committed you need to ask three questions:

i.   Do you have a person using or threatening unlawful violence? If 'Yes',

ii. Is it towards a real person at the scene? If 'Yes',

iii. Would a hypothetical person of reasonable firmness (who does not have to be or even be likely to be) present at the scene fear for his/her personal safety?

If the answer to any of these three questions is 'No' there is no affray.

See *Investigators' Manual*, para 3.6.4

Racially and Religiously Aggravated Offences

For the purposes of your examination there are three questions to ask when deciding whether an offence is racially or religiously aggravated.

Question 1

Is the offence capable of being racially or religiously aggravated?

One of the most common errors that students make when considering what a racially or religiously aggravated offence is, is to confuse the definition of what makes an offence racially or religiously aggravated (under s 28 of the Crime and Disorder Act 1998), with the definition of a *'racist incident'* (as per the Stephen Lawrence enquiry). A *'racist incident'* is 'any incident which is perceived to be racist by the victim or any other person'. This definition can be applied to any offence or indeed any incident and is entirely unrelated to that under s 28 of the Act.

The purpose of this legislation is to provide the court with the ability to sentence offenders to a lengthier term of imprisonment thus reflecting the serious nature of the racially or religiously aggravating factors of the offence.

EXERCISE 16.5

There are four categories of offence that can be racially or religiously aggravated under the Crime and Disorder Act 1998. What are they?

1. _____

2. _____

3. _____

4. _____

Explanation 16.5

Your answer may have looked something like this:

1. Assaults.

2. Criminal damage.

3. Public order offences.

4. Harassment.

One way to remember this is with the mnemonic **CHAP**.

        C   Criminal damage

        H   Harassment

        A   Assaults

        P   Public order offences

You now need to identify what *particular* offences within those headings are subject to the legislation.

EXERCISE 16.6

What particular offences are capable of being racially or religiously aggravated under the Crime and Disorder Act?

Criminal damage

1. _____

Harassment

1. _____

2. _____

Assault

1. _____

2. _____

3. _____

Public order offences

1. _____

2. _____

3. _____

Remember that you cannot get longer than 'life' so aggravated criminal damage (s 1(2) of the Criminal Damage Act 1971) and s 18 wounding (Offences Against the Person Act 1861) will never be racially or religiously aggravated in terms of increasing the sentence available.

Your answer should have looked like this:

Explanation 16.6

Criminal damage

1. 'Simple' criminal damage (s 1(1) of the Criminal Damage Act 1971).

Harassment (note that these two offences *are not on your syllabus* but are correctly mentioned in the Manual when discussing this topic)

1. Harassment (s 2 of the Protection from Harassment Act 1997).

2. Putting people in fear of violence (s 4 of the Protection from Harassment Act 1997).

Assaults

1. Common Assault (s 39 of the Criminal Justice Act 1988).

2. Actual bodily harm (s 47 of the Offences Against the Person Act 1861).

3. Wounding or grievous bodily harm (s 20 of the Offences Against the Person Act 1861).

Public order offences (note that these three offences *are not on your syllabus* but are correctly mentioned in the Manual when discussing this topic)

1. Causing fear or provocation of violence (s 4 of the Public Order Act 1986).

2. Intentional harassment, alarm, or distress (s 4A of the Public Order Act 1986).

3. Causing harassment, alarm, or distress (s 5 of the Public Order Act 1986).

Let us say that the offence you are being questioned on is one of the offences that is capable of being racially or religiously aggravated.

Question 2

Has the defendant committed the offence?

Before an offence becomes racially or religiously aggravated you must ask if the defendant is guilty of the basic offence. You do not need to concern yourself with the public order offences as they are not on your syllabus but all the other offences are. You must consider if the defendant has a defence, e.g. in 'simple' damage, does the defendant have a lawful excuse or permission? In assaults, does the defendant have 'consent'? Remember that you are judge and jury in an examination and you should make a decision based on the facts as they are presented to you. If the defendant has not committed the basic offence then it does not matter what he/she has said or done; the offence *cannot* be racially or religiously aggravated.

Question 3

Let us presume that the offence is one capable of being racially or religiously aggravated and the defendant has no defences and is guilty of the basic offence. You should now ask:

Is the offence racially or religiously aggravated?

This final question involves an understanding of s 28 of the Crime and Disorder Act.

E

EXERCISE 16.7

Answer the following questions on s 28.

When (in time) does an offence become racially or religiously aggravated?

_____

_____

There are two ways the offence can become racially or religiously aggravated; what are they?

1. _____

2. _____

Explanation 16.7

The time period is:

Immediately before, during, or after

There is no statutory definition of what these terms actually mean so you should approach them from a common sense angle. However, in the Criminal Damage section of your Manual, the case of *DPP v Parry* [2004] EWHC 3112 states that comments made 20 minutes after the defendant had caused damage *would not* qualify as 'immediately after'.

The offence can become racially or religiously aggravated if either

1. the offender *demonstrates* hostility towards the victim or

2. the offence is *motivated* by hostility towards the victim.

The demonstration or motivation must be based on the victim's membership or presumed membership of a racial or religious group.

E

EXERCISE 16.8

Decide whether or not the below groups of people would or would not be covered by s 28 of the Act.

Group	would	would not
Sikhs		
The English		
Traditional Gypsies		
Catholics		
The French		
Rastafarians		
Travellers		
Catholics		
Muslims		
Atheists		

Explanation 16.8

This exercise may cause you some concern as after all, you are a police officer not an anthropologist! The relevant sections in your Manual describe racial groups, religious, and other racial groups in some detail and it is easy to become confused by seemingly complex explanations as to who is what and why. Rather than try to remember who is covered, choose the easier alternative and remember *who is not* covered. Since the Anti-terrorism, Crime and Security Act 2001, religions have been incorporated into the legislation meaning that nearly all types of person will be covered. Your Manual makes one exception stating that:

'Traditional "gypsies" *(as opposed to travellers)* are capable of being a racial group'

In other words, everybody **BUT TRAVELLERS** would be covered by the legislation. So unless the victim is a traveller the offence can be racially or religiously aggravated (if all the other elements are satisfied). So your list from Exercise 16.8 would look like this:

Group	would	would not
Sikhs	X	
The English	X	
Traditional Gypsies	X	
Catholics	X	
The French	X	
Rastafarians	X	
Travellers		X
Catholics	X	
Muslims	X	
Atheists	X	

Remember that police officers are entitled to the protection this legislation offers.

See *Investigators' Manual*, paras 3.7 to 3.7.8

Conclusion

Now that you have finished this section of the Workbook you should have a good understanding of the offences of violent disorder and affray and have a greater awareness of what makes an offence racially or religiously aggravated. Remember that questions on the latter often come in two parts so make sure you apply the law in relation to both to get the question correct.

Now that you have finished the Workbook section on 'Public Order Offences and Racially and Religiously Aggravated Offences' you should attempt the 'Recall Questions' before re-reading the relevant section in the Manual and making your second attempt at the multiple-choice questions. The answers to these questions are printed in the 'Answers Section' at the rear of the Workbook.

Recall Questions

Try and answer the below questions. Do not allow yourself to continue until you have answered the questions to your satisfaction.

- How can a defendant commit an offence of violent disorder?

- Where can all public order offences be committed?

- What happens if one of three defendants charged with violent disorder is acquitted?

- How can a defendant commit an offence of affray?

- With regard to the term 'violence', why is affray different to all other public order offences?

- What are the three questions you should ask regarding a possible offence of affray?

- What does the mnemonic **CHAP** stand for?

- What specific offences can be racially and religiously aggravated under ss 28 to 32 of the Crime and Disorder Act 1998?

- When can an offence (in time) be racially or religiously aggravated?

- What are the two ways in which a defendant might illustrate racial or religious hostility?

- Who **IS NOT** covered by this legislation?

Kidnapping and False Imprisonment

Aim

The aim of this section is for you to be able to explain and distinguish between the offences of kidnapping and false imprisonment.

Objectives

At the end of this section you should be able to:

1. Outline the offence of kidnapping.
2. Outline the offence of false imprisonment.
3. Distinguish between the offences of kidnapping and false imprisonment.
4. Apply your knowledge to multiple-choice questions.

Introduction

The offences of kidnapping and false imprisonment are closely related. This close relationship may cause you difficulty in your examination if you do not understand the individual offences and their differences. This section is designed to provide you with that knowledge.

Multiple-choice Questions

> Begin this section of the Workbook by answering the below multiple-choice questions. Mark your answer in the 'First Attempt' box. Then read and complete the exercises in the 'Kidnapping and False Imprisonment' section. Once you are satisfied that your knowledge is of a good standard, return to these questions and mark your answer in the 'Second Attempt' box. The answers to these questions can be found in the 'Answers Section' at the rear of the Workbook.

MCQ 17.1   NICKLIN is going through a difficult divorce after his wife left him and moved in with POYNER. NICKLIN intends to force his wife to come back to him and drives to POYNER's address, where he speaks to his wife at the front door of the house. NICKLIN asks his wife to sit with him in his car on the false pretext of trying to sort out some of their differences. NICKLIN's wife agrees and walks to the car with him. After several minutes the two begin to argue and NICKLIN's wife attempts to get out of the car. NICKLIN grabs hold of her and locks the car doors. He then drives the car 200 metres along the road, before unlocking the doors and letting his wife out.

At what stage, if at all, does NICKLIN first commit the offence of kidnapping?

A When his wife agrees to walk with him to his car.

B When he grabs hold of his wife and locks the car doors.

C When he drives her 200 metres along the road.

D NICKLIN does not commit the offence, as a husband cannot kidnap his wife.

First Attempt	
Second Attempt	

MCQ 17.2 TIs ROW and BROWNSWORD are arguing about the offence of false imprisonment. Both officers make statements in relation to the offence.

Only one of the statements is correct; which one is it?

A This offence can only be committed if the defendant intends to restrain a person's freedom of movement.

B An unlawful arrest may amount to an offence of false imprisonment.

C The courts have held that in order for an offence of false imprisonment to be committed, any restraint must be more than momentary.

D False imprisonment is triable either way and punishable with a maximum sentence of ten years' imprisonment.

First Attempt	
Second Attempt	

MCQ 17.3 UDALL is walking through a park looking for someone to sexually assault. He plans to take his victim back to his house to carry out the assault. He sees YOUNG and ACTON (boyfriend and girlfriend) taking some drugs near a tree and approaches them. UDALL falsely states that he is a plain-clothes police officer searching for drugs. He tells YOUNG that he has been cautioned and his punishment is to stay in the same spot for 30 minutes, but tells ACTON that she will have to come with him to the police station. YOUNG remains next to the tree while ACTON, who believes UDALL is a police officer, walks several metres with him. As ACTON and UDALL are walking together, ACTON asks to see UDALL's warrant card. UDALL panics and runs away.

Which of the below statements is correct?

A UDALL has kidnapped ACTON and falsely imprisoned YOUNG.

B UDALL has kidnapped ACTON, but has not falsely imprisoned YOUNG because no force was used.

C UDALL has attempted to kidnap ACTON and falsely imprisoned YOUNG.

D   UDALL has not kidnapped ACTON as she was not taken to UDALL's house, but has falsely imprisoned YOUNG.

First Attempt	
Second Attempt	

False Imprisonment (Common Law)

E

EXERCISE 17.1

Examine the below comments and decide whether they are 'true' or 'false'.

1. False imprisonment can only be committed intentionally.

   True / False

2. An offence of false imprisonment is complete when the victim's freedom of movement is restrained.

   True / False

3. The offence of false imprisonment is complete even though the restraint may be momentary only.

   True / False

4. A physical assault is a necessary ingredient of the offence of false imprisonment.

   True / False

5. An offence of false imprisonment may take place anywhere so long as the victim is prevented from moving from a particular place.

   True / False

Explanation 17.1

There is nothing complicated about this offence.

False imprisonment is committed by unlawfully restraining the freedom of the victim and may be committed either intentionally or recklessly. As soon as the freedom of the victim is restrained, the offence is committed and this restraint need only be momentary. There is no requirement for a physical assault to take place and the offence can be committed anywhere.

Therefore, comments 1 and 4 are false and comments 2, 3, and 5 are true.

See *Investigators' Manual*, para 3.4

Kidnapping (Common Law)

E

> **EXERCISE 17.2**
>
> There are four points to prove when considering the offence of kidnapping. What are they? (Do not worry about the order of the points to prove.)
>
> A person is guilty of kidnapping if
> ↓
> _____
> ↓
> _____
> ↓
> _____
> ↓
> _____

Explanation 17.2

Your answer should have included:

A person is guilty of kidnapping if
↓
he takes or carries away another person
↓
by force or fraud
↓
without the consent of the person taken or carried away
↓
and without lawful excuse

Kidnapping is an aggravated form of false imprisonment. It can be committed by any person against any person, i.e. there are no exceptions; a husband can kidnap his wife, a father can kidnap his child.

For the offence of kidnapping think of all the elements of false imprisonment, but also think of the offender causing some form of *movement of the victim* by taking or carrying them away (whether this movement is achieved by force or fraud is immaterial). Do not concern yourself about the distance that the victim has been moved (in *R v Wellard* (1978) 67 Cr App R 364, a distance of 100 yards was held to be 'ample evidence' of such movement), as any distance will suffice. Once movement occurs, the offence is committed.

It is important to remember that the offence can be committed by the use of fraud. This is well illustrated by the case of *R v Metcalfe* ((1983) 10 CCC (3d) 114). The victim entered the vehicle of the accused, a former acquaintance, in which a friend of the accused was also sitting. The victim was driven to a garage in the belief that he was either going to talk about 'old times' or alternatively was going to be given drugs. In fact the accused and his friend were planning to lure the victim to the garage where he was to be confined and held to ransom. In refusing the appeal, Nemets C.J.B.C. said: 'In my opinion the offence of kidnapping was complete on the victim's entry into the car. His agreement to go with the abductors was no consent in law. It was obtained by a fraudulent stratagem. Fraud was used as a substitute for force.'

Therefore, *as soon* as the victim is moved from one point to another (by force *or* by fraud) the offence is committed.

Remember that consent can be removed at any time. If a victim willingly accompanies the offender (no force or fraud is used by the offender at this stage) and a point is reached where the victim removes that consent, any further movement of the victim by the offender (by force or fraud) will constitute an offence.

See *Investigators' Manual*, para 3.5

Conclusion

> Although the offences of kidnapping and false imprisonment are relatively uncommon and only briefly mentioned in the *Investigators' Manual*, you would be ill advised to exclude them from your revision. This short section should have assisted you in under-standing and differentiating between the two offences.

Now that you have finished this Workbook section, you should attempt the 'Recall Questions' before re-reading the relevant section in the Manual and making your second attempt at the multiple-choice questions. The answers to these questions can be found in the 'Answers Section' at the rear of the Workbook.

Recall Questions

Try and answer the questions below. Do not allow yourself to continue until you have answered the questions to your satisfaction.

- What are the points to prove for an offence of kidnapping?

- What is the sentence for an offence of kidnapping?

- What are the points to prove for an offence of false imprisonment?

- What type of 'recklessness' is required for an offence of false imprisonment?

- What are the differences between an offence of kidnapping and an offence of false imprisonment?

18 | Misuse of Drugs

Aim

The aim of this section is to explain some of the offences and defences under the Misuse of Drugs Act 1971.

Objectives

At the end of this section you should be able to:

1. State the meaning of the term 'possession'.
2. Identify the points to prove for the offence of possession of a controlled drug contrary to s 5(2) of the Misuse of Drugs Act 1971.
3. Identify the points to prove for the offence of possession with intent to supply a controlled drug contrary to s 5(3) of the Misuse of Drugs Act 1971.
4. Identify when an offence of supplying a controlled drug contrary to s 4(3) of the Misuse of Drugs Act 1971 has been committed.
5. Outline the defences available under s 5 of the Misuse of Drugs Act 1971.
6. Outline the defences available under s 28 of the Misuse of Drugs Act 1971.
7. Apply your knowledge to multiple-choice questions.

Introduction

The Misuse of Drugs Act 1971 seems to be under constant review but it is still the mainstay of legislation regulating drugs offences. Although the abuse and illegal distribution of controlled drugs creates crimes in their own right, you will be aware of the effect that drug-related crime has on society in general. Even if you are not dealing with drug offences per se, it is likely that some of your time is taken up by dealing with offences linked to drug crime. The widening availability and consequent falling price of some drugs may see you dealing with more drug-related offences in the future. For example, in some locations, it is easier and cheaper to obtain a 'bag' of cocaine (a Class A drug) than it is to obtain cannabis resin (this is still a Class C drug at the time of writing). It is widely recognized that each part of the country has its own particular problems with different controlled drugs and what may be a common problem in one part of the country may not be the same elsewhere. Therefore, this section of the Workbook concentrates on several of the main offences as well as basic terms and defences available under the Act.

Multiple-choice Questions

> Begin this section of the Workbook by answering the below multiple-choice questions. Mark your answer in the 'First Attempt' box. Then read and complete the exercises in the 'Misuse of Drugs' section. Once you are satisfied that your knowledge is of a good standard, return to these questions and mark your answer in the 'Second Attempt' box. The answers to these questions can be found in the 'Answers Section' at the rear of the Workbook.

MCQ 18.1   RUSH is at a party being held in the house of a well-known drug dealer. He is speaking to some friends when BALLARD slips several Ecstasy tablets into RUSH's jacket pocket without RUSH's knowledge. A short while later, RUSH leaves the party, but as he walks out of the front door the police raid the premises and RUSH is detained by PC YOUNG. PC YOUNG searches RUSH under the powers granted by s 23(2) of the Misuse of Drugs Act 1971 and finds the Ecstasy tablets in RUSH's outer jacket pocket. RUSH says, 'That's not mine, I've never seen those pills before!'

Considering the concept of 'possession' alone, which of the below statements is correct?

A   You do not have to show anything other than the fact that RUSH had the drugs in his physical control.

B   To prove possession you need to show that RUSH had the Ecstasy in his physical control and that he knew of its presence.

C   Physical control is not required to prove possession, but knowledge of the drugs presence is.

D   You would need to show that RUSH had physical control of the drug, along with the facts that he knew of its presence and that it was a controlled drug.

First Attempt	
Second Attempt	

MCQ 18.2   DC WALLIS (an undercover police officer) has arranged to meet GARWOOD outside a pub to buy £500.00 worth of cocaine from him. GARWOOD drives on to the pub car park and as he gets out of his car he is arrested by DC WALLIS for an offence of possession of a controlled drug with intent to supply. GARWOOD is searched and a large amount of drugs paraphernalia is found in his possession (clingfilm, paper, scales, and contact details). In GARWOOD's pocket is £6,000.00 in cash and a large amount of cocaine. Later investigation of GARWOOD's financial status reveals a large amount of unexplained wealth in his bank account.

In relation to the offence of possession with intent to supply (contrary to s 5(3) of the Misuse of Drugs Act 1971), which of the below statements is correct?

A   Possession with intent to supply a controlled drug to an undercover police officer would not amount to an offence under this section.

B Possession of the drugs paraphernalia (clingfilm, paper, scales, and contact details) can be used to prove the offence of possession with intent to supply.

C In proving an offence of possession with intent to supply, the prosecution can adduce evidence of GARWOOD's unexplained wealth.

D The presence of large sums of money with the seized drugs cannot be used to prove an intention to supply a controlled drug.

First Attempt	
Second Attempt	

MCQ 18.3 DIXON is walking to a railway station and finds a small plastic bag on the pavement containing what he believes to be cannabis resin. He puts it in his pocket and continues to walk to the railway station, intending to hand the drug in to a police station inside the railway station. As he gets to the railway station he decides that he will hand the drug in the next day and catches a train home. The next day DIXON arrives at the railway station and begins to make his way to the police station. A ticket collector asks for his ticket and, as DIXON pulls out the ticket from his pocket, the packet containing the drug falls to the floor. The police are called and PC JACK arrives to deal with the situation. PC JACK suspects the packet contains cannabis and arrests DIXON for possession of the drug.

Which of the below statements is correct?

A PC JACK should not have arrested DIXON for the offence of possession of a controlled drug, as cannabis resin is a Class C drug and it is not an offence to possess it.

B DIXON has committed the offence of possession of a controlled drug, as he did not take reasonable steps to deliver the drug to a person lawfully entitled to take custody of it as soon as possible after taking possession of it.

C Although DIXON commits the offence of possession he will have a defence under s 5(4)(b) of the Misuse of Drugs Act 1971, as when he took possession of the drug it was solely for the purpose of delivering it to a person lawfully entitled to take custody of it.

D DIXON has committed the offence of possession of a controlled drug and does not have a defence because he did not take reasonable steps to destroy the drug.

First Attempt	
Second Attempt	

MCQ 18.4 DAWSON is convicted of an offence of supplying a controlled drug (contrary to s 4(3) of the Misuse of Drugs Act 1971).

Which of the below comments is correct with regard to the imposition of a travel restriction order on DAWSON under the Criminal Justice and Police Act 2001?

A If an order is made it will last for a minimum period of three years.

B DAWSON could not be subject to such an order, as he has not committed an offence involving the importation/exportation of a controlled drug.

C An order can be made, but only if DAWSON is sentenced to more than four years' imprisonment.

D If an order is made against DAWSON it cannot be suspended in any circumstances.

First Attempt	
Second Attempt	

Possession

E

> **EXERCISE 18.1**
>
> Examine the below scenarios and provide an answer based on whether the named person has 'possession' or not. Do not concern yourself as to whether an offence has been committed. Think about *'possession'* alone.
>
> 1. WHITE is a drug dealer who keeps a large quantity of cannabis hidden under his bed at his home address. WHITE is out of his house and dealing in drugs when he is arrested.
>
>   When WHITE is arrested, does he have possession of the cannabis hidden under his bed?
>
>   Yes / No
>
> 2. THORLEY approaches a drug dealer and asks to buy some heroin. The dealer tells THORLEY that he has some heroin in his car parked 100 metres away. THORLEY gives the dealer £100.00 and asks him to go to his car and get the drug.
>
>   Does THORLEY have possession of the heroin when the cash exchanges hands?
>
>   Yes / No
>
> 3. SHENTON has arranged for his drug dealer to send him 50 LSD tablets through the post. SHENTON leaves his house to go to work and, 30 minutes later, a postal worker puts the letter containing the drugs through SHENTON's front door letterbox.
>
>   Would SHENTON be in possession of the LSD tablets once they had been posted through his front door?
>
>   Yes / No
>
> 4. PULCELLA lives in a block of flats. The front door of his flat is insecure and, without PULCELLA's knowledge, his neighbour (who is a drug dealer) hides several hundred Ecstasy tablets inside a settee in PULCELLA's living room.
>
>   Does PULCELLA have possession of the Ecstasy tablets once the drug dealer has hidden them inside his settee?
>
>   Yes / No

5. LARTER has been suffering from headaches in the afternoon. He picks up several aspirins from a flatmate's bedside table and goes to work. The tablets are in fact Ecstasy tablets.

   When LARTER picks up the Ecstasy tablets thinking they are aspirin, does he possess the Ecstasy?

   Yes / No

6. JILBERT is a delivery driver. He parks outside an address and removes a parcel with the words 'Fragile—Contains Glass' printed on it, to deliver to the address. The parcel actually contains a large amount of cannabis resin.

   When JILBERT delivers the parcel, does he have possession of the cannabis resin?

   Yes / No

7. FERGUSON owns a flat where she and her boyfriend live. FERGUSON's boyfriend has a friend who is a drug dealer. The drug dealer visits the flat regularly and uses cannabis while he is there. FERGUSON realizes that the drug dealer is highly likely to bring drugs into her house. The police raid the flat and find some cannabis in a drawer in the kitchen. There is no proof that the cannabis actually belongs to FERGUSON.

   Does FERGUSON possess the cannabis in these circumstances?

   Yes / No

Explanation 18.1

Possession has been described as a neutral concept. When you are considering possession *alone* it might be better to think of it as the 'tough luck' principle. To prove possession you need

i. physical control of it, and
ii. knowledge of its presence.

So if you have something (and that means anything) in your physical control and you know that you have that something, then it's tough luck if it turns out to be a drug and you didn't know that. Do not worry about whether the person who possesses it is innocent or not, that is what the defences under this Act are for. This approach will help solve some of the above scenarios, but you also need to know what 'physical control' actually means.

1. Tough luck, WHITE—you have possession. Actual physical custody of the drug is not required but physical control is. WHITE has physical *control* of the drugs at his home address. Think about the situation where a dealer is arrested and then a search of his house is carried out later on; if he/she was the only occupant and you found drugs there you would charge him/her with an offence in relation to those drugs because he/she has possession of them.

2. THORLEY does not have possession. This is because THORLEY does not have physical control over the drug as yet. At this stage only the drug dealer has possession.

3. Tough luck, SHENTON—you have possession. Normally you cannot possess something unless you are aware that you have control over it. This is an exception to that rule because even though SHENTON is unaware that the LSD has arrived, it was delivered to his address in *response to a request from him* (*R v Peaston* (1978) 69 Cr App R 203(CA)).

4. PULCELLA does not have possession. As explained in the SHENTON scenario, you cannot have possession if you are unaware that you have control over it. The drugs have been placed in PULCELLA's flat without his knowledge so he cannot be aware that he has control over them. The same reasoning would apply if drugs were placed in someone's pocket, car, etc. without their knowledge—they are unaware of its presence—they do not have possession.

5. Tough luck, LARTER—you have possession. LARTER has physical control over the tablets and he knows of their presence. It *IS TOTALLY IRRELEVANT* that he does not know that what he has is in fact a controlled drug.

6. Tough luck, JILBERT—you have possession for the same reason as LARTER.

7. FERGUSON does not have possession. This follows the ruling in *Adams v DPP* [2002] EWHC 438 (Admin), where the court stated that where knowledge of possession of the drug was limited to the fact that a visitor had brought drugs into the defendant's home intending to take them, that was not sufficient evidence from which it was appropriate to infer that she had control over the drugs.

There is only one other issue in relation to possession:

Quantity—if the quantity is 'visible, tangible, and measurable' it can be possessed. If it is too small to even know about it, it cannot be possessed.

See *Investigators' Manual*, paras 3.8.2 to 3.8.2.5

Having established what possession actually is, you will now examine three chief offences relating to the concept.

Possession of a Controlled Drug

You should now be in a position to say that you understand the concept of 'possession'.

If that is the case then you only need to add one factor to be able to identify the points to prove for the offence of possession of a controlled drug.

Possession (as explained above)

+

The defendant knows that he/she is in possession of something which is, in fact, a prohibited or controlled substance

The only other factor that should be considered is sentencing. A clue to the sentencing comes from the section itself.

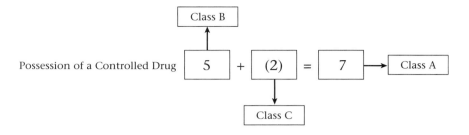

See *Investigators' Manual*, para 3.8.5.5

Possession with Intent to Supply

You should now be in a position to say that you understand the offence of possession of a controlled drug.

If that is the case then you only need to add one factor to be able to identify the points to prove for the offence of possession of a controlled drug with intent to supply.

Possession of a controlled drug/substance (as explained above)

+

The intention that he/she will supply that drug/substance to another

E

EXERCISE 18.2

The offence of possession with intent to supply is more complex than mere possession. Examine the below scenario and answer the questions that follow it.

PC CLOUGH takes part in a drugs raid and during the raid she finds a large amount of cannabis resin hidden in a wardrobe. PC CLOUGH places a small amount of the cannabis resin in a drugs bag and secretes the rest in her jacket. This is because PC CLOUGH is also a drug dealer who has been taking drugs from other searches and from those she has arrested for drugs offences to sell on the streets. PC CLOUGH arrested FLINT for possession of a controlled drug some time ago and after he witnessed her removing the majority of his drugs for herself, he informed the police about what he saw. An undercover operation has been mounted to obtain evidence of PC CLOUGH's drug dealing activities. DC JOY (an undercover police officer) has made contact with PC CLOUGH in her drug dealing capacity and PC CLOUGH has told him that she can supply him with £10,000.00 worth of cannabis resin. The night before the deal is due to take place, the police raid PC CLOUGH's home address and arrest her for possession with intent to supply (amongst other offences). Her house is searched and the police recover approximately £10,000.00 worth of cannabis resin. A search of the room where the resin was stored reveals the following:

i.   a large amount of clingfilm,
ii.   several sets of scales,

iii.   a book containing details of who PC CLOUGH sells drugs to and the quantities they buy,

iv.   a large amount of tin foil,

v.   a dozen 'Rizla' cigarette paper packs,

vi.   £15,000.00 in various note denominations, and

vii.   bank account details showing that PC CLOUGH has over £50,000.00 placed in three different bank accounts in her name.

When PC CLOUGH is interviewed she states that as a police officer she has lawful possession of the drugs and that the arrest is unlawful.

1. What effect will the fact that she is a police officer have with regard to the offence of possession with intent to supply and why?

_____

_____

2. Will the fact that PC CLOUGH possessed the drugs with intent to supply them to an undercover officer have an impact on the case?

Yes / No

3. Of the seven items seized during the search, which would be relevant evidence to show that PC CLOUGH is an active drugs dealer generally and which could be used to prove a charge of possession with intent to supply?

Active Drugs Dealer	Proof of the Charge

Explanation 18.2

1. The fact that the defendant is a police officer has no effect as the lawfulness of possession is irrelevant; what matters is the lawfulness of the intended supply.

2. No. Possession with intent to supply a controlled drug to a person who is in fact an undercover police officer amounts to an offence.

3. Your completed table should have looked like this:

Active Drugs Dealer	Proof of the Charge
The clingfilm	£15,000.00 in cash
The scales	Bank account details of the £50,000.00
The book containing drug deal details	
The tin foil	
The 'Rizla' papers	

Drug dealing paraphernalia will not prove an intention to supply.

See *Investigators' Manual*, para 3.8.5.6

Supplying a Controlled Drug

E

EXERCISE 18.3

This offence can be committed in three ways. What are they?

1. _____

_____

2. _____

_____

3. _____

_____

Explanation 18.3

The ways in which the offence can be committed are as follows:

To supply or offer to supply a controlled drug

To be concerned in the supplying of such a drug

To be concerned in the making to another of an offer to supply

'To be concerned' means to provide some kind of identifiable assistance such as telephoning a contact or similar helpful act.

E

EXERCISE 18.4

In this exercise you are only required to consider the 'supply' element of the offence. Examine the scenarios and decide whether there has been a supply.

1. KENDRICK is a registered drug addict who legally possesses a controlled drug. He is on a walking holiday with his fiancée when he decides he needs to administer the drug. He takes enough of the drug for his usual dose and leaves the remainder of the drug with his fiancée while he administers his dose out of sight behind some bushes.

   Does KENDRICK supply his fiancée with a controlled drug?

   Yes / No

   Why / Why not?

   _____

   _____

   _____

2. MOSSON is a drug dealer who carries out his business outside a pub called 'The Anchor'. MOSSON is drinking in 'The Anchor' when he receives a call on his mobile from SWAIN requesting a supply of heroin. MOSSON does not trust SWAIN and asks WILLIAMS (who is also drinking in the pub) to look after the bulk of his heroin until he comes back from the deal with SWAIN. WILLIAMS agrees and holds onto the drugs. Thirty minutes later, MOSSON returns and WILLIAMS hands back the drugs.

   When WILLIAMS hands the drugs back to MOSSON, does he supply?

   Yes / No

   Why / Why not?

   _____

   _____

   _____

3. What would the situation be if, instead of asking WILLIAMS to look after the drugs, MOSSON produced a gun and said, 'I'll blow your head off if you don't look after this for me!' and when MOSSON returned to the pub, WILLIAMS handed the drugs to him?

   _____

   _____

   _____

Explanation 18.4

The term 'supply' (for the purposes of this Act) means to furnish a drug to another so that *the other* can use it for his/her own purposes and thereby gain a benefit. It is not merely the physical transfer of the drug from one person to another.

1. KENDRICK is not supplying. It does not matter that his possession of the drug is legal, what is important is what his fiancée is getting by receiving the drug from him in the first place and in this situation she is getting nothing whatsoever, i.e. she receives no benefit from the activity. If KENDRICK had given her the drug for her own use she *would* be benefiting and consequently KENDRICK would supply to his fiancée.

2. WILLIAMS does supply. This is because handing the drugs back to MOSSON enables MOSSON to sell the drugs to his customers. This is a benefit to MOSSON and, therefore, WILLIAMS supplies.

3. WILLIAMS would still supply, as MOSSON would receive exactly the same benefit as at 2 (see *R v Panton* [2001] EWCA Crim 611).

This can be a little confusing; see if the below diagram helps you.

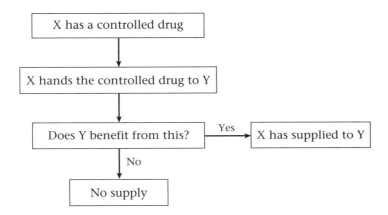

Please remember that when an *offer* is made to supply a controlled drug the offence is complete *at that point*.

- It does not matter whether the defendant has actually got any drugs.
- It does not matter if the defendant intends to carry out the offer or not.
- It does not matter who the offer is made to.
- *The only thing that does matter is that the offer was made.*

See *Investigators' Manual*, paras 3.8.5.2 to 3.8.5.3

Defence to Unlawful Possession

E

EXERCISE 18.5

Section 5 of the Misuse of Drugs Act 1971 creates a defence to unlawful possession. Examine the below scenarios and decide whether the defence exists or not and justify your answer.

1. LOOMES is a teacher and, while he is making his way to a class, he finds a pupil smoking a cannabis joint. LOOMES confiscates the cannabis joint in order to prevent the pupil from continuing to commit an offence with it. LOOMES places the cannabis joint in a locked drawer in his office.

   If the drug were to be found in LOOMES's desk drawer, would he have a defence under s 5?

   Yes / No

   Why / Why not?

   _____

   _____

2. MAYBURY finds what she suspects to be LSD in her daughter's bedroom. To prevent her daughter committing an offence, she takes the item and decides to ask one of her work colleagues for his opinion as to whether the item is LSD. The following day she takes it into her workplace for that purpose. MAYBURY decides that if her colleague thinks the item is LSD then she will destroy it. On her way to work, the police stop MAYBURY and the LSD is found in her possession.

   Does MAYBURY have a defence under s 5 in these circumstances?

   Yes / No

   Why / Why not?

   _____

   _____

3. RAINES is a youth worker. He finds several hypodermic needles containing what he suspects to be heroin in a street. He picks them up and decides that he will take them to his local police station.

   If RAINES were found in possession would he be able to use a defence under s 5?

   Yes / No

   Why / Why not?

   _____

   _____

Explanation 18.5

Only RAINES would be able to use the defence available under s 5 of the Act.

1. LOOMES has confiscated the drug to prevent an offence taking place or continuing to take place and that would satisfy the first part of the defence under s 5(4)(a). However, *as soon as possible* after taking possession of the drug he must either destroy it or deliver it to the custody of someone lawfully entitled to possess it and this has not been done.

2. MAYBURY has confiscated the drug for the right reason and intends to destroy it, but this is not done *as soon as possible*.

3. RAINES has taken possession of the drug with a view to handing it to someone entitled to possess it as soon as possible.

See *Investigators' Manual*, para 3.8.4.1

General Defence under s 28

E

EXERCISE 18.6

The defences under s 28 are applicable to six offences. Name four of them.

1. _____

2. _____

3. _____

4. _____

Explanation 18.6

Three of the offences that are covered by the defence have been dealt with in this section, i.e. unlawful possession, possession with intent to supply, and unlawful supply. The other offences covered are unlawful production, unlawful cultivation of cannabis, and offences connected with opium.

Now that you have identified the offences that the defence is relevant to, you need to understand how to apply its provisions.

E

EXERCISE 18.7

In the scenarios below, state whether s 28 would provide the named person with a defence and explain your decision.

1. JAMES shares a flat with RAFFERTY and the two men often share each other's clothing. One evening, JAMES decides to go out and get a takeaway meal and puts on RAFFERTY's coat. The police stop JAMES on his way to the takeaway and find several Ecstasy tablets in the coat pocket. JAMES thought the coat was empty and has no knowledge of their presence.

   Would a defence be open to JAMES?

   Yes / No

Why / Why not?

_____

_____

_____

2. In scenario 5 of Exercise 18.1, you examined circumstances surrounding LARTER as below:

   LARTER has been suffering from headaches in the afternoon. He picks up several aspirins from a flatmate's bedside table and goes to work. The tablets are in fact Ecstasy tablets.

   Would a defence be open to LARTER?

   Yes / No

   Why / Why not?

   _____

   _____

3. PEACOCK approaches his dealer and buys £50.00 of heroin from him. PEACOCK is stopped by the police and the drug is found in his possession. Analysis of the drug shows that it is not heroin, it is in fact 'speed' (amphetamine).

   Would a defence be open to PEACOCK?

   Yes / No

   Why / Why not?

   _____

   _____

Explanation 18.7

There are three defences under s 28. Broadly speaking they are:

- lack of knowledge (by the defendant) of some fact alleged by the prosecution;
- a general lack of knowledge about the drug in question; and
- a conditional belief about the drug in question.

1. JAMES would have a defence. He could use the defence under s 28(2) because he neither knew nor suspected nor had reason to suspect a fact alleged by the prosecution. The fact would be possession.

2. LARTER would have a defence if he proved that he neither believed nor suspected or had reason to suspect that the substance or product was a controlled drug.

3. PEACOCK would not have a defence. Proving that the drug in question was a different controlled drug to the one he thought it was will not lead to acquittal.

There is a good example of the remaining defence in your _Investigators' Manual_.

Remember that the Misuse of Drugs Regulations 2001 provide for certain people to be exempt from committing offences of possession and supply.

See *Investigators' Manual*, paras 3.8.4.2 to 3.8.4.5

Conclusion

There are a large number of offences and regulations contained within the Misuse of Drugs section in your *Investigators' Manual* and it has not been possible to cover them all in detail in this section of the Workbook. You should remember that this material is equally testable as anything you have dealt with. That said, you should now be in a position to answer questions on some of the more common offences and defences and you should have a good understanding of the concept of 'possession'. This knowledge should assist you in your further study of drug-related material.

Before you make your second attempt at the multiple-choice questions at the beginning of this section, you should answer the 'Recall Questions' and then re-read the 'Misuse of Drugs' section in the *Investigators' Manual* to reinforce your knowledge on this subject. The answers to these questions are printed in the 'Answers Section' at the rear of the Workbook.

After you have made your second attempt at the multiple-choice questions you may wish to answer the 'Drug Offence Scenarios' that follow the 'Recall Questions'.

It is suggested that you answer these scenario questions IMMEDIATELY AFTER you have made your second attempt at the multiple-choice questions, but BEFORE you check your answers to those multiple-choice questions.

Recall Questions

Try and answer the questions below. Do not allow yourself to continue until you have answered the questions to your satisfaction.

- Name three 'Class A' drugs.

- What is cannabis?

- Explain what is required to show 'possession'.

- What groups of people might be exempt from drug offences under the Misuse of Drugs Regulations 2001?

- What are the two defences available under s 5 of the MODA 1971?

- What are the defences available under s 28 of the MODA 1971?

- What offences does s 28 of the MODA 1971 relate to?

- What are the maximum prison sentences for possession of a controlled drug?

- How could you use evidence recovered in a search of a drug dealer's house to assist you in proving a charge of possession with intent to supply?

Part 3: Assaults, Drugs, Firearms, and Defences

- Define the offence of supplying a controlled drug.

- What powers do the police possess under s 23 of the MODA 1971?

Drug Offence Scenarios

In order to provide you with an opportunity to test your knowledge relating to this material, some scenarios have been produced for you to consider. The scenarios deal with some of the offences and defences you have studied in this section, along with other legislation covered in the *Investigators' Manual*. You should consider each scenario and write down your answer on a piece of paper. The solutions to these scenarios follow the answers to the multiple-choice questions for the Misuse of Drugs in the 'Answers Section' at the rear of the Workbook.

SBQ 18.1   Mrs GRUNDY suffers from acute arthritic pain. She has heard that using cannabis is a good method for relieving this pain and carries out some research via the Internet into the drug. She discovers that she can buy seeds from a country outside the UK and this will enable her to grow cannabis plants at her home. She orders these seeds and when they arrive she keeps them at her home where she is the sole occupant. She knows that cannabis is a controlled drug and that possession of it is illegal.

What offence(s), if any, would Mrs GRUNDY commit and why? (Include any knowledge you have in relation to what cannabis is in your answer.)

SBQ 18.2   After receiving the seeds, Mrs GRUNDY decides to plant them in plant pots. She regularly waters and feeds the plants until they mature into large plants that contain the leaves and flowering tops of the cannabis plant.

What offence(s), if any, would you now consider and why?

SBQ 18.3   Mrs GRUNDY is a non-smoker. She decides that she will make a cake containing the dried leaves from the cannabis plant because she believes that the drug will still work if digested. Again, she is aware that cannabis is a controlled drug. A lifelong friend of hers, Mrs SWAIN, visits Mrs GRUNDY and during her visit Mrs GRUNDY offers her a slice of the cake. Mrs GRUNDY does this because she knows that Mrs SWAIN also suffers from arthritic pain. Mrs SWAIN is unaware of the contents of the cake.

What offence(s), if any, are committed by this activity and why?

SBQ 18.4   COLT lives alone in a flat. A search warrant (under s 23 of the Misuse of Drugs Act 1971) is executed at his flat just as he is consuming drugs. The police find COLT with a syringe in his hand; the syringe contains Amphetamine Sulphate (a controlled drug). This substance had been prepared for injection.

There is no question about possession, but what class of substance is COLT in possession of?

SBQ 18.5   COLT's flat is searched and a pack of tablets are found. There should be 32 tablets in the pack but five are missing. These tablets are labelled 'MST 50 mg' (Morphine Sulphate Tablets 50 mg in strength and consequently a controlled drug). They are issued against a prescription to Mrs Susan COLT, who is COLT's mother. The date the tablets were dispensed is 20 days prior to the search.

What offence(s), if any, does COLT commit and why?

SBQ 18.6   Had COLT taken the tablets directly to his mother after collecting them, would he have a defence to possession of the tablets?

SBQ 18.7   Imagine that you had cause to deal with COLT as he left the chemists with the prescribed morphine tablets for his mother. You carried out a lawful search of his person and discovered the tablets. What authority would you have to enter the chemists and demand that the pharmacist show you records relating to the supply of those drugs to COLT?

SBQ 18.8   You receive specific information that a known drugs dealer in your police area is in possession of a pill-making machine that he intends to use to convert amphetamine powder into amphetamine pills. He has only just acquired this machine and has made some enquiries about obtaining the necessary amphetamine powder. You decide to make an application for a search warrant under s 23 of the Misuse of Drugs Act 1971 to search for and recover the machine.

Would a warrant be granted?

19 │ Firearms and Gun Crime

Aim

The aim of this section is to supply you with an overview of offences relating to the criminal use of firearms.

Objectives

At the end of this section you should be able to:

1. Explain what a firearm is under s 57 of the Firearms Act 1968.
2. Identify when an offence under s 16 of the Firearms Act 1968 (possession with intent to endanger life) has been committed.
3. Point out relevant issues in an offence under s 16A of the Firearms Act 1968 (possession with intent to cause fear of violence).
4. Outline the offence under s 17(1) of the Firearms Act 1968 (using a firearm to resist arrest).
5. Point out relevant issues in an offence under s 17(2) of the Firearms Act 1968 (possessing a firearm while committing or being arrested for a Schedule 1 offence).
6. Outline the offence under s 18(1) of the Firearms Act 1968 (having a firearm with intent to commit an indictable offence or resist arrest).
7. Define the offence of having a firearm in a public place contrary to s 19 of the Firearms Act 1968.
8. Identify when a convicted person can possess a firearm.
9. State the police powers under s 47 of the Firearms Act 1968.
10. Apply your knowledge to multiple-choice questions.

Introduction

There are very few people who find the study of firearms law easy. At this stage of your revision you should have read the firearms section of your Manual and you will be aware that this contains lengthy and complicated lists of what constitutes a certain type of firearm. The additional lists of exemptions compound this difficulty. One approach (although this is not guaranteed to be successful all of the time) is to examine the exceptions rather than the rule and you will see this approach adopted in part of this section of the Workbook.

The section concentrates on the criminal use of firearms, as this is a particularly relevant area of law for Trainee Investigators.

Multiple-choice Questions

> Begin this section of the Workbook by answering the below multiple-choice questions. Mark your answer in the 'First Attempt' box. Then read and complete the exercises in the 'Firearms' section. Once you are satisfied that your knowledge is of a good standard, return to these questions and mark your answer in the 'Second Attempt' box. The answers to these questions can be found in the 'Answers Section' at the rear of the Workbook.

MCQ 19.1 ROBE is a drugs dealer and he is becoming concerned that KNIGHT, a rival dealer, is taking over his area. ROBE drives around looking for KNIGHT in order to warn him off. He sees KNIGHT dealing drugs on a street corner and loses his temper because KNIGHT is dealing in his area again. ROBE drives his car towards KNIGHT, intending to kill him by running him over. KNIGHT manages to jump out of the way and is uninjured, but ROBE loses control of his car and it crashes into a wall. When the police arrive, they find ROBE unconscious in his car. They search his car and find a revolver hidden in the glove box of the car.

Does ROBE commit the offence of possession of a firearm with intent to endanger life (contrary to s 16 of the Firearms Act 1968)?

A   No, the firearm was not the means by which KNIGHT's life was endangered.

B   Yes, he had possession of a firearm at the time of endangering KNIGHT's life.

C   No, because KNIGHT was uninjured as a result of the attack.

D   Yes, as there is no need for the firearm to be produced or shown to KNIGHT.

First Attempt	
Second Attempt	

MCQ 19.2 Section 17(2) of the Firearms Act 1968 creates a specific offence of possessing a firearm while committing or being arrested for a Schedule 1 offence.

Which of the below statements is correct in respect of this offence?

A   Theft (contrary to s 1 of the Theft Act 1968) is not a Schedule 1 offence.

B   Simple damage (contrary to s 1(1) of the Criminal Damage Act 1971) is not a Schedule 1 offence.

C   The offence of wounding (contrary to s 18 of the Offences Against the Person Act 1861) is not a Schedule 1 offence.

D   Rape (contrary to s 1 of the Sexual Offences Act 2003) is not a Schedule 1 offence.

First Attempt	
Second Attempt	

MCQ 19.3   MOSELEY is visiting his friend CHAMBERS. CHAMBERS asks MOSELEY if, on his way home, he will be passing 'The Swan' pub. When MOSELEY states that he will be, CHAMBERS asks MOSELEY to drop a package containing several fishing rods off to the licensee of 'The Swan', KILBURN. MOSELEY agrees and takes the package, which actually contains an unloaded shotgun. On his way to the pub, MOSELEY is stopped by PC FRENCH and the contents of the package are discovered.

Considering the offence under s 19 of the Firearms Act only (having a firearm/imitation firearm in a public place), which of the following comments is correct?

A   This offence is 'absolute' and MOSELEY's possession of the unloaded shotgun is all that is required.

B   MOSELEY would not commit the offence because the shotgun is unloaded.

C   An offence under s 19 cannot be committed by being in possession of a shotgun, loaded or unloaded.

D   The offence is not committed because MOSELEY had no knowledge that the package actually contained a firearm.

First Attempt	
Second Attempt	

MCQ 19.4   FOULGER is planning to burgle an office on an industrial estate and as part of his plan he drives to the road where the office is situated, parks his car, and walks toward the offices to make a note of the security arrangements that are in place. FOULGER always carries a Magnum 44 firearm when he is out of his house and this occasion is no exception. The gun is tucked into his trousers with FOULGER's T-shirt pulled over the top of the firearm. The gun is not loaded. FOULGER walks around the office on the pavement making notes as he does so, but a member of staff at the office becomes suspicious of FOULGER's behaviour and calls the police. PC NASH attends the scene and stops FOULGER in the street. The officer notices the shape of the firearm underneath FOULGER's clothing.

Considering PC NASH's powers under s 47 of the Firearms Act 1968, which of the below comments is correct?

A   If PC NASH has reasonable cause to suspect that FOULGER has a firearm with him in a public place he may require him to hand over the firearm.

B   PC NASH can only use his powers under s 47 of the Act if he reasonably believes that FOULGER has a firearm in a public place.

C   PC NASH can only require the firearm to be handed over if he reasonably suspects it is loaded or reasonably suspects FOULGER has ammunition for the firearm in his possession.

D   PC NASH cannot request that the firearm be handed over unless he reasonably suspects that FOULGER is committing or about to commit a relevant offence for the purposes of this section.

First Attempt	
Second Attempt	

Firearm

In order to understand offences relating to the criminal use of firearms, you must be able to understand what a firearm actually is. The definition of a firearm is provided by s 57 of the Firearms Act 1968.

Complete Exercises 19.1 and 19.2 before referring to their joint Explanation 19.1 and 19.2.

E

EXERCISE 19.1

Write down what you can remember about the definition of the word 'firearm'.

_____

_____

_____

_____

E

EXERCISE 19.2

Use the information you have just written down to help you decide whether the below items would, could, or would not be classed as a 'firearm' for the purposes of s 57 of the Firearms Act 1968. Place a mark in the box you consider to be appropriate.

Description	Would	Could	Would Not
A telescopic sight			
The trigger of a prohibited weapon			
An imitation revolver			
A signalling pistol			
A silencer			
A flash eliminator			
A prohibited weapon			
An air pistol			
The barrel of a prohibited weapon			

Explanation 19.1 and 19.2

Let's begin with the definition of the word 'firearm'.

A lethal barrelled weapon of any description

from which any shot, bullet, or missile can be discharged and includes any prohibited weapon, whether it is such a lethal weapon as aforesaid or not; and

any component part of such a lethal or prohibited weapon; and

any accessory to any such weapon designed or adapted to diminish the noise or flash caused by firing the weapon

You probably remembered the fact that a firearm is a 'lethal barrelled weapon', but did you remember the other parts of the definition? Depending on how much you remembered, it would obviously affect your decisions in the table. Your finished table should have looked as below.

Description	Would	Could	Would Not
A telescopic sight			X
The trigger of a prohibited weapon	X		
An imitation revolver		X	
A signalling pistol		X	
A silencer		X	
A flash eliminator		X	
A prohibited weapon	X		
An air pistol		X	
The barrel of a prohibited weapon	X		

The low-lighted items have all been held to be lethal barrelled weapons, but this will not always be the case. This is one of those areas of the law where it is better to make a presumption in favour of the item being a 'firearm'. Rather than trying to remember what a firearm *is*, it might be easier to remember what a firearm *is not*.

A firearm *is not*

- a telescopic sight, or
- a silencer or accessory *on its own*.

You should examine your *Investigators' Manual* to understand the exceptions with regard to silencers and accessories.

See *Investigators' Manual*, paras 3.9.1 to 3.9.2.2

Possession with Intent to Endanger Life

E

EXERCISE 19.3

Examine the scenario below and provide answers where requested.

HALLORAHAN discovers that his wife is having an affair with COURT and decides to confront COURT to sort the matter out. He places several items into his car and drives to COURT's house, intending to kill him if COURT does not finish the affair. HALLORAHAN has a number of items with him:

i. an imitation firearm (an AK-47 machine gun) in the boot of his car;
ii. a 9mm Beretta pistol, held in a shoulder holster worn by HALLORAHAN; and
iii. a 12-gauge shotgun that HALLORAHAN has placed on the front passenger seat of his car.

HALLORAHAN has placed the shotgun in his car, intending to get his friend, JAGO, to come with him and use the shotgun to kill COURT.

1. Which of the three items does HALLORAHAN have in his 'possession'?

_____

_____

2. Which of the three items could be used to commit an offence under s 16 of the Firearms Act 1968?

_____

_____

3. What is your opinion of the fact that HALLORAHAN has brought the shotgun, intending to get a friend he has not even approached yet to use it to kill COURT?

_____

_____

4. HALLORAHAN is obviously not going to kill COURT if he finishes the affair with HALLORAHAN's wife. How would this affect the offence?

_____

_____

HALLORAHAN gets to JAGO's house but he is not in. He drives to COURT's house but as he pulls onto COURT's drive, COURT sees him and runs away before HALLORAHAN even gets out of his car.

5. COURT has not been injured. Does this make a difference to whether the offence has been committed or not?

Yes / No

HALLORAHAN decides he has had enough and takes out the Beretta pistol, intending to kill himself with the firearm.

6. What does the law say with regard to the life endangered being that of the defendant?

7. At what point of this scenario, if at all, does HALLORAHAN first commit the offence under s 16 of the Act?

Explanation 19.3

1. The term 'possession' does not require HALLORAHAN to have actual physical possession of the items. Therefore, HALLORAHAN has possession of all three items. Possession does not even require the knowledge of the existence of the firearm and as long as the defendant knows that they have *something* then that is enough. However, in order to commit an offence under s 16, the firearm *must* be the means by which life is endangered and you can hardly endanger life with something that you do not know exists.

2. The Beretta pistol and the shotgun. You cannot commit this offence with an imitation firearm because life *cannot be* endangered with a *fake* firearm. An imitation firearm for the purposes of the criminal use of firearms offences (ss 16, 16A, 17(1), 17(2), and 18(1)) is anything that has the appearance of a firearm (but not fingers!).

3. The offence is complete if a person has a firearm in his possession with intent to enable another to endanger life. It does not matter that JAGO has not been approached and would not matter if he was and refused. *This is an offence of intent.*

4. This would be a conditional threat, but that would not alter the fact that the offence has been committed (*R v Bentham* [1973] QB 357). *This is an offence of intent.*

5. It does not. *This is an offence of intent.*

6. The life endangered must be the life of another and not the defendant's.

7. At the beginning of the scenario, when he has the guns (the Beretta and the shotgun) in his possession with intent to kill COURT.

See *Investigators' Manual*, para 3.9.6.1

Possession with Intent to Cause Fear of Violence

E

EXERCISE 19.4

Consider the offence of possession with intent to cause fear of violence as you read the below scenario. When you have finished reading, complete the tasks that follow the scenario.

HANSON is continually having parties in his garden and this is disturbing GILBERT (HANSON's neighbour), who finds the noise unbearable. One night GILBERT decides he is going to do something about the problem. He knows that HANSON is a violent individual and he will need to protect himself in some way before confronting him, so he puts an imitation firearm, which has the appearance of a Walther PPK pistol, in his jacket pocket.

GILBERT goes round to the HANSON's house and knocks on the door. Moments later the door is answered by HANSON's girlfriend, KILNER. As it is KILNER and not HANSON who has answered the door, GILBERT does not produce the imitation firearm. Instead, and intending to make KILNER fear that violence will be used against HANSON, he says to KILNER, 'Turn the music down or I'll break your boyfriend's arm!' KILNER does not believe GILBERT and tells him to go away before slamming the door in his face.

1. Think of the offence under s 16A only. You should be able to identify four issues from this scenario that will effect your decision in deciding whether or not an offence has been committed. What are they?

   i. _____

   ii. _____

   iii. _____

   iv. _____

2. Take each issue that you have identified in turn and state what effect it has regarding the offence.

   i. _____

   ii. _____

   iii. _____

   iv. _____

3. What is your conclusion regarding the scenario?

   _____

Explanation 19.4

1. You should have identified the following issues from the scenario:

   i. GILBERT has possession of an imitation firearm. Does this offence apply to imitation firearms?

    ii. The threat of violence is delivered to KILNER. Can the intention to cause fear of violence be delivered to a third party who would not be subject to violence if the threat were carried out?

    iii. The imitation firearm was not produced or used to make the threat. Would this have any effect regarding this offence?

    iv. KILNER did not believe GILBERT's threat. Does the fact that the person who receives the threat does not believe it make any difference?

2. Dealing with each issue in turn, you should have arrived at similar answers to the below:

    i. The offence can be committed, as it applies to imitation firearms as well as firearms.

    ii. The partial intention of the defendant must be to cause *any* person to believe that unlawful violence will be used against them *or another person*. The threat against HANSON can be delivered to KILNER.

    iii. While the firearm need not be produced or shown to anyone, the firearm or imitation must be the means for the threat. Possession of a firearm while making a general threat to someone who does not know of its presence (KILNER) is unlikely to fall within this section.

    iv. This is an offence of intention. Whether KILNER believes GILBERT is immaterial.

3. This information should lead you to the conclusion that GILBERT has not committed the offence under s 16A of the Act.

See Investigators' Manual, para 3.9.6.2

Using a Firearm to Resist Arrest

EXERCISE 19.5

Look at the following statements and decide whether they are true or false.

1. Using an imitation firearm as a means to resist arrest would constitute an offence under this section.

   True / False

2. This offence requires proof of 'possession' of the firearm.

   True / False

3. This offence requires proof that the defendant made some actual use of a firearm to resist arrest.

   True / False

4. DC SMITH is in the process of arresting NAYLOR for an offence of theft when his friend, BARKER, approaches the officer and points a silencer at him. She tells DC SMITH to let NAYLOR go. BARKER commits the offence under s 17(1).

   True / False

Explanation 19.5

1. True. However, the imitation firearm *must* be complete. Using imitation component parts to resist arrest would not constitute an offence.

2. False.

3. True. Proof of possession is not required, but proof that some use of a firearm or imitation firearm to resist arrest is.

4. False. Remember that a silencer *on its own* is not a firearm.

See *Investigators' Manual*, para 3.9.6.3

Possessing a Firearm while Committing or Being Arrested for a Schedule 1 Offence

This offence sometimes causes difficulty because of the problems associated with identifying what a Schedule 1 offence is. The **DART** mnemonic in your *Investigators' Manual* might help you remember what is included.

E

> **EXERCISE 19.6**
>
> Consider the below circumstances. Identify and deal with the key issues as they occur in the scenario.
>
> NORWOOD owes £2,000.00 to CAPE, but has refused to pay back the money he owes on several occasions. CAPE has lost patience with NORWOOD and drives to NORWOOD's house to get the money. CAPE has an imitation Browning pistol in the glove box of his car which he considers using to threaten NORWOOD with, but then decides he does not need to and leaves it in his car which he parks outside NORWOOD's house. He knocks at the door, which is opened by NORWOOD's wife moments later. As soon as the door is opened, CAPE says, 'Give me some cash or you'll get a beating!' NORWOOD's wife has no idea who CAPE is or that her husband owes him money and thinking she is being robbed, she hands over £500.00 from her purse. CAPE, who believes that he has a right in law to the money and thinks he is doing nothing wrong, gets back into his car and drives off, but not before NORWOOD's wife writes down his registration number. Mrs NORWOOD reports the incident as a robbery.
>
> 1. Think of the offence under s 17(2) only. You should be able to identify four issues from this scenario that will affect your decision in deciding whether or not an offence has been committed. What are they?
>
>   i. _____
>
>   _____
>
>   ii. _____
>
>   _____

iii. _____

_____

iv. _____

_____

2. Take each issue that you have identified in turn and state what effect it has regarding the offence.

i. _____

_____

ii. _____

_____

iii. _____

_____

iv. _____

_____

3. What is your conclusion regarding the scenario so far?

_____

_____

Police enquiries trace CAPE through the registration number of his car. The police attend CAPE's house and arrest him for the offence of robbery. CAPE's house is searched and the imitation Browning pistol is found in CAPE's bedroom.

4. Think of this part of the scenario in isolation. Has CAPE committed the offence under s 17(2)?

Yes / No

CAPE is charged with robbery and possession of a firearm whilst being arrested for a Schedule 1 offence and pleads not guilty to both offences. At his trial he is found not guilty of the robbery because there was no theft (belief in a right in law, s 2(1)(a) of the Theft Act 1968).

5. What effect will the finding of 'not guilty' have with regard to the charge of possessing a firearm while committing a Schedule 1 offence?

_____

_____

Explanation 19.6

1. You should have identified the following issues from the scenario:

   i.   CAPE has an imitation firearm. Can the offence be committed with an imitation firearm?

   ii. CAPE leaves the imitation firearm in the glove box of his car. Does this qualify as 'possession'?

   iii. The offence that Mrs NORWOOD believes has been committed is one of robbery. Is robbery a Schedule 1 offence?

   iv. CAPE believes he has a legal right to the money and has done nothing wrong. Is this a robbery?

2. Dealing with each issue in turn, you should have arrived at similar answers to the below:

   i.   This offence can be committed with an imitation firearm (imitation in the general sense).

   ii. Remember that possession is wide and that you do not have to prove that CAPE actually had the imitation firearm with him. In his car a short distance away would constitute possession.

   iii. Robbery is a Schedule 1 offence (coming under the **T** of **DART** as 'Theft, robbery, burglary, blackmail, and TWOC—Theft Act 1968).

   iv. This is an important point. CAPE has not committed a robbery because there is no theft.

3. If there is no dishonesty there is no theft. If there is no theft there is no robbery. If a robbery has not been committed, CAPE cannot commit the offence under s 17(2). He needs to have a firearm/imitation firearm in his possession at the time of committing a Schedule 1 offence and he clearly *has not* committed a Schedule 1 offence.

4. The imitation firearm is in CAPE's possession and he has been arrested for a Schedule 1 offence; therefore, he commits the offence under s 17(2). You might be confused as to how this can be if he has not actually committed the robbery and that is understandable. If it helps, think of the 'arrest' as a neutral part of the proceedings and ask 'has CAPE been arrested for a Schedule 1 offence?' The answer is 'Yes'. Whereas the answer to 'has CAPE *actually* committed a Schedule 1 offence?' is 'No'.

5. In light of the explanation at 4, you should realize that the finding of 'not guilty' will not affect the charge under s 17(2).

See *Investigators' Manual*, para 3.9.6.4

Having a Firearm with Intent to Commit an Indictable Offence or Resist Arrest

EXERCISE 19.7

Read the below scenario and answer the questions based on its circumstances.

SALISBURY is planning to rob a Post Office in a small village. He drives into the village and parks a short distance from the Post Office. SALISBURY has a 9 mm Beretta pistol hidden underneath the front driver's seat of his car, but he does not intend to use it during the course of the robbery, as his primary reason for having the pistol is to protect himself. SALISBURY begins walking towards the Post Office, but is arrested by the police who have been tipped-off about his plan.

Has SALISBURY committed the offence under s 18(1)?

Yes / No

Why / Why not?

_____

_____

_____

Explanation 19.7

SALISBURY commits the offence. The fact that he has a firearm (or imitation firearm) with him when intending to commit an indictable offence is all that is required. There does not have to be a connection between the firearm and the indictable offence the defendant is intending to commit.

The second part of the offence deals with the defendant resisting arrest or preventing the arrest of another.

Examine the below scenario then attempt Exercise 19.8.

PC LEY approaches AIDEY, who is trespassing on private land with a loaded shotgun in his possession. PC LEY arrests AIDEY for the offence of trespassing on land with a firearm under s 20(2) of the Act, but AIDEY points the shotgun at the officer and says, 'You're not arresting me, mate'.

E

EXERCISE 19.8

Consider the circumstances regarding PC LEY and AIDEY.

Would AIDEY commit an offence under s 18?

Yes / No

Why / Why not?

_____

_____

_____

Explanation 19.8

AIDEY would commit this offence. AIDEY has actually made use of the firearm but, as has already been mentioned, this is not necessary. All that is required is that he has the firearm with him.

See *Investigators' Manual*, para 3.9.6.6

Having a Firearm/Imitation Firearm in a Public Place

E

EXERCISE 19.9

Write down as much of the definition of this offence as you can.

A person commits an offence if

↓

↓

↓

↓

↓

↓

Explanation 19.9

Your answer should have contained the below detail:

A person commits an offence if
↓
without lawful authority or reasonable excuse (proof of which lies on him)
↓
he has with him in a public place
↓
a loaded shotgun
↓
an air weapon (whether loaded or not)
↓
any other firearm (whether loaded or not) together with ammunition suitable for use in that firearm or
↓
an imitation firearm

This is an 'absolute' offence and it does not matter if the person does not know that they actually have a firearm with them.

Try remembering it by using the mnemonic **FAIL**.

F	Firearm together with ammo for it
A	Air weapon
I	Imitation firearm
L	Loaded shotgun

Absolute **fail**ure in a public place is not allowed without lawful authority or reasonable excuse.

See *Investigators' Manual*, para 3.9.6.7

Possession of Firearms by Convicted Persons

E

EXERCISE 19.10

How long, if at all, would the named person be prohibited from possessing a firearm and (if there is a period of disqualification) when would it begin from?

RIPLEY was sentenced to 12 months' imprisonment for theft, but only served six months of her sentence.

Period:

Run from:

MATHER was sentenced to four months' imprisonment for assault, but was released after serving two months' imprisonment.

Period:

Run from:

GREGSON was sentenced to three years' imprisonment for robbery and served two years.

Period:

Run from:

FENNA was sentenced to ten years' imprisonment for a s 18 wounding. He served his full sentence.

Period:

Run from:

DOLAN was sentenced to five years' imprisonment for fraud and served three years.

Period:

Run from:

Explanation 19.10

Look at the below list and see if this assists you.

three years or more = banned for life

three months up to three years = banned for five years

Whatever the period of disqualification is, it begins on the day of release

$3 \times 3 = 5$

See *Investigators' Manual*, para 3.9.7

Police Powers (s 47)

E

EXERCISE 19.11

Consider the below scenarios and decide what course of action is open to the named police officer under s 47 of the Firearms Act 1968.

1. PC TRENT is on uniform patrol in a public place when she sees LINGUARD walking towards her carrying a shotgun. The shotgun is loaded.

   Can PC TRENT require TRENT to hand over the shotgun for examination?

   Yes / No

2. PC TRENT is on uniform patrol in a public place when she sees LINGUARD walking towards her carrying a shotgun. The shotgun is not loaded.

   Can PC TRENT require TRENT to hand over the shotgun for examination?

   Yes / No

3. PC TRENT is on uniform patrol in a public place when she sees LINGUARD walking towards her carrying a shotgun.

   Can PC TRENT detain and search LINGUARD in the exercise of her powers under s 47 of the Act?

   Yes / No

4. PC TRENT is on uniform patrol in a public place when she sees LINGUARD walking towards her carrying a shotgun. LINGUARD gets into a Ford Escort car that begins to drive towards the officer.

   Can PC TRENT stop and search the vehicle under s 47 of the Act?

   Yes / No

5. PC TRENT is on uniform patrol when she is called to a private school's playing fields where LINGUARD is shooting rabbits with a shotgun. LINGUARD is a trespasser.

Can PC TRENT require TRENT to hand over the shotgun?

Yes / No

6. PC TRENT is on uniform patrol when she is called to a house where there has been a report of a suspicious person in a private garden. When she arrives she sees LINGUARD cleaning his shotgun in the garden, which turns out to be his property. The call was made in good faith but was incorrect.

Can PC TRENT require TRENT to hand over the shotgun?

Yes / No

7. DC PARKER (dressed in plain clothes) is taking a witness statement from JONES when he sees KITSON walking down the street outside JONES's house with a shotgun. The shotgun is not loaded.

Can DC PARKER require KITSON to hand over the shotgun?

Yes / No

What will happen if KITSON says 'No'?

Explanation 19.11

Section 47 is a common sense power and works as follows:

A constable

can stop, search, and detain a person or vehicle and enter any place to do so

if he has reasonable cause to suspect

they have a firearm with them in a public place

and require them to hand over the firearm for examination

Where the person is not in a public place it is exactly the same, but the officer must have reasonable cause to suspect the person is:

Trespassing with a firearm in a building or

Trespassing with a firearm on land

1. Yes.

2. Yes.

3. Yes.

4. Yes.

5. Yes.

6. No.

7. Yes. If KITSON says 'No' a summary offence is committed.

See *Investigators' Manual*, para 3.9.8

Conclusion

This part of the Workbook has sought to provide you with an understanding of offences relating to the criminal use of firearms, as well as some associated subjects. You should be aware that there are a number of firearms issues that can only be addressed by reading the appropriate section in your *Investigators' Manual*.

Now that you have finished this section, you should attempt the 'Recall Questions' before re-reading the relevant section in the Manual and making your second attempt at the multiple-choice questions. The answers to these questions are printed in the 'Answers Section' at the rear of the Workbook.

Recall Questions

Try and answer the questions below. Do not allow yourself to continue until you have answered the questions to your satisfaction.

- What IS NOT a firearm?

- Explain when a silencer could be classed as a firearm.

- What is an imitation firearm?

- What is the only offence that you have studied in this section where the offence cannot be committed with an imitation firearm?

- Can fingers be an imitation firearm?

- What does the term 'possession' mean?

- What are the two offences that deal with firearms and resisting arrest?

- What differences are there between the two offences?

- Outline the offence of possession of a firearm with intent to endanger life.

- What does the mnemonic **DART** stand for?

- What does the mnemonic **FAIL** stand for?

- What does 3 × 3 equal and why?

- What are your powers under s 47 of the Firearms Act 1968?

PART FOUR

Sexual Offences

20 | Sexual Offences

Aim

The aim of this section is to provide you with an insight into ss 1 to 4 of the Sexual Offences Act 2003 and their associated topics.

Objectives

At the end of this section you should be able to:

1. State when victims of sexual offences are entitled to anonymity.
2. Define the offence of rape contrary to s 1 of the Sexual Offences Act 2003.
3. Explain the issues surrounding consent under ss 74, 75, and 76 of the Sexual Offences Act 2003.
4. Outline the meaning of the terms 'sexual' and 'touching'.
5. Identify when offences under ss 1 to 4 of the Sexual Offences Act 2003 have been committed.
6. Apply your knowledge to multiple-choice questions.

Introduction

Your examination syllabus covers some, but not all, of the Sexual Offences Act 2003. In this first section you will examine some of the more common sexual offences, along with issues relating to consent and the terms 'sexual' and 'touching'. The fact that the 'Sexual Offences' section in your Manual is small in comparison to the other sections of the Manual should not be misinterpreted as meaning that this section is unimportant. There is a strong chance you will be asked a significant number of questions relating to this legislation.

Multiple-choice Questions

Begin this section of the Workbook by answering the below multiple-choice questions. Mark your answer in the 'First Attempt' box. Then read and complete the exercises in the 'Sexual Offences' section. Once you are satisfied that your knowledge is of a good standard, return to these questions and mark your answer in the 'Second Attempt' box. The answers to these questions can be found in the 'Answers Section' at the rear of the Workbook.

MCQ 20.1   ABBOTT is the victim of an offence of sexual activity with a child (an offence under s 9 of the Sexual Offences Act 2003). DC COLES is investigating the offence and interviews ABBOTT. During the interview, ABBOTT expresses concern about her details becoming known to the public.

What response should DC COLES give?

A   ABBOTT will be entitled to anonymity until she is 16 years old.

B   ABBOTT will be entitled to anonymity until she is 18 years old.

C   ABBOTT will be entitled to anonymity until she is 21 years old.

D   ABBOTT will be entitled to anonymity throughout her lifetime.

First Attempt	
Second Attempt	

MCQ 20.2   EMERY and her common-law husband JOYCE are both serial sex offenders. They kidnap PORTER while she is walking her dog in a park and drag her into a nearby hut, where they sexually abuse her. During the attack, EMERY forces her fingers into PORTER's anus. Moments later, JOYCE forces his fingers into PORTER's vagina before forcing his penis into PORTER's mouth and ejaculating.

At what point, if any, is the offence of rape first committed?

A   When EMERY forces her fingers into PORTER's anus.

B   When JOYCE forces his fingers into PORTER's vagina.

C   When JOYCE forces his penis into PORTER's mouth.

D   The offence of rape is not committed in these circumstances.

First Attempt	
Second Attempt	

MCQ 20.3   MATELIN was born a male, but has had hormone treatment to create breasts and has had gender reassignment surgery to replace the penis with a surgically constructed vagina. While walking along a street, MATELIN is approached from behind by SUTTON who pushes MATELIN into a nearby alleyway. SUTTON digitally penetrates MATELIN's surgically constructed vagina and then digitally penetrates MATELIN's anus.

Does SUTTON commit an offence of assault by penetration (contrary to s 2 of the Sexual Offences Act 2003)?

A   Yes, but only when he digitally penetrates MATELIN's anus.

B   No, although the offence can be committed by either sex, the victim must be female.

C   Yes, when he penetrates MATELIN's surgically constructed vagina.

D No, this offence can only be committed when penetration is carried out with something other than a part of the body.

First Attempt	
Second Attempt	

MCQ 20.4 WALTON has a fetish for feet. He gets a job at a shoe shop in order to satisfy his desires and obtains sexual gratification every time he touches a customer's foot when he is helping them to try on a pair of shoes. WALTON realizes that shop customers would not consent to him touching their feet if they knew he was obtaining sexual gratification as a consequence.

Considering the offence of sexual touching (contrary to s 3 of the Sexual Offences Act 2003) only, which of the below statements is correct?

A WALTON does not commit the offence because a reasonable person would not regard his fetish as being 'sexual'.

B The fact that WALTON obtains sexual gratification from the touching means that it is 'sexual' and as a consequence he commits the offence.

C The offence is not committed in these circumstances because WALTON has not touched a sexual organ or orifice.

D WALTON commits the offence because he did not believe that his victims would consent to the activity.

First Attempt	
Second Attempt	

MCQ 20.5 OAKEY is walking home when she is attacked by KNOTT and JEVONS. KNOTT holds a knife to OAKEY's face and tells her that unless she masturbates JEVONS, he will cut her eyes out. OAKEY masturbates JEVONS and is then forced to insert her fingers in JEVONS's anus by KNOTT. JEVONS is a willing participant in the acts.

Which of the below statements is correct with regard to the offence of causing a person to engage in sexual activity without consent?

A Because OAKEY was forced to penetrate JEVONS's anus, this offence could be punished with life imprisonment.

B KNOTT only commits the offence because he forces OAKEY to insert her fingers in JEVONS's anus.

C The maximum sentence that KNOTT could receive would be ten years' imprisonment.

D The offence is not committed because JEVONS was a willing participant.

First Attempt	
Second Attempt	

Anonymity

EXERCISE 20.1

Examine the below scenarios and decide

i.   whether the victim would be entitled to anonymity owing to the nature of the offence;

ii. whether the age of the victim impacts on anonymity; and

iii. if they are entitled to anonymity, how long would it be for?

1. MANSFIELD is a 32-year-old victim of an offence of rape.

   Is MANSFIELD entitled to anonymity because of the nature of the offence?

   Yes / No

   Does MANSFIELD's age impact on anonymity?

   Yes / No

   How long, if at all, would MANSFIELD be entitled to anonymity for?

   _____

2. RILEY is a 14-year-old victim of a child sex offence.

   Is RILEY entitled to anonymity because of the nature of the offence?

   Yes / No

   Does RILEY's age impact on anonymity?

   Yes / No

   How long, if at all, would RILEY be entitled to anonymity for?

   _____

Explanation 20.1

The best approach to take with regard to whether anonymity will be provided or not is to presume that it will be. There is only one applicable time period—anonymity is for life.

See *Investigators' Manual*, para 4.1.3

Rape

EXERCISE 20.2

Examine the below scenario and then answer the questions, giving a short reason for your answer where appropriate.

FORSYTH (a 27-year-old male) is in a pub when he sees STEWART (an 18-year-old female). FORSYTH introduces himself to STEWART and buys her a drink and they talk for a while. There are no seats available inside the pub so the two walk outside into a deserted garden area and continue to talk. Several minutes later FORSYTH and STEWART begin to kiss and FORSYTH fondles STEWART's breasts with her consent. FORSYTH pushes STEWART to the floor so that she is kneeling down in front of him. He unzips his trousers and pushes his erect penis towards STEWART's mouth. STEWART says, 'No don't, I don't want to, I don't like oral sex.' FORSYTH ignores STEWART and pushes his penis into her mouth. Moments later FORSYTH takes off his trousers and pants and forces STEWART to lie down. As he does this, STEWART says, 'Don't do it you bastard!' FORSYTH pulls down STEWART's pants and attempts to put his penis in her vagina, but STEWART resists and punches FORSYTH in the face. FORSYTH retaliates and punches STEWART in the face several times. He tells STEWART he will kill her if she does not let him have sexual intercourse with her. STEWART believes FORSYTH and stops resisting. FORSYTH penetrates STEWART's vagina with his penis but does not ejaculate. Several minutes later, FORSYTH takes his penis out of STEWART's vagina, dresses, and leaves.

1. What is the definition of rape?

A person (A) commits an offence of rape if

↓

_____

↓

_____

↓

_____

↓

_____

2. At what point, if at all, is the offence of rape first committed by FORSYTH?

_____

_____

3. The fact that FORSYTH did not ejaculate would cause difficulty for the prosecution if FORSYTH were ever charged with an offence of rape.

True / False

Explanation 20.2

1. The definition of rape is:

A person (A) commits an offence of rape if

he intentionally penetrates the vagina, anus, or mouth of another person (B)

with his penis

B does not consent to the penetration; and

A does not reasonably believe that B consents

2. The offence is first committed when FORSYTH puts his penis into STEWART's mouth.

3. It is not necessary to prove ejaculation in a prosecution for rape.

Try remembering the definition by using the mnemonic **VAMPIRE**:

V	Vagina
A	Anus
M	Mouth
P	Penis penetrated
I	Intentionally and with no
R	Reasonable belief in consent and
H/Sh **E**	He/She does not consent to the penetration

This is the **only** offence where the offender **must** be male—*Remember, rape can only be committed by a penis*!

All other sexual offences on your syllabus can be committed by **both** sexes.

Consent and Presumptions

Let's return to the scenario involving FORSYTH and STEWART.

STEWART leaves the pub in a state of shock. She makes her way back to her flat and, having given the incident considerable thought, she decides that she will contact the police and make a complaint of rape against FORSYTH. She visits her local police station and reports the offence. DS NORTHWAY and several officers on her crew deal with the case. One of those officers is TI LAPWORTH. TI LAPWORTH is instructed to obtain a statement of complaint from STEWART. STEWART gives an account of the incident at the pub to the officer.

E

EXERCISE 20.3

Concentrate on the issue of consent under s 74 of the Sexual Offences Act 2003. What should TI LAPWORTH be considering when STEWART tells her about the incident?

_____

_____

_____

_____

_____

Explanation 20.3

TI LAPWORTH should note that, although STEWART was a willing partner at first, she did not consent to oral sex and was forced into the act. Sexual intercourse was obtained by threatening STEWART. Section 74 states that consent must be 'true' consent, not simply a submission induced by fear or fraud and that a person consents when they have the freedom and capacity to make that choice.

A statement of complaint is obtained from STEWART and she is medically examined to obtain evidence of the offence. DS NORTHWAY's team carry out a number of enquiries during which CCTV evidence from a security system at the pub is recovered. The CCTV is of high quality and shows the attack from start to finish. FORSYTH is identified from the footage and is arrested two days after the incident and interviewed about the offence. During the interview, FORSYTH maintains that STEWART had consented to oral and sexual intercourse with him and that he had not assaulted her.

E

EXERCISE 20.4

Consider the provisions under s 75 of the Sexual Offences Act 2003 (Evidential Presumptions About Consent) and answer the below questions.

The existence of certain specified circumstances (under s 75(2)) may allow the court to presume that the victim did not consent to the act and the defendant did not reasonably believe the complainant consented.

Rather than ask you to write down what these circumstances are, let's see if you recognize any of them in the below scenarios. Say whether the presumption can be made. We will start with FORSYTH.

A. FORSYTH was using violence against STEWART immediately before he had sexual intercourse with her.
   The presumption can/cannot be made.
B. RABIN approached LAWLOR who was pushing a pram containing her two-month-old baby. RABIN produced a knife and told LAWLOR he would stab her child to death that instant if she did not have sexual intercourse with him. LAWLOR had sexual intercourse with RABIN.
   The presumption can/cannot be made.

C. HUGHES has kidnapped EDGE and keeps him locked in a garage. HUGHES asks EDGE if he could have anal sex with him and EDGE replies 'Yes'. HUGHES penetrates EDGE's anus with his penis.

The presumption can/cannot be made.

D. HARPER goes to a party and has too much to drink. She goes into a bedroom and falls unconscious on a bed. KITSON enters the bedroom and decides to have sexual intercourse with HARPER while she is unconscious.

The presumption can/cannot be made.

E. COELLO is mute and because she is paralysed from the neck down she is confined to a wheelchair. INGLEY approaches her and asks her for sexual intercourse. When she does not reply, INGLEY takes her out of her wheelchair and has sexual intercourse with her.

The presumption can/cannot be made.

F. PICKFORD places a date-rape drug into ROBSON's drink, causing her to be stupefied. PICKFORD takes ROBSON to his flat and has sexual intercourse with her.

The presumption can/cannot be made.

Explanation 20.4

In all the above scenarios (A to F), the presumption could be made. This is a *rebuttable* presumption as the defendant does have the opportunity to challenge the presumption by producing sufficient evidence to raise an issue as to whether the victim consented, or as to whether the defendant reasonably believed the complainant consented.

Try to remember the circumstances of s 75(2) by thinking 'Sex **SLAVE**'.

S	Substance to stupefy
L	Locked up (unlawfully detained)
A	Asleep/unconscious
V	Violence or fear of violence to that person or another
E	E-mobilised (physically disabled)

The final section dealing with presumptions about consent is s 76 of the Act.

E

EXERCISE 20.5

Examine the below scenarios and state whether a presumption under s 76 would be drawn.

1. TIPPIN is a music teacher. He tells WIGLEY, one of his students, that if she has sexual intercourse with him it will improve her singing voice. As a result, WIGLEY allows TIPPIN to have sexual intercourse with her.

The presumption can/cannot be made.

Why / Why not?

_____

_____

2. John and James FELTHOUSE are twin brothers and have been seeing their respective girlfriends for six months. They decide it would be funny to exchange girlfriends for the evening. The brothers exchange girlfriends and have sexual intercourse with them, each pretending to be the other brother. The girlfriends are unaware that they have slept with a different brother.

The presumption can/cannot be made

Why / Why not?

_____

_____

Explanation 20.5

Think about s 76 as the 'fraud' presumption; consent has been obtained because of a lie. The presumption would be made in both examples.

1. WIGLEY has been told that having sexual intercourse will improve her voice. She has been lied to as to the nature of the act.

2. The girlfriends have slept with the brothers because they have impersonated a person known personally to the complainant.

This presumption is *irrebuttable*.

Remember that the issues surrounding consent under ss 74, 75, and 76 apply to all the offences under ss 1 (Rape), 2 (Assault by Penetration), 3 (Sexual Assault by Touching), and 4 (Causing Sexual Activity Without Consent) of the Act.

See *Investigators' Manual*, paras 4.3 to 4.3.4

'Touching' and 'Sexual'

E

EXERCISE 20.6

Before you examine the offences under ss 2, 3, and 4 of the Act, you must understand the terms 'touching' and 'sexual'. Answer the below questions with regard to those terms after reading the below scenario.

FARREL (a 21-year-old male) and HALLARD (a 20-year-old female) are common-law husband and wife. They place an advertisement in a local paper stating that they have a second-hand designer wedding dress for sale. LLOYD (a 30-year-old female) contacts them and arranges to visit their house to inspect the wedding dress. The truth is that FARREL and HALLARD do not have a dress for sale. They have placed the advertisement in the paper in an attempt to lure a lone female to their house, where they plan to sexually assault and murder their victim. At the arranged time, LLOYD arrives and is shown into the lounge of the house by HALLARD. HALLARD asks LLOYD if she would like a cup of tea and LLOYD replies that she would. HALLARD makes LLOYD a drink and the two women talk about weddings for several minutes before LLOYD asks to see the wedding dress. HALLARD tells LLOYD that the dress is in a wardrobe in her upstairs bedroom and suggests that she view the dress there. LLOYD agrees and the two women go upstairs. HALLARD walks through the bedroom door followed by LLOYD. As LLOYD walks into the bedroom and past the door, FARREL (who has been hiding behind the bedroom door) approaches LLOYD from behind and places a chloroform soaked rag to her mouth and nose. LLOYD struggles but is quickly rendered unconscious. When LLOYD wakes up she is still in the bedroom and fully clothed, but she is tied to a chair by her feet and hands and has been gagged. FARREL and HALLARD are both fully clothed and sitting on a bed watching her.

1. FARREL walks over to LLOYD and strokes her skirt. He does not actually touch her body. While he does this he says to LLOYD, 'Fancy a shag?'

   Is this 'touching'?

   Yes / No

   Why / Why not?

   _____

   _____

   Is this 'sexual'?

   Yes / No

   Why / Why not?

   _____

   _____

2. FARREL moves his hand onto LLOYD's leg and strokes her leg through her skirt saying, 'Go on, will you shag me?'

   Is this 'touching'?

   Yes / No

   Why / Why not?

   _____

   _____

   Is this 'sexual'?

   Yes / No

   Why / Why not?

   _____

   _____

3. HALLARD picks up a riding crop from the bed. She walks over to LLOYD and stands next to her. She rubs the end of the riding crop against LLOYD's breasts and says, 'I'm going to fuck you.'

Is this 'touching'?

Yes / No

Why / Why not?

_____

_____

Is this 'sexual'?

Yes / No

Why / Why not?

_____

_____

4. FARREL takes off his jeans and masturbates his penis against LLOYD's arm (through her blouse). He does not say anything.

Is this 'touching'?

Yes / No

Why / Why Not?

_____

_____

Is this 'sexual'?

Yes / No

Why / Why not?

_____

_____

Explanation 20.6

1. This would be regarded as 'touching' and 'sexual'. This is because 'touching' has been held to include touching a person's clothing (*R v H*, *The Times*, 8 February (2005)). It would be 'sexual' as, although this act is not sexual by its very nature (failing the first part of the definition of the term), it would fall into the second half, i.e. it becomes sexual because of the circumstances and FARREL's intention.

2. This would be regarded as 'touching' and 'sexual'. This is because the definition of 'touching' includes touching through anything (the skirt). It is 'sexual' for the same reason as point 1.

3. This would be regarded as 'touching' and 'sexual'. The definition of 'touching' includes touching with anything else (the riding crop). It is 'sexual' for the same reason as point 1.

4. This would be regarded as 'touching' and 'sexual'. It is 'touching' because the definition includes touching with any part of the body and through anything. It is 'sexual' because a reasonable person would always consider masturbation to be sexual by its very nature.

See *Investigators' Manual*, paras 4.2.1 and 4.2.2

Offences Under ss 2, 3, and 4 of the Act

FARREL and HALLARD subject LLOYD to a horrific sexual attack lasting a number of hours. At the end of the attack they leave LLOYD naked, gagged, and tied to a bed. They tell LLOYD they will be back in an hour to further abuse her and then kill her. After FARREL and HALLARD leave, LLOYD struggles violently to escape her bonds. She manages to free one of her hands and from there she is able to remove her gag and free herself. She tries to escape through the bedroom door but it is firmly locked. She runs to the window and pulling back the curtains she bangs on the window and screams for help.

While LLOYD was being attacked, her fiancé, JARVIS, had become concerned for her welfare. He tried to ring LLOYD on her mobile phone but received no reply. LLOYD had told JARVIS where she was going and so JARVIS drove to FARREL and HALLARD's house. He saw LLOYD's car parked near to the house and believing that LLOYD was still looking at the wedding dress, he decided to join her. As he walked towards the front door he saw his naked fiancée banging on an upstairs window and heard her scream for help.

JARVIS forces the front door of the house and runs into the house and upstairs. He kicks open the bedroom door and finds LLOYD in the bedroom. She tells JARVIS what has happened and JARVIS gets her out of the house and contacts the police. The police attend and after speaking to LLOYD and JARVIS, they lie in wait for FARREL and HALLARD to return. When they do, they are arrested.

LLOYD provides the police with a precise account of the incident, stating exactly what happened during her ordeal.

E

EXERCISE 20.7

Below is a table listing the actions of FARREL and HALLARD. For each action choose *one* offence you think has been committed e.g a tick in box 2 for an offence of assault by penetration.

	Action	1	2	3	4
1	FARREL penetrates LLOYD's vagina with a vibrator				
2	HALLARD orders LLOYD to masturbate FARREL				
3	FARREL makes LLOYD penetrate HALLARD's vagina with her tongue				

	Action	1	2	3	4
4	FARREL penetrates LLOYD's vagina with his penis				
5	HALLARD penetrates LLOYD's vagina with a glass bottle				
6	FARREL penetrates LLOYD's vagina with his tongue				
7	FARREL penetrates LLOYD's anus with a vibrator				
8	HALLARD kisses LLOYD's buttocks				
9	FARREL penetrates LLOYD's anus with his penis				
10	FARREL penetrates LLOYD's anus with his finger				
11	FARREL forces LLOYD to penetrate HALLARD's vagina with a vibrator				
12	HALLARD penetrates LLOYD's anus with her tongue				
13	HALLARD forces LLOYD to penetrate her own vagina with her own fingers				
14	HALLARD penetrates LLOYD's anus with a knife				
15	FARREL compels LLOYD to lick HALLARD's vagina				
16	FARREL penetrates LLOYD's mouth with his penis				
17	FARREL fondles LLOYD's breasts				

Explanation 20.7

If you have your *Investigators' Manual* with you, you should turn to the pages dealing with the offences under ss 1 to 4 of the Act. This may help you understand this exercise.

Section 1—Rape—Numbers 4, 9, and 16.

You should remember that this offence is triggered by the offender penetrating the victim's vagina, anus, or mouth with **his penis**.

Section 2—Assault by Penetration—Numbers 1, 5, 6, 7, 10, and 14.

As rape is the only offence that can only be committed by a man, this offence can be committed by FARREL and HALLARD. It involves the sexual penetration of the vagina or anus of the victim with a part of the offender's body, or indeed with anything whatsoever.

Section 3—Sexual Touching—Numbers 8 and 17.

You should have been able to identify these offences after the exercises in relation to both terms.

Section 4—Causing Sexual Activity Without Consent.

Where the offender(s) cause another person to engage in sexual activity involving some sort of penetration, the maximum penalty is increased from ten years' imprisonment to life imprisonment.

Your completed table should look like the one below.

	Action	1	2	3	4
1	FARREL penetrates LLOYD's vagina with a vibrator		X		
2	HALLARD orders LLOYD to masturbate FARREL				X
3	FARREL makes LLOYD penetrate HALLARD's vagina with her tongue				X
4	FARREL penetrates LLOYD's vagina with his penis	X			
5	HALLARD penetrates LLOYD's vagina with a glass bottle		X		
6	FARREL penetrates LLOYD's vagina with his tongue		X		
7	FARREL penetrates LLOYD's anus with a vibrator		X		
8	HALLARD kisses LLOYD's buttocks			X	
9	FARREL penetrates LLOYD's anus with his penis	X			
10	FARREL penetrates LLOYD's anus with his finger		X		
11	FARREL forces LLOYD to penetrate HALLARD's vagina with a vibrator				X

	Action	1	2	3	4
12	HALLARD penetrates LLOYD's anus with her tongue		X		
13	HALLARD forces LLOYD to penetrate her own vagina with her own fingers				X
14	HALLARD penetrates LLOYD's anus with a knife		X		
15	FARREL compels LLOYD to lick HALLARD's vagina				X
16	FARREL penetrates LLOYD's mouth with his penis	X			
17	FARREL fondles LLOYD's breasts			X	

See *Investigators' Manual*, paras 4.3 and 4.4 to 4.4.3

Conclusion

Now that you have finished this section, you should be able to differentiate between the offences created by ss 1 to 4 of the Sexual Offences Act 2003. You should be capable of identifying consent issues under the three appropriate sections and you should also be able to explain the terms 'sexual' and 'touching', which are of crucial importance to this category of offence. These abilities will not only assist you to answer questions on the subject in the NIE, but should prove to be of practical use in the workplace.

Now that you have finished the Workbook section on 'Sexual Offences', you should attempt the 'Recall Questions' before re-reading the relevant section in the Manual and making your second attempt at the multiple-choice questions. The answers to these questions are printed in the 'Answers Section' at the rear of the Workbook.

Recall Questions

Try and answer the questions below. Do not allow yourself to continue until you have answered the questions to your satisfaction.

- Who is entitled to anonymity and for how long?
- What is the definition of rape (can you remember the mnemonic)?
- What does s 74 of the Sexual Offences Act 2003 say about consent?
- List the six circumstances where a rebuttable presumption of consent may be raised by s 75(2) of the Act.
- What would need to be proved for this section to apply?

- What does the law say with regard to surgically constructed body parts?

- What are the two circumstances where an irrebuttable presumption about consent can be raised?

- What does the term 'sexual' mean?

- What does the term 'touching' mean?

- What is the *actus reus* of an offence under s 2 of the Sexual Offences Act 2003?

- When could you receive life imprisonment for committing an offence under s 4 of the Sexual Offences Act 2003?

- What is s 4 of the Sexual Offences Act 2003 about?

21 | Child Sex Offences

Aim

The aim of this section is to explain criminal offences relating to the sexual abuse of children.

Objectives

At the end of this section you should be able to:

1. Explain the offences connected with sexual activity with a child (ss 9 and 10 of the Sexual Offences Act 2003).

2. State when an offence of sexual activity in the presence of a child (s 11 of the Sexual Offences Act 2003) has taken place.

3. Identify key points from the offence of causing a child to watch a sex act (s 12 of the Sexual Offences Act 2003).

4. State when an offence under s 13 of the Sexual Offences Act 2003 (child sex offences committed by children or young persons) may be committed.

5. Outline the offence of arranging or facilitating the commission of a child sex offence (contrary to s 14 of the Sexual Offences Act 2003).

6. Outline the offence of meeting a child following sexual grooming (contrary to s 15 of the Sexual Offences Act 2003).

7. Identify the exceptions to aiding, abetting, or counselling an offence involving or directed towards children.

8. Identify common factors relating to offences under ss 9 to 15 of the Sexual Offences Act 2003.

9. Outline the offences connected with indecent photographs of children (s 1 of the Protection of Children Act 1978 and s 160 of the Criminal Justice Act 1988).

10. Apply your knowledge to multiple-choice questions.

Introduction

This section deals with offences under ss 9 to 15 of the Sexual Offences Act 2003, as well as legislation covering indecent photographs of children. It highlights the fact that not all the offences covered in your syllabus have their own individual paragraph reference, rather they are mentioned in the 'keynote' areas that explain the law in action. This, in turn, emphasizes the importance of the 'keynote' areas for your revision.

Multiple-choice Questions

Begin this section of the Workbook by answering the below multiple-choice questions. Mark your answer in the 'First Attempt' box. Then read and complete the exercises in the 'Child Sex Offences' section. Once you are satisfied that your knowledge is of a good standard, return to these questions and mark your answer in the 'Second Attempt' box. The answers to the questions are printed in the 'Answers Section' at the rear of the Workbook.

MCQ 21.1   COLCOUGH (a 19-year-old male) approaches LEENEY (a 14-year-old schoolgirl wearing school uniform) while she is waiting for her mother to pick her up outside the gates of her school. COLCOUGH begins talking with LEENEY and after several minutes he asks her if he can fondle her breasts. LEENEY agrees but before COLCOUGH can do anything, LEENEY's mother arrives, picks her daughter up, and drives off.

Which of the below statements is correct with regard to the offence of inciting a child to engage in sexual activity (contrary to s 10 of the Sexual Offences Act 2003)?

A   COLCOUGH does not commit the offence because LEENEY consented to the activity.

B   The fact that there was no sexual activity between COLCOUGH and LEENEY does not matter; COLCOUGH has committed the offence.

C   COLCOUGH does not commit the offence because he is under 21 years of age.

D   COLCOUGH commits the offence and, because LEENEY is under 16 years old, the offence is complete.

First Attempt	
Second Attempt	

MCQ 21.2   MOORWOOD is a paedophile and derives sexual pleasure from masturbating in front of children. He visits a park and hides in some bushes near to a set of swings where SANDARS (a 14-year-old boy) is playing. MOORWOOD comes out from behind the trees, drops his trousers, and begins masturbating.

With regard to the offence of sexual activity in the presence of a child (s 11 of the Sexual Offences Act 2003), which of the below comments is correct?

A   MOORWOOD must be at least 16 years old to commit this offence.

B   Sexual gratification does not form part of this offence.

C   The offence is not committed in these circumstances as SANDARS is over the age of 13.

D   It is not necessary to show that the child was in fact aware of the activity in every case.

First Attempt	
Second Attempt	

MCQ 21.3   TURNER (a 45-year-old male) is in his study at his home and is using the Internet to search for pornographic images. He is looking at a site where there are a number of still images of cartoon men and women having sexual intercourse. His nephew, MARTIN (who is 16 years

old), walks into the study and sees the images. TURNER asks MARTIN if he would like to see some more of the images and MARTIN replies that he would. TURNER shows MARTIN more of the still cartoon images and obtains sexual gratification from showing them to MARTIN.

Considering the offence under s 12 of the Sexual Offences Act 2003 (causing a child to watch a sexual act) only, which of the below comments is correct?

A TURNER does not commit the offence because the images are still cartoons and not real life moving images.

B TURNER does not commit the offence because MARTIN is 16 years old.

C It does not matter that the images are still or that they are cartoons, TURNER commits the offence.

D The offence is not committed because TURNER was originally viewing the pictures on his own and did not intentionally show them to MARTIN in the first instance.

First Attempt	
Second Attempt	

MCQ 21.4 TREVENA (a 15-year-old female) is approached by POWELL (a 35-year-old male) at her 15th birthday party. POWELL tells TREVENA that he will take her on an all-expenses paid trip to the USA as a surprise birthday present. TREVENA tells POWELL she will think about his offer. The next day, POWELL visits a travel agent and books the trip. POWELL intends to have sexual intercourse with TREVENA when they arrive in the USA (an offence contrary to s 9 of the Sexual Offences Act 2003). The next day TREVENA phones POWELL and tells him she will not be going with him on the holiday.

Does POWELL commit an offence contrary to s 14 of the Sexual Offences Act 2003 (arranging or facilitating a child sex offence)?

A Yes, because the offence is complete whether or not sexual activity actually takes place.

B No, because POWELL planned to commit the offence outside the United Kingdom.

C Yes, but only if TREVENA had agreed to leave the country with POWELL.

D No, because he planned to commit the offence rather than arranging that another person should do so.

First Attempt	
Second Attempt	

MCQ 21.5 HENSON is 18 years old and his girlfriend, JEFFERSON, is 17 years old. They have lived together for two years and have sex on a regular basis in a flat that they rent. One evening the couple are watching a DVD when HENSON produces a digital camera. He suggests to JEFFERSON that they have a bath and he will take pictures of her, to which she consents. They go to the bathroom and he takes pictures of her getting undressed and lying in the bath. HENSON takes off his clothes, puts the camera on a cabinet, sets a timer device and takes a picture of them both naked in the bath. The next day he shows all the pictures to his male friend at work.

At what point, if at all, does HENSON commit an offence contrary to s 1 of the Protection of Children Act 1978?

A When he takes the photograph of JEFFERSON.

B When he joins JEFFERSON in the bath and photographs them in the bath.

C When he shows his friend the photographs at work.

D The offence is not committed in these circumstances.

First Attempt	
Second Attempt	

Sexual Activity with a Child

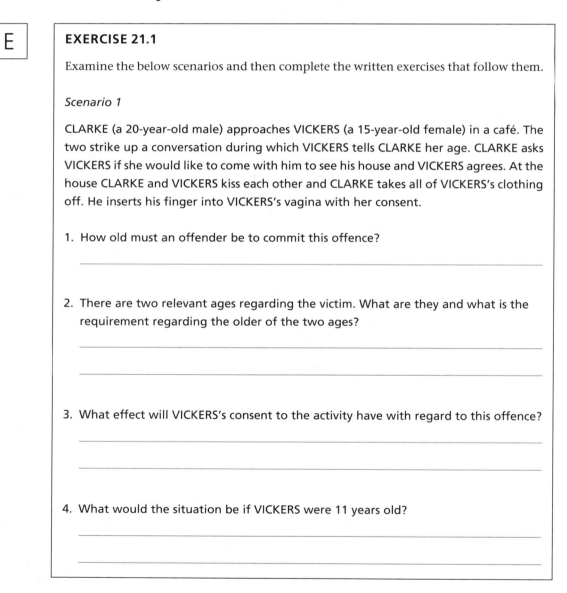

E

EXERCISE 21.1

Examine the below scenarios and then complete the written exercises that follow them.

Scenario 1

CLARKE (a 20-year-old male) approaches VICKERS (a 15-year-old female) in a café. The two strike up a conversation during which VICKERS tells CLARKE her age. CLARKE asks VICKERS if she would like to come with him to see his house and VICKERS agrees. At the house CLARKE and VICKERS kiss each other and CLARKE takes all of VICKERS's clothing off. He inserts his finger into VICKERS's vagina with her consent.

1. How old must an offender be to commit this offence?

    _____

2. There are two relevant ages regarding the victim. What are they and what is the requirement regarding the older of the two ages?

    _____

    _____

3. What effect will VICKERS's consent to the activity have with regard to this offence?

    _____

    _____

4. What would the situation be if VICKERS were 11 years old?

    _____

    _____

Scenario 2

CLARKE (a 20-year-old male) approaches VICKERS (a 15-year-old female) in a café. The two strike up a conversation during which VICKERS tells CLARKE her age. CLARKE asks VICKERS if she would like to come with him to see his house and VICKERS agrees. At the house CLARKE and VICKERS continue talking to each other and during the conversation CLARKE asks VICKERS if she would like him to put his finger in her vagina. VICKERS says, 'I don't know.' CLARKE replies, 'Go on, you'll enjoy it once I've started.'

1. Think about what CLARKE has done. What offence does CLARKE commit in these circumstances?

2. VICKERS replies 'no' and walks out of the house. Does it make any difference that no sexual activity has taken place?

   Yes / No

3. Imagine that instead of just chatting in the café, CLARKE asked VICKERS to come to his house and have sexual intercourse with his friend, FINCH. What effect would this have?

Explanation 21.1

Scenario 1

1. The offender must be at least 18 (18+).

2. The two ages are under 16 (−16) and under 13 (−13). If the victim is under 16 you have to show that the offender did not reasonably believe that the victim is 16 or over.

3. The fact that the victim (whatever their age) consents does not matter.

4. You may have found this question difficult to answer, so do not worry if that was the case. It was included because it is an obvious question to ask when you study child sex offences and there is no answer contained in your Manual. If VICKERS were 11 years old then it would appear that CLARKE has committed the offence under s 9 of the Act. However, you may have realised that the activity would also constitute an offence under s 2 of the Act (see previous section on 'Sexual Offences'), as all that would need to be proved is the intentional sexual penetration and the child's age. So which offence would be charged? Where a child is under 13, one of the relevant offences under ss 5 to 8 of the Act would normally be charged. The penalties for these offences are higher, reflecting the fact that a child under 13 cannot legally consent to sexual activity. However,

occasionally the offence might be used where the child is under 13. An example would be where a person was charged with the offence of sexual activity with a child, all parties believing the child to be 13 or over, and it then became known in the course of the trial that the child was actually under 13. The extension of the offence to children under 13 means that the trial could continue with the original charge when necessary.

Scenario 2

1. CLARKE is encouraging VICKERS to engage in sexual activity that would constitute an offence under s 9 of the Act. There is a specific offence of causing or inciting someone to commit the offence under s 10 of the Act.

2. No. Incitement (see 'Incomplete Offences' section) is all about trying to get someone to commit an offence. If VICKERS actually did something then the substantial offence would be committed. The offence exists to punish the pre-substantive offence conduct and so the fact that no sexual activity has taken place is immaterial.

3. The offence would still be committed, as the s 10 offence is about incitement to commit the offence with the defendant (CLARKE) or a third person (FINCH).

In the process of completing exercises relating to ss 9 and 10 of the Act, you will have unconsciously obtained information relating to the offences dealt with in ss 11 and 12. As you continue, see if you can see these connections.

See *Investigators' Manual*, para 4.5.1

Sexual Activity in the Presence of a Child

E

EXERCISE 21.2

Try answering the below questions to form the basis of the definition of this offence. Your answers should have between one and four words in them (other than the answers to questions 6 and 7, where you will have more words in the answer).

1. What age does the offender have to be?

2. What state of mind is required?

3. What must the offender do?

4. What kind of act must it be?

5. What is the purpose of the act?

6. He engages in the activity when?

_____

7. What has the offender got to know or believe?

_____

8. What age brackets must the victims fall into?

i. _____

ii. _____

Explanation 21.2

How far away were your answers from the actual definition of the offence?

A person aged *18 or over* (A) commits an offence if

↓

he *intentionally*

↓

engages in an activity

↓

the activity is *sexual*

↓

for the purpose of *obtaining sexual gratification*, he engages in it

↓

when *another person (B) is present or is in a place from which A can be observed*

and

knowing or believing *that B is aware, or intending that B should be aware,*
that he is engaging in it and

↓

B is *under 16* and A *does not reasonably believe that B is 16 or over* or

B is *under 13*

EXERCISE 21.3

Examine the below scenarios and decide whether an offence under s 11 has been committed. Give a short reason for your answer.

1. GAUNT (a 25-year-old male) is standing outside a portacabin, used as a changing room for under 16s who play football on a nearby field. GAUNT drops his trousers and to obtain sexual gratification he begins masturbating towards the portacabin, believing that there are children inside who can see him. The portacabin is in fact empty.

Section 11 offence committed?

Yes / No

Why / Why not?

_____

_____

_____

2. COPELAND and his girlfriend BONE (both 37 years old) are having a picnic in a secluded area of a campsite. They both believe they are alone and cannot be seen and begin to have sexual intercourse together. Unknown to either of them, NICHOLLS (an 11-year-old) is watching them.

Section 11 offence committed?

Yes / No

Why / Why not?

_____

_____

_____

3. THORNLEY (a 48-year-old male) is sitting in a steam room in a gym when PRICE (a 12-year-old female) walks in and sits opposite THORNLEY. THORNLEY pulls down his trunks and begins masturbating towards PRICE, believing she can see him and in order to gain sexual gratification. Unknown to THORNLEY, PRICE cannot see what he is doing because of the amount of steam in the room.

Section 11 offence committed?

Yes / No

Why / Why not?

_____

_____

_____

Explanation 21.3

1. This would not constitute an offence, as you must show that a person under 16 is present or is in a place from which the defendant can be observed.

2. This would not constitute an offence because neither COPELAND nor BONE knew, believed, or intended that a child should be aware that they were engaged in that activity.

3. This would constitute an offence, as it is not necessary to show that a child was in fact aware of the activity in every case. If you work through the definition you can see that

THORNLEY has intentionally engaged in sexual activity for the purpose of sexual gratification when another person (PRICE) is present and believing that PRICE is aware that he is engaging in it.

See *Investigators' Manual*, para 4.5.2

Causing a Child to Watch a Sex Act

E

EXERCISE 21.4

You should be able to answer the below questions based on your study of this section so far.

1. How old must the offender be?

_____

2. What age brackets do the victims fall into?

_____

The correct answers to the above questions have been placed in the appropriate place within the definition of this offence (set out below), along with some hints as to the missing sections. Can you fill in the gaps?

A person aged 18 or over (A) commits an offence if
↓

for the purpose of _____
↓

he intentionally causes _____

_____

_____
↓

the activity is _____
↓

and either

i. B is under 16 and A does not reasonably believe that B is 16 or over; or
ii. B is under 13

Explanation 21.4

Your answer should have contained the following:

A person aged 18 or over (a) commits an offence if

for the purpose of *obtaining sexual gratification*

he intentionally causes *another person (B) to watch a third person engaging in an activity, or to look at an image of any person engaging in an activity*

the activity is *sexual*

and either

   i.   B is under 16 and A does not reasonably believe that B is 16 or over; or

   ii. B is under 13

E

EXERCISE 21.5

Concentrating on the activity of the third person and the word 'image', answer the below questions (take it that all the other elements of the offence are satisfied).

1. The activity that the child watches can be live or recorded.

   True / False

2. There is a requirement that the child needs to be in close physical proximity to the sexual act.

   True / False

3. Which of the below would or would not qualify as an 'image' for the purposes of this offence?

	Image	Not an image
A film		
A photograph		
A magazine		
A 3-dimensional sculpture		
A cartoon		
A computer-generated picture		

Explanation 21.5

1. True.

2. False. For example, an offender could show a child a live image via webcam where the actual activity is taking place hundreds of miles away.

3. All of these examples would qualify.

See *Investigators' Manual*, para 4.5.3

Child Sex Offences Committed by Children or Young Persons

This offence is mentioned in the 'Keynote' areas explaining ss 9, 11, and 12 of the Act. The intention of this part of the Workbook is to draw your attention to the existence of the section.

You will have seen that in all of the offences examined so far (ss 9, 10, 11, and 12) the age of the offender is always 18+. What happens when someone aged less than 18 commits one of these acts?

Section 13 deals with this situation by saying that the person will still commit an offence. However, the maximum sentence for an offender who is less than 18 is five years' imprisonment.

Arranging or Facilitating the Commission of Child Sex Offences

E

EXERCISE 21.6

Look at the below scenarios. Has an offence under this section been committed?

MARCOU operates a sex-tourism business. HOPE approaches MARCOU and asks him if he can arrange for a 14-year-old girl to be made available to him to have sexual intercourse with. MARCOU tells HOPE that he can, but the abuse will have to take place in Thailand. HOPE tells MARCOU to go ahead with the arrangements and MARCOU books flights and a hotel for HOPE, and also makes arrangements for a 14-year-old girl to be made available to HOPE when he arrives in Thailand. MARCOU makes these arrangements in the belief that HOPE will have sexual intercourse with the girl when he visits Thailand. A week before HOPE is due to fly out to Thailand he is involved in a car accident and breaks his leg. He contacts MARCOU and tells him that he can no longer make the trip and to cancel all the arrangements.

1. Who, if anyone, has committed the offence under s 14?

   _____

   Why / Why not?

   _____

   _____

   _____

   _____

2. This offence can only be committed if the activities are to take place in the United Kingdom.

   True / False

3. Arranging what 'relevant offences' would trigger the commission of this offence?

    i.   _____

    ii.   _____

    iii.   _____

    iv.   _____

    v.   _____

4. Does the fact that MARCOU only 'believed' that HOPE was going to have sexual intercourse with a 14-year-old girl make any difference?

    Yes / No

5. HOPE never travelled to Thailand. What effect, if any, will this have on the case?

    _____

Explanation 21.6

1. HOPE and MARCOU have both committed the offence.
   The title of the offence tells you a lot about it, but it is unlikely to be enough for you to answer questions.

A person commits this offence when they:

intentionally

↓

arrange or facilitate something

↓

that they intend to do

↓

intend another to do or

↓

believe that another person will do

↓

in any part of the world

↓

and doing so will involve the commission of an offence under ss 9 to 13

You can see from the definition how both men would commit the offence.

2. False.

3. The five trigger offences are those that you have studied so far in this section of the Workbook, i.e. offences under ss 9 to 13.

4. No—see the definition.

5. None at all. The offence is complete whether or not the sexual activity actually takes place.

See Investigators' Manual, para 4.5.4

Meeting a Child Following Sexual Grooming

E

EXERCISE 21.7

Study the scenarios set out below. Answer the questions and provide an explanation for your answers where you are asked.

Scenario 1

HOLLIS (a 20-year-old male) has a full-time job working as a section supervisor in a supermarket. He is in charge of a number of staff, some of who are part-time. One of the part-time workers is SUMPTER (a 15-year-old female), who works in the supermarket on Saturdays. HOLLIS is aware that SUMPTER has a 'crush' on him and one Saturday she approaches him and asks him to go to a works party with her on the following Friday. HOLLIS agrees to go with SUMPTER and intends to have sexual intercourse with her at the party. HOLLIS phones SUMPTER on Thursday night and they talk about the party. On the Friday morning he phones her again and asks if he should take some condoms with him. SUMPTER tells HOLLIS that taking condoms will not be necessary as she will not have sexual intercourse with him; however, she will give him oral sex. HOLLIS travels to the party but SUMPTER does not turn up, as she is unwell.

1. What age should the offender be?

2. What about the age of the victim?

3. How many times must the offender have met or communicated with the other person?

4. Does the fact that SUMPTER made the initial contact have any bearing on the case?

   Yes / No

5. The communication by the defendant with the other person must have some form of sexual content in it.

   Yes / No

6. What is a 'relevant offence'?

7. SUMPTER did not turn up to the party. What effect(s) will this have?

_____

8. Does HOLLIS commit the offence?

Yes / No

Why / Why not?

_____

_____

_____

_____

_____

Scenario 2

KIRK (a 14-year-old male) lives next door to REDROW (an 18-year-old female). KIRK goes on holiday with his family to Spain for two weeks and REDROW is due to join them for the final week of the holiday. In the first week of his holiday, KIRK receives several text messages from REDROW telling him that she loves him and that she wants to have sexual intercourse with him when she arrives in Spain. KIRK sends several messages back to REDROW telling her that they do not have any type of relationship together and there is absolutely no chance whatsoever that they will have any sort of sexual contact. REDROW ignores these messages and when she flies out to Spain, she does so with the intention of having sexual intercourse with KIRK.

1. Can a female commit this offence?

Yes / No

2. The communications were sent from the United Kingdom to Spain. Does this make a difference?

Yes / No

3. REDROW was travelling to Spain intending to have sexual intercourse in that country. Does this make a difference?

Yes / No

4. There is no chance that REDROW could do as she intended. Does this make a difference?

Yes / No

5. Does REDROW commit the offence?

Yes / No

```
┌─────────────────────────────────────────────────────────────────┐
│   Why / Why not?                                                  │
│                                                                   │
│   ───────────────────────────────────────────────────────────    │
│                                                                   │
│   ───────────────────────────────────────────────────────────    │
│                                                                   │
│   ───────────────────────────────────────────────────────────    │
│                                                                   │
│   ───────────────────────────────────────────────────────────    │
│                                                                   │
└─────────────────────────────────────────────────────────────────┘
```

Explanation 21.7

Scenario 1

1. 18+

2. −16

3. Twice.

4. None at all.

5. False. There may be explicit sexual content in the communications, but there is no requirement that this must be the case. The communications could be completely inoffensive.

6. Any of the offences covered by Part I of the Sexual Offences Act 2003 (the sexual offences you have studied in your Manual).

7. It will have no effect. The intended offence does not have to take place, as this offence is all to do with the intentions of the offender when meeting or travelling to meet the other person.

8. Yes. HOLLIS has communicated with SUMPTER on a least two previous occasions and travelled to the party with the intention of having oral sex with SUMPTER (an offence under s 9 of the Act), who is under 16 years of age.

Scenario 2

1. Yes. Remember that the only offence that cannot be committed by a female is rape.

2. No. The meetings or communications can have taken place in any part of the world.

3. No. The meeting can take place in any part of the world.

4. No. Remember that this is an offence that is all about the *intention* of the offender.

5. Yes. REDROW has communicated with KIRK on at least two occasions and is travelling with the intention of having sexual intercourse with KIRK (an offence under s 9 of the Act), who is under 16 years of age.

See *Investigators' Manual*, para 4.5.4

Common Factors

s 9	s 10	s 11	s 12	s 13	s 14	s 15
↓	↓	↓	↓	↓	↓	↓
Offender 18+	Offender 18+	Offender 18+	Offender 18+	*Offender UNDER 18*	*ANY AGE*	Offender 18+
↓	↓	↓	↓	↓	↓	↓
Victim −16	Victim −16	Victim −16	Victim −16	Victim −16	Victim −16	Victim −16
↓	↓	↓	↓	↓		
Victim −13	Victim −13	Victim −13	Victim −13	Victim −13		

Exceptions to Aiding, Abetting, or Counselling

In certain circumstances a person acting in the interests of a child may appear to be aiding, abetting, or counselling one of the offences in the 'Child Sex Offences' section of your *Investigators' Manual*.

This will *not* be the case if the person is acting to protect, prevent, or promote the:

- **S** Safety of the child (protect)
- **T** Transmitted sexual infection (protect)
- **E** Emotional well-being (promote)
- **P** Pregnancy (prevent)

and not for the purpose of:

- **C** Causing or encouraging the sexual activity
- **O** Obtaining sexual gratification
- **P** Participation

See *Investigators' Manual*, para 4.5

Indecent Photographs of Children

Legislation in relation to indecent photographs of children is dealt with by the Protection of Children Act 1978 and the Criminal Justice Act 1988.

Remember that a person will be a 'child' for the purposes of both of these Acts if it appears from the evidence as a whole that he/she was, at the material time, under the age of 18.

Protection of Children Act 1978 s 1

E

EXERCISE 21.8

Answer the below questions relating to this legislation. Do not attempt to provide word for word answers; short notes/descriptions will be fine.

1. Apart from photographs, what other material is dealt with in this section?

   _____

2. There are four ways that a defendant can commit the offence. What are they?

   i. _____

   ii. _____

   iii. _____

   iv. _____

3. There are two defences to this offence. What are they?

   i. _____

   ii. _____

4. The 'Marriage and other relationship' section provides a defence, but the defendant will have to satisfy four criteria. What are they?

   i. _____

   ii. _____

   iii. _____

   iv. _____

5. There are exceptions for criminal proceedings whereby a defendant is not guilty if he/she proves that:

   i. _____

   ii. _____

   iii. _____

6. Using the information you have from the above answers to assist you, examine the below scenarios and decide whether the defendant has committed an offence. Give reasons for your answers.

Scenario 1

CUTLER is a delivery driver. He takes a sealed package from an office to the home address of GARGAN. He is stopped by the police as he walks towards GARGAN's house. The package contains indecent pseudo-photographs of children.

Offence committed?

Yes / No

Why / Why not?

_____

_____

_____

Scenario 2

FRIPP takes a photograph of his 17-year-old girlfriend, McQUEEN, who he is living with in an enduring family relationship. The photograph is taken with McQUEEN's consent. In the photograph McQUEEN is naked and sitting with her legs astride FRIPP's friend, LOGAN.

Offence committed?

Yes / No

Why / Why not?

_____

_____

_____

Explanation 21.8

You will probably not have been able to answer all of the questions from 1 to 5, but you should have had some knowledge of the subject. If you had filled in these questions you would have a note form of the offence and defences for this offence.

Photos and Pseudo-Photographs

Take or permit or make

Distribute

Possess with a view to distribute

Advertising that you distribute or show

Defence if there is a legitimate reason for possession/distribution

Defence if had not seen/did not know/no cause to suspect

Not guilty if

Child over 16 and

defendant and child were married or living in an enduring family relationship and

photo of child alone or child + defendant but no 3rd party and

child consented

Exception if

Making photo/pseudo-photo to prevent/detect/investigate crime/criminal proceedings

Member of Security Service and making was necessary function

Member of GCHQ and making was a necessary function

With this information you could answer the scenarios.

Scenario 1

No offence. The material is indecent and CUTLER is distributing it, but he has a defence as he has not seen the pseudo-photographs.

Scenario 2

Offence committed. FRIPP has only satisfied three of the four requirements for a defence under s 1A of the Act. As his friend LOGAN is in the picture, the offence is committed.

Criminal Justice Act 1988 s 160

This is the same as the offence under s 1 of the Protection of Children Act except:

It relates to *POSSESSION*

There is an extra defence—*photo/image sent to him without request and not kept for an unreasonable time*

The exceptions for crime/Security/GCHQ *do not apply*

See *Investigators' Manual*, paras 4.5.7 to 4.5.9

Conclusion

One of the major issues that Trainee Investigators are concerned with regarding child sex offences under the Sexual Offences Act 2003 are the relevant ages for the offences. Having completed the exercises in this section, you should appreciate the similarities between some of these offences and as a consequence you should be confident regarding the age requirements. You should also see the connections with the previous section examining 'Sexual Offences', as the terms 'touching' and 'sexual' are significant components of many of the offences you have examined. You should now possess a good knowledge of most of the child sex offences applicable to the National Investigator's Examination syllabus (familial and protection issues aside).

You should now attempt the 'Recall Questions' before re-reading the relevant section in the Manual and making your second attempt at the multiple-choice questions. The answers to these questions are printed in the 'Answers Section' at the rear of the Workbook.

Recall Questions

Try and answer the below questions. Do not allow yourself to continue until you have answered the questions to your satisfaction.

- When would a person be exempt from aiding, abetting, or counselling a child sex offence?

- What section deals with offenders who are under 18 years of age?

- What is the definition of the offence of sexual activity with a child under 16?

- What happens if a child consents to a s 9 (SOA 2003) offence?

- What must you show to prove an offence of engaging in sexual activity in the presence of a child (s 11, SOA 2003)?

- What is an 'image' for the purposes of a s 12 (SOA 2003) offence?

- What is a 'relevant offence' for the purposes of the offence of arranging or facilitating the commission of a child sex offence (s 14, SOA 2003)?

- What is the definition of the offence of meeting a child following sexual grooming (s 15, SOA 2003)?

- What is the relevant age for the offence under s 15?

- What is required if a defendant wishes to use the exception regarding marriage to a charge of possessing an indecent photograph of a child?

- What are the two defences to a charge of taking an indecent photograph of a child?

22 | Preparatory Offences

Aim

The aim of this section is to give you a thorough understanding of the 'Preparatory Offences' found under ss 61, 62, and 63 of the Sexual Offences Act 2003.

Objectives

At the end of this section you should be able to:

1. Define and explain the offence of committing a criminal offence with intent to commit a sexual offence (s 62 of the Sexual Offences Act 2003).
2. Define and explain the offence of trespass with intent to commit a relevant sexual offence (s 63 of the Sexual Offences Act 2003).
3. Define and explain the offence of administering a substance with intent (s 61 of the Sexual Offences Act 2003).
4. Apply your knowledge to multiple-choice questions

Introduction

Although these offences are dealt with relatively quickly in your Manual you will have realized by now that this is not indicative of your examiners' approach to the material. As preparatory offences are never far from the headlines, particularly the offence of administering a substance with intent, you can safely assume that questions on this area of the Sexual Offences Act 2003 may find their way into your examination in 2009.

Multiple-choice Questions

Begin this section of the Workbook by answering the below multiple-choice questions Mark your answer in the 'First Attempt' box. Then read and complete the exercises in the 'Preparatory Offences' section. Once you are satisfied that your knowledge is of a good standard, return to these questions and mark your answer in the 'Second Attempt' box. The answers to these questions can be found in the 'Answers Section' at the rear of the Workbook.

MCQ 22.1   FOXALL (an adult male) goes to a nightclub where he sees WALKER (an adult female) standing at the bar. He asks her if she would like a drink and she asks for an orange juice. FOXALL buys WALKER an orange juice, but before he gives it to WALKER he asks a member of bar staff to add a double vodka to the drink. FOXALL's motive is to stupefy WALKER so that he can commit an offence of sexual touching (contrary to s 3 of the Sexual Offences Act 2003) against her. WALKER does not notice her orange juice has been 'spiked' and after FOXALL has bought her three more 'spiked' drinks she becomes very drunk. She staggers towards the toilets and FOXALL follows her intending to fondle her breasts, but before he can touch WALKER she falls over. A member of staff comes to her aid and FOXALL decides to leave.

Does FOXALL commit an offence contrary to s 61 of the Sexual Offences Act 2003 (administering a substance with intent)?

A   No, as the offence of sexual touching has not been committed.

B   Yes, but this is an attempt to commit the offence.

C   No, as alcohol is not a 'substance'.

D   Yes, in the circumstances all the elements of the offence are present.

First Attempt	
Second Attempt	

MCQ 22.2   HUBBALL (a 56-year-old male) wants to sexually assault a female (committing an offence of sexual assault by touching contrary to s 3 of the Sexual Offences Act 2003 in the process). He is walking in a park when he sees PARTON (a 19-year-old female) place her pedal cycle against a tree and walk off into some nearby woods. HUBBALL decides to immobilize the bike so that it cannot be ridden and plans to sexually assault PARTON when she returns and is examining her bike. HUBBALL jumps on the front wheel of the bike to buckle it and smashes the chain mechanism.

Considering the offence of committing a criminal offence with intent to commit a sexual offence (contrary to s 62 of the Sexual Offences Act 2003) only, which of the below statements is correct?

A   HUBBALL commits the offence when he causes criminal damage to PARTON's pedal cycle.

B   Sexual assault by touching is not a relevant sexual offence for the purposes of this offence.

C   HUBBALL would only commit the offence if he committed an offence of kidnapping or false imprisonment.

D   This offence is only committed when the criminal offence committed is one involving physical violence.

First Attempt	
Second Attempt	

MCQ 22.3 ROCHESTER breaks into a house owned by NICHOLL. ROCHESTER searches the house for any property worth stealing and while he is searching he looks out of a window and sees NICHOLL in the back garden of her house, hanging some washing on a line. ROCHESTER decides to rape NICHOLL in the back garden, but as he is making his way through the house he is disturbed by NICHOLL's husband and runs away from the scene.

Does ROCHESTER commit an offence in relation to s 63 of the Sexual Offences Act 2003 (trespass with intent to commit a relevant sexual offence)?

A   Yes, as he was a trespasser and intended to commit a relevant sexual offence.

B   No, because he does not intend to commit the offence in the premises in which he is a trespasser.

C   Yes, but he will have to attempt to commit the relevant offence.

D   No, because when he entered as a trespasser he did not intend to commit a relevant sexual offence.

First Attempt	
Second Attempt	

Committing an Offence with Intent to Commit a Sexual Offence

E

EXERCISE 22.1

Write down anything you know about this offence.

_____

_____

_____

_____

_____

_____

Explanation 22.1

Did you include the definition in the above exercise? This is one of those offences where the title of the offence represents 95 per cent of the definition.

A person commits an offence under this section if

he commits any offence

with the intention of committing a relevant sexual offence

E

EXERCISE 22.2

Read the below scenario and use the information from the previous exercises to assist you to answer the questions.

BABB approaches GLADSTONE in a pub and begins chatting to her. Several minutes after they begin to talk to each other, BABB decides that he wants to have sex with GLADSTONE. However, it seems that he will be disappointed as, although GLADSTONE accepts a drink from him, she begins to talk to INMAN (another man standing at the bar). BABB feels insulted and annoyed by this rejection and decides that he will rape GLADSTONE at the first opportunity. BABB notices that GLADSTONE is wearing an expensive wristwatch and when the opportunity arises he manages to steal the watch from her wrist without her knowledge. His plan is that when GLADSTONE notices the wristwatch is missing he will help her look for it and then suggest that he escort her to a nearby police station to report it lost. As soon as they are outside the pub he will kidnap her and rape her. When GLADSTONE notices the wristwatch is missing BABB offers to help her look for it. GLADSTONE thanks BABB, but tells him not to bother as the watch was a cheap fake and then leaves the pub with INMAN.

1. Would the theft of the watch qualify as 'any offence'?

   Yes / No

2. What is a 'relevant sexual offence' and give an example of an excluded sexual offence?

   _____

   _____

   _____

   _____

3. Does there have to be an immediate link between the offence committed and the relevant sexual offence?

   Yes / No

4. What difference would it make if instead of stealing GLADSTONE's wristwatch, BABB waited for her to leave the pub and as she did he kidnapped her intending to rape her?

   _____

   _____

5. GLADSTONE left without BABB even getting close to the commission of the planned offence of rape. What effect will this have?

   _____

   _____

6. Does BABB commit the offence?

Yes / No

Explanation 22.2

As you will see, there is nothing complicated about this offence.

1. Yes, and for that matter so would *absolutely any other criminal offence.*

2. This is an area where it is better to remember the exception rather than the rule. If the intended sexual offence is not covered by the Sexual Offences Act 2003, then it is not a relevant offence. Your Manual gives a good example of this, stating that offences under the Protection of Children Act 1978 would not qualify. Therefore, committing a criminal offence with intent to take an indecent photograph of a child (s 1 of the Protection of Children Act 1978) would not constitute an offence under s 62.

3. No.

4. If the criminal offence is one of kidnap or false imprisonment, the maximum sentence is increased from ten years to life.

5. None whatsoever. Remember that this offence and the offences under s 61 (administering a substance with intent) and s 63 (trespass with intent to commit a relevant sexual offence) are all *preparatory offences*. The whole point of these offences is to cater for behaviour that falls short of the intended end offence in the mind of the offender. If the offender actually had raped or sexually assaulted his/her victim before the preparatory offence was committed, then you would charge them with the substantive offence and these offences would be a complete waste of time.

6. Yes.

See *Investigators' Manual*, para 4.7.1

Trespass with Intent to Commit a Relevant Sexual Offence

E

EXERCISE 22.3

Following the example from the previous offence, what do you think the definition of this offence is?

A person commits an offence if

↓

_____

↓

_____

↓

_____

Explanation 22.3

You might not have got the last line, but your answer should have looked similar to this.

A person commits an offence if

he is a trespasser on any premises

he intends to commit a relevant sexual offence on the premises; and

he knows that, or is reckless as to whether, he is a trespasser

E

EXERCISE 22.4

Answer the below questions.

1. What is a 'relevant sexual offence' for the purposes of this offence?

_____

_____

2. Which of the below would or would not be classed as 'premises' for the purposes of this offence?

Example	Premises	Not Premises
A semi-detached house		
A tent		
A portacabin used as an office		
An abandoned houseboat		
A car		

3. A person is a trespasser if they are on the premises without the owner's consent.

   True / False

4. This offence requires that the substantive sexual offence is at least attempted.

   True / False

5. The defendant must intend to commit the relevant offence on the premises.

   True / False

Explanation 22.4

1. A 'relevant sexual offence' for this offence is exactly the same as a 'relevant sexual of-fence' for the purposes of the offence under s 62 of the Act (committing a criminal offence with intent to commit a sexual offence).

2. Your answers should have looked like this:

Example	Premises	Not Premises
A semi-detached house	X	
A tent	X	
A portacabin used as an office	X	
An abandoned houseboat	X	
A car	X	

Open spaces or gardens would not be classed as 'premises'.

3. True.

4. False, this is a preparatory offence.

5. True. The premises where the offender is a trespasser must also be the intended location of the relevant sexual offence. If the offender is a trespasser in premises, but intends to commit the relevant sexual offence elsewhere, the offence is not made out.

See *Investigators' Manual*, para 4.7.2

Administering a Substance with Intent

EXERCISE 22.5

Examine the below scenarios and decide whether an offence has been committed or not. Give reasons for your answers.

1. DELEHAY is in a nightclub drinking from a bottle of beer. HURLSTON places GHB (a date-rape drug) into DELEHAY's bottle of beer without her knowledge, intending to stupefy her so that he can rape her. DELEHAY drinks the beer and passes out.

Section 61 offence committed?

Yes / No

Why / Why not?

_____

_____

_____

_____

2. KANSAL and RAVENHALL are in a nightclub drinking double vodka. KANSAL is sexually attracted to RAVENHALL and thinks that RAVENHALL might be more likely to have sexual intercourse with him if he bought her triple vodka. He suggests that they should have stronger drinks and RAVENHALL agrees. KANSAL buys RAVENHALL a number of triple vodka drinks, intending to make her more susceptible to his advances. Owing to the effects of the triple vodka drink, RAVENHALL agrees to have sexual intercourse with KANSAL.

   Section 61 offence committed?

   Yes / No

   Why / Why not?

   _____

   _____

   _____

   _____

3. TUCKWELL is working behind a bar in a pub when YASIN walks in. TUCKWELL has always liked YASIN, but she has constantly spurned his advances. When YASIN asks for a coke, TUCKWELL puts rohypnol (a date-rape drug) into her drink. He intends the drug to overpower YASIN so that he can commit an offence of assault by penetration (contrary to s 2 of the Sexual Offences Act 2003) against her. YASIN drinks the coke and becomes ill.

   Section 61 offence committed?

   Yes / No

   Why / Why not?

   _____

   _____

   _____

   _____

4. RIPPON and YOUNG (two females) are attracted to SHELLAM (a male) who works in the same office as they do. One evening when the three are working overtime, RIPPON approaches SHELLAM from behind and places a cloth impregnated with chloroform over his face. SHELLAM falls unconscious to the floor. RIPPON has done

this with the intention of enabling YOUNG to commit an offence of sexual touching (contrary to s 3 of the Sexual Offences Act 2003) against SHELLAM.

Section 61 offence committed?

Yes / No

Why / Why not?

_____

_____

_____

_____

Explanation 22.5

Before the exercises are explained it would be a good idea to refresh your memory in relation to the definition of this offence.

A person commits an offence if he

intentionally administers a substance to, or causes a substance to be taken by, another person (B)

knowing that (B) does not consent, and

with the intention of stupefying or overpowering (B)

so as to enable any person to engage in a sexual activity that involves (B)

1. An offence has been committed. HURLSTON has intentionally administered a substance to DELEHAY intending to rape her.

2. An offence has not been committed. Although alcohol is a substance for the purposes of this offence it has not been administered with the requisite intention, i.e. to stupefy or overpower. It would be an offence to add alcohol to 'spike' a drink where the victim did not know that they were consuming alcohol, or where the victim knew they were drinking alcohol but their drink was 'spiked'. It would not cover KANSAL encouraging RAVENHALL to get drunk so that KANSAL could have sex with her because RAVENHALL knew what she was drinking.

3. An offence has been committed. Remember that the reason for the substance being administered or being caused to be taken is to enable a person to engage in *sexual activity*, i.e. any sexual activity.

4. An offence has been committed. It is easy to become focused on date-rape cases, but remember that the substance can be administered in any way and not necessarily through a drink. The offence can be committed by a male or female and can be committed in order to enable some person (not necessarily the person who administered the substance) to engage in sexual activity with the victim.

See *Investigators' Manual*, para 4.7.3

Conclusion

Now that you have concluded this section of the Workbook, you should be conscious of the fact that there is more to these offences than meets the eye. Having said that, there is no need to make them out to be complex and lengthy affairs because that is plainly not the case. Completing this section should put you in a strong position to deal with any questions relating to these offences.

Before you attempt the 'Recall Questions', have a look at the sexual offence summaries overleaf which provide you with a brief summary of 'Sexual Offences'. Once you have completed the 'Recall Questions', re-read the relevant section in the Manual and make your second attempt at the multiple-choice questions. The answers to these questions are printed in the 'Answers Section' at the rear of the Workbook.

Recall Questions

Try and answer the below questions. Do not allow yourself to continue until you have answered the questions to your satisfaction.

- What is the definition of the offence under s 62 of the Sexual Offences Act 2003?

- What is a 'relevant sexual offence' for the purposes of ss 62 and 63 of the Sexual Offences Act 2003?

- What does the term 'premises' mean?

- What is a 'substance' for the purposes of s 61 of the Sexual Offences Act 2003?

- What is the definition of the offence under s 63 of the Sexual Offences Act 2003?

Sexual Offences Act 2003—Offence Summaries

Sexual offences

Section 1 Rape	→	Male offender **VAMPIRE** ss 74, 75, 76 apply
Section 2 Assault by Penetration	→	Penetrating vagina or anus with anything ss 74, 75, 76 apply
Section 3 Sexual Touching	→	Sexual touching without consent ss 74, 75, 76 apply
Section 4 Causing Sexual Activity	→	Intentionally cause sexual activity Penetration = life ss 74, 75, 76 apply

Section 5 Rape Victim U13	→
Section 6 Assault by Penetration Victim U13	→
Section 7 Sexual Touching Victim U13	→
Section 8 Causing Sexual Activity Victim U13	→

Anonymity, consent, sexual, touching and conduct

Anonymity → Presume anonymity for life

Section 74
Consent → Must be 'true' no fear or force
Agree by choice
Freedom and capacity to choose

Section 75
Evidential Presumptions → Rebuttable
Sex **SLAVE**

Section 76
Conclusive Presumptions → Irrebuttable
Deception or Impersonate

Section 78
Sexual → Sexual by nature
May be sexual + circumstances or purpose
No exotic fetishes

Section 79
Touching → Any body part, with anything, through anything

Criminal Conduct → Penetration is a continuing act
No need for ejaculation
Surgically constructed = real

Child sex offences

Section 9
Sexual Activity with Child → Section 16
Sexual Activity with Child
Position of Trust → Offender 18+
Victim U16 or U13
Consent is irrelevant

Section 10
Inciting Section 9 → With defendant or 3rd party
No need for sexual activity

Section 11
Sexual Activity in Presence of Child → Section 18
Sexual Activity in Presence of Child
Position of Trust → Offender 18+
Victim U16 or U13
For sexual gratification
Child must be there

Section 12
Causing Child to Watch a Sexual Act → Section 19
Causing a Child to Watch a Sexual Act
Position of Trust → Offender 18+
Victim U16 or U13
For sexual gratification
Watch 3rd person or image

Section 13
Child Sex Offence Committed by U18 → Same offences as s 9 to 12
Offender U18
Max five years' imprisonment

Section 14
Arranging or Facilitating Child Sex Offences → Arranging or facilitating s 9 to 13
Any part of the world
No need for sexual activity

Section 15
Meeting a Child Following Sexual Grooming → Offender 18+
Victim U16
Met or communicated twice
Any part of the world for sex offence

Preparatory offences

Section 61
Administer Substance with Intent →
- Any substance
- Any sexual offence
- Enable any person to engage in activity
- No need for ulterior sex offence to take place

Section 62
Commit Criminal Offence with Intent to Commit Sexual Offence →
- Any criminal offence
- Any sex offence covered by SOA 2003
- Kidnap or False imprisonment = Life
- No need for ulterior sex offence to take place

Section 63
Trespass with Intent to Commit a Relevant Sexual Offence →
- Premises = any structure or vehicle
- Offence must take place in premises
- Any sex offence covered by SOA 2003
- No need for ulterior sex offence to take place

PART FIVE

Answers Section

Answers Section

1. State of Mind and Criminal Conduct

Answers to Multiple-choice Questions

MCQ 1.1 Answer **C**—After the decision in *R v G & R* [2003] 3 WLR 1060, objective recklessness has all but been consigned to history. This makes answers A and B incorrect (as B is objective recklessness). Answer D is fabricated.

Investigators' Manual, para 1.1.4.2

MCQ 1.2 Answer **A**—These facts are very similar to the case of *R v Smith* [1959] 2 QB 35. It is only in exceptional circumstances that medical treatment will break the chain of causation (*R v Jordan* (1956) 40 Cr App R 152), making answer C incorrect. Following the 'but for' test, the fact that LOVATT received poor treatment and was dropped several times on the way to the hospital will not affect GRICE's liability, making answers B and D incorrect.

Investigators' Manual, paras 1.2.4 to 1.2.5

MCQ 1.3 Answer **C**—Drug dealers are not generally liable for the ultimate deaths of their victims (*R v Dalby* [1982] 1 WLR 425 and *R v Armstrong* [1989] Crim LR 149), making answer A incorrect. You must take your victim as you find them, making answer B incorrect (*R v Blaue* [1975] 1 WLR 1411) and answer D incorrect (*R v Haywood* (1908) 21 Cox CC 692).

Investigators' Manual, para 1.2.5

MCQ 1.4 Answer **A**—Although not frequent, there have been instances where the courts have held an offence does not require any *mens rea* to be proved. Answer B is incorrect as in some rare cases, absolute liability can be imposed. Answer C is incorrect as 'intent' is not defined by law as it varies according to the offence being committed. Answer D is incorrect as 'objective' recklessness has effectively been eliminated by the decision in *R v G & R* [2003] 3 WLR 1060.

Investigators' Manual, paras 1.1.2 to 1.1.4.2

MCQ 1.5 Answer **C**—When proving *actus reus* you must show that the defendant's conduct was voluntary and that it occurred while the defendant still had the required *mens rea*.

Investigators' Manual, para 1.1.2

2. Incomplete Offences

Answers to Multiple-choice Questions

MCQ 2.1   Answer **D** — Answer A is incorrect as there can be a conspiracy where a husband and wife are involved in the offence, just as long as they are not the only two parties to the conspiracy. An abandoning of the agreement altogether will not prevent a statutory conspiracy being committed, making answer B incorrect. Just because SALE happens to work at the bank will not prevent a conspiracy taking place, making answer C incorrect.

Investigators' Manual, para 1.3.3.1

MCQ 2.2   Answer **C** — At points 'A' and 'B', BLACKMAN's activities are 'merely preparatory'. At point 'C' he 'embarks on the crime proper' and has gone beyond mere preparation, making answer D incorrect.

Investigators' Manual, para 1.3.4

MCQ 2.3   Answer **A** — You cannot attempt a summary only offence. However, if the offence is a summary only offence solely because of a statutory limit imposed in some cases (e.g. criminal damage to property of low value), then the offence can be attempted, making answer B incorrect. You *can* attempt the factually impossible, making answer C incorrect. Answer D is incorrect, as MYCROFT's actions have gone beyond mere preparation.

Investigators' Manual, para 1.3.4

MCQ 2.4   Answer **C** — This question checks whether you know the exceptions regarding the Criminal Attempts Act 1981. You cannot attempt to conspire, making answer A incorrect. You cannot attempt to counsel, making answer B incorrect, and you cannot attempt to procure the commission of an offence, making answer D incorrect.

Investigators' Manual, para 1.3.4

MCQ 2.5   Answer **A** — Vehicle interference is committed when a person interferes with a motor vehicle or trailer with the intention that they or some other person will steal the vehicle or trailer, steal anything in the motor vehicle or trailer or commit TWOC (s 12(1) of the Theft Act 1968. The intention to commit criminal damage will not support a charge of vehicle interference, making answers B, C and D incorrect.

Investigators' Manual, para 1.3.4.1

3. The Regulation of Investigatory Powers Act (RIPA) 2000

Answers to Multiple-choice Questions

MCQ 3.1   Answer **C** — A C.H.I.S. is someone who establishes or maintains a relationship with another person for the covert purpose of obtaining information or providing access to information or who covertly discloses information obtained by the use of such a relationship. This will not cover members of the public who contact the police and supply general information to them, making answer A incorrect. Answer B is incorrect as the definition will not cover instances where members of the public have come across information in the ordinary course of their jobs and who suspect criminal activity and then pass that information to the police. However, once the police begin to direct the person, for example by asking them to develop the information in some way to enhance it, that person could then become a C.H.I.S. making answer D incorrect.

Investigators' Manual, para 1.4.5.1

MCQ 3.2   Answer **D** — C.H.I.S. authorizations can cover activity carried out in the United Kingdom or elsewhere.

Investigators' Manual, para 1.4.5.2

MCQ 3.3   Answer **B** — In the case of the police services in England and Wales and in normal circumstances, the authorizing officer for C.H.I.S. is a superintendent or above. Authorization will last for 12 months.

Investigators' Manual, paras 1.4.5.2 and 1.4.5.3

MCQ 3.4   Answer **B** — Intrusive surveillance deals with surveillance on residential premises or private vehicles, making answers A and C incorrect as this is taking place in factory premises. The activity would be covered by the Act, making answer D incorrect, as this is a specific operation that is covert and likely to result in the obtaining of private information about a person.

Investigators' Manual, para 1.4.6.4

MCQ 3.5   Answer **A** — This is one of the exceptions to the normal rules relating to surveillance. Intercepting communications by telephone will be directed surveillance if the communication is sent or intended to be received by someone who has *consented* to its interception and there is no interception warrant.

Investigators' Manual, para 1.4.6.1

MCQ 3.6   Answer **D** — Urgent authorization for directed surveillance can be granted by an officer of inspector rank or above. It must be in writing and will last for a period of three days (72 hours).

Investigators' Manual, para 1.4.6.2

MCQ 3.7   Answer **D** — Intrusive surveillance authorizations last for three months.

Investigators' Manual, para 1.4.6.5

4. Code 'B', Entry, Search, and Seizure

Answers to Multiple-choice Questions

MCQ 4.1   Answer **B** — When the detained person is in police custody at a designated police station, a s 18 search is authorized by an officer of the rank of inspector or above, making answer D incorrect. Answer A is incorrect as the search can take place if the officer has reasonable grounds to suspect that evidence relating to the indictable offence for which the person has been arrested or to some other indictable offence which is connected to or similar to that offence will be on the premises. Answer C is incorrect because theft is an either way offence which means that it is indictable.

Investigators' Manual, para 1.5.3.1

MCQ 4.2   Answer **A** — Section 32 allows an officer to search an arrested person for anything which might be evidence relating to the offence, making answer D incorrect. A search of the bed-sit and communal lounge in the house can only take place if DC AHMED has reasonable grounds for believing (*not suspecting*) that there is evidence for which the search is permitted on those premises. Therefore, answers B and C are incorrect.

Investigators' Manual, paras 1.5.3.2 and 1.5.3.3

MCQ 4.3   Answer **B** — Section 17 of PACE is a power to enter and search in order to arrest not to search for evidence, making answer D incorrect. The power can be executed by an officer in plain clothes in these circumstances, making answer A incorrect. Whether the occupier has been spoken with or not will not stop this power being used, making answer C incorrect.

Investigators' Manual, para 1.5.3.5

MCQ 4.4   Answer **D** — Section 19 is a power of seizure and does not provide a power to search, making answer C incorrect. The power can be used when a constable reasonably believes that the item has either been obtained in the consequence of an offence or is evidence in relation to an offence he/she is investigating or any other offences and it is necessary to seize the item to prevent it being lost, damaged, altered, or destroyed, making answer B incorrect. Answer A is incorrect as the power can only be used when the officer is 'lawfully' on the premises. DC DYER has been told to leave and is no longer 'lawfully' on the premises and is a trespasser and cannot then seize any property he may find.

Investigators' Manual, para 1.5.4.1

MCQ 4.5   Answer **B** — Answer A is incorrect as a s 8 warrant can permit entry on a number of occasions. Answer C is incorrect as the warrant may be a 'specific premises' warrant or an 'all premises' warrant. Answer D is incorrect as possession of a warrant under s 8 does not authorize police officers to seize all material found on relevant premises to be taken away and 'sifted' somewhere else (*R v Chesterfield Justices, ex parte Bramley* [2000] 2 WLR 409.

Investigators' Manual, para 1.5.2.3

5. Codes 'C', 'D', and 'E' Case Study

Answers to Multiple-choice Questions

MCQ 5.1   Answer **C** — A person, including a parent or guardian, should not be an appropriate adult if they are

i.   suspected of involvement in the offence, or
ii. the victim, or
iii. a witness, or
iv. involved in the investigation.

In addition, if the person has received admissions prior to attending to act as an appropriate adult, they will be prevented from acting in that capacity. If a juvenile's parent is estranged from the juvenile (as with BOYD), they should not be asked to act as the appropriate adult if the juvenile expressly and specifically objects to their presence.

Code 'C' Notes for Guidance 1B

MCQ 5.2   Answer **A** — The custody officer should record any comment the detainee makes in relation to the arresting officer's account, but shall not invite comment; this makes answer C incorrect. The custody officer shall not put specific questions to the detainee regarding their involvement in any offence, nor in respect of any comments made in response to the arresting officer's account, making answers B and D incorrect.

Code 'C' 3.4

MCQ 5.3   Answer **D** — Detained people may be allowed to speak to a person on the telephone for a reasonable time. However, the right can be delayed if the detainee is in custody for an indictable offence (as well as being detained under the Terrorism Act 2000), making answer B incorrect. The authorization required is that of an officer of the rank of inspector or above. If the facility is allowed, then the person making the phone call should be informed that the call may be listened to and may be given in evidence, making answer C incorrect. Answer A is fabricated, as whether the person is a juvenile or not makes no difference to the denial or delay of the facility.

Code 'C' 5.6 to 5.7

MCQ 5.4   Answer **B** — A solicitor or appropriate adult must be permitted to consult a detainee's custody record as soon as practicable after their arrival at the station and at any other time whilst the person is detained. Arrangements for this access must be agreed with the custody officer and may not unreasonably interfere with the custody officer's duties.

Code 'C' 2.4

MCQ 5.5   Answer **A** — If video cameras are installed in the custody area, notices shall be prominently displayed showing cameras are in use. Any request to have the video cameras switched off shall be refused.

Code 'C' 3.11

MCQ 5.6   Answer **B** — If it appears a person does not understand the caution, the person giving it should explain it in his or her own words.

Code 'C' Notes for Guidance 10D

MCQ 5.7   Answer **A** — If the suspect refuses to sign their disagreement then the refusal should be recorded. It does not matter who records this refusal.

Code 'C' Notes for Guidance 11E

MCQ 5.8   Answer **C** — If the interviewer considers a solicitor acts in a way that the interviewer is unable properly to put questions to the suspect, the interviewer will stop the interview and consult an officer not below superintendent rank, if one is readily available, and otherwise an officer not below inspector rank not connected with the investigation.

Code 'C' 6.10

MCQ 5.9   Answer **D** — A detainee who wants legal advice may not be interviewed unless the detainee changes their mind about wanting legal advice. In these circumstances the interview may be started or continued without delay, provided that the detainee agrees to do so in writing or on tape and an officer of inspector rank or above has enquired about the detainee's reasons for their change of mind and gives authority for the interview to proceed.

Code 'C' 6.6 (d)

MCQ 5.10   Answer **B** — If a solicitor arrives at the station to see a particular person, that person must, unless Annex B applies, be so informed whether or not they are being interviewed and asked if they would like to see the solicitor. This applies even if the detainee has declined legal advice or, having requested it, subsequently agreed to be interviewed without receiving advice. This makes answers A and C incorrect. The detainee should be asked if they would like to see the solicitor regardless of the legal advice already received, making answer D incorrect.

Code 'C' 6.15

MCQ 5.11   Answer **B** — Meal breaks should normally last at least 45 minutes.

Code 'C' Notes for Guidance 12B

MCQ 5.12   Answer **C** — Shorter breaks after two hours should last at least 15 minutes.

Code 'C' Notes for Guidance 12B

MCQ 5.13   Answer **D** — If the suspect leaves the interview room during a break, then the tapes shall be removed from the tape recorder and the procedures for the conclusion of an interview followed. If the suspect leaves the interview room, then it is immaterial whether an interviewer or solicitor or both remain. This makes answers A and B incorrect. If the suspect remains in the interview room during the short break, then there is no need to remove the tapes and the same tapes can be used when the interview recommences, making answer C incorrect.

Code 'E' 4.12 to 4.14

MCQ 5.14   Answer **A** — The suspect shall initially be offered a video identification parade, making answer D incorrect. The choice is that of the officer in charge of the case (in consultation with the identification officer), making answer B incorrect. The suspect and his/her solicitor are allowed to make representations as to why another procedure should be used, making answer C incorrect.

Code 'D' 3.14

MCQ 5.15   Answer **B** — In these circumstances the interviewer should call an officer of at least inspector rank, or if not available the custody officer, into the interview room and ask him/her to sign the master tape seal.

Code 'E' 4.18

6. Special Warnings

Answers to Multiple-choice Questions

MCQ 6.1   Answer **B** — Answers A and C are incorrect as, although the necklace was not found on DOOLEY's person or in or on his clothing or footwear, this would not preclude the giving of a special warning to DOOLEY in these circumstances. Answer D is incorrect, as it does not matter who gives the special warning to DOOLEY.

Investigators' Manual, para 1.8.7

MCQ 6.2   Answer **D** — Special warnings *do apply* to 'no comment' interviews, making answer B incorrect. Answer C is incorrect, as the presence of a solicitor is immaterial as long as the suspect has had the opportunity to consult one. Answer A is incorrect, as SINGH was not arrested 'at a place at or about the time the offence was committed'.

Investigators' Manual, para 1.8.8

MCQ 6.3   Answer **D** — Answers A, B, and C are all incorrect as all of these are requirements when delivering a special warning to a suspect. Answer D is correct, as the suspect *does not* have to be cautioned at the conclusion of the special warning.

Investigators' Manual, para 1.8.7

7. Administration of Justice

Answers to Multiple-choice Questions

MCQ 7.1   Answer **A** — The offence can be committed in 'judicial proceedings' which includes courts, tribunals, or persons hearing evidence on oath, making answer B incorrect. The offence can be committed by a witness or an interpreter, making answer C incorrect. The offence is punishable with seven years' imprisonment, making answer D incorrect.

Investigators' Manual, para 1.14.1

MCQ 7.2   Answer **C** — A charge of perverting the course of justice does not require the authorization of the Director of Public Prosecutions (DPP), making answer A incorrect. Answer B is incorrect, as destroying or concealing evidence are just two ways this offence can be committed; there are numerous other ways available as long as there is a positive act by the defendant. The offence can involve intimidating witnesses, but can also involve the destruction, concealment, or falsification of evidence, making answer D incorrect.

Investigators' Manual, para 1.14.2

MCQ 7.3   Answer **A** — The fact that the threat is made to MOSS or is made otherwise than in the presence of the victim is immaterial, making answers B and D incorrect. The fact that the original offence is an assault makes no difference to the commission of the offence, making answer C incorrect.

Investigators' Manual, para 1.14.3.1

MCQ 7.4   Answer **B** — Where the sentence for the original offence is 14 years, this offence would be punishable with a sentence of seven years' imprisonment, making answers A, C, and D incorrect.

investigators' Manual, para 1.14.5

MCQ 7.5   Answer **B** — There is no limitation placed on the sentence for the offence the defendant has assisted, making answer A incorrect. This offence cannot be attempted, making answer C incorrect. The consent of the DPP and not the Attorney General is required before a prosecution is brought, making answer D incorrect.

Investigators' Manual, para 1.14.5

MCQ 7.6 Answer **D** — Permission to prosecute for the offence is required from the DPP, making answer A incorrect. This does not make C correct as although the prosecuting permission is correctly identified in the answer (from the DPP), PALTRY *has not* committed the offence. Answer B is incorrect as the offence applies to all 'relevant' offences and does not exclude offences on the grounds of length of sentence. As PALTRY has only received reasonable compensation for her loss she does not commit the offence.

Investigators' Manual, para 1.14.6

8. Theft

Answers to Multiple-choice Questions

MCQ 8.1 Answer **D** — Section 2 of the Theft Act 1968 states that a person will not be treated as dishonest if

(a) he appropriates property in the belief that he has the right in law to deprive the other of it (answer A); or,

(b) if he appropriates property in the belief that he would have the other's consent if the other knew of the appropriation and the circumstances of it (answer C); or

(c) he appropriates property in the belief that the person to whom the property belongs cannot be discovered by taking reasonable steps (answer B).

A person *may* be dishonest notwithstanding that he is willing to pay for the property.

Investigators' Manual, para 2.1.2

MCQ 8.2 Answer **C** — The fact that gambling debts are not legally enforceable is immaterial, making answer A incorrect. The belief on the part of the defendant need only be honestly held; there is no requirement for the belief to be reasonable, making answer D incorrect. Section 2(1)(a) of the Theft Act 1968 (appropriating property in the belief that there is a right in law to deprive the other of it) means that WISEDALE is not dishonest, making answer B incorrect.

Investigators' Manual, para 2.1.2

MCQ 8.3 Answer **A** — The ruling in *R v Ghosh* [1982] QB 1053 states that where s 2 of the Theft Act does not assist the jury, they should decide
- whether, according to the ordinary standards of reasonable and honest people, what was done was 'dishonest; and if it was
- whether the defendant himself must have realised that what was done was dishonest by those standards.

Investigators' Manual, para 2.1.3

MCQ 8.4 Answer **B** — If SMITH buys the car in good faith and gives value for it (i.e. a reasonable price), but then discovers it has been stolen, her refusal to return it to GOODALL will not, without more, attract liability for theft (see s 3(2) of the Theft Act 1968). This makes answers A and C incorrect. Answer D is incorrect, as the same property can be stolen on more than one occasion.

Investigators' Manual, para 2.1.4

MCQ 8.5 Answer **D** — A person cannot steal land or things forming part of the land and severed from it by him, except if a person is not in possession of land and they appropriate anything forming part of the land by severing it or causing it to be severed (s 4(2)(b) of the Theft Act 1968). This makes answer B incorrect. If you are in possession of land under a tenancy, then things forming part of that land to be used with it are 'property' capable of being stolen. However, s 4(2)(c) of the Theft Act 1968 states that this relates to fixtures and structures let to be used with the land (e.g. fireplaces, fitted kitchens, sheds, etc.). Answers A and C are incorrect, as a tenant cannot steal the land of which he/she stands possessed *nor things forming part of the land (i.e. the rhododendron bush)*.

Investigators' Manual, para 2.1.5

MCQ 8.6 Answer **A** — This question relates to s 5(3) of the Theft Act 1968, which states: *where a person* (DELACY) *receives property from or on account of another* (the mortgage funds from BOOTH) *and is under an obligation to retain and deal with that property or its proceeds in a particular way* (using the money for the mortgage), *the property or proceeds shall be regarded* (as against him) *as belonging to the other* (i.e. the mortgage money still belongs to BOOTH). The mortgage funds only ever belong to BOOTH, making answers B, C, and D incorrect.

Investigators' Manual, para 2.1.7

MCQ 8.7 Answer **B** — The intention to permanently deprive can be met by treating a thing as one's own to dispose of, regardless of the other's rights. The storyline of this question is as per *DPP v J* (2002) LTL 20 February. The Administrative Court held that a person who took something and dealt with it for the purpose of rendering it useless in this way demonstrated the intention of treating the article as his/her own to dispose of (remember that you would still need the other elements of theft to prove the offence, e.g. dishonesty). There is no need for the property to be totally destroyed, making answer A incorrect. Answers C and D are both incorrect, as BUSH has permanently deprived NEWALL of the headphones in these circumstances.

Investigators' Manual, para 2.1.10

MCQ 8.8 Answer **D** — Land can be stolen e.g. by a trustee or other representative (see s 4(2)(a)), making answer A incorrect. A tamed wild creature will be regarded as property (s 4(4)), making answer B incorrect. Answer C is incorrect as although a cheque is of very little value in itself, it still has value and is property. Human bodies cannot be stolen (*Doodeward* v *Spence* (1908) 6 CLR 406).

Investigators' Manual, paras 2.1.5 and 2.1.6

9. Burglary and Aggravated Burglary

Answers to Multiple-choice Questions

MCQ 9.1 Answer **D** — The sentence for burglary when the building/part of a building is a dwelling is 14 years' imprisonment.

Investigators' Manual, para 2.2.1

MCQ 9.2 Answer **A** — Burglary is triable on indictment if the 'ulterior' offence is so triable, OR if the offence is committed in a dwelling and violence was used.

Investigators' Manual, para 2.2.1

MCQ 9.3 Answer **D** — Abstracting electricity is not theft, so at point A there can be no intent for the purposes of burglary. Once inside, REDGRAVE can only commit burglary in the garage by stealing or causing GBH or attempting either. Criminal damage is not a 'trigger' offence, so answer B is incorrect. TWOC is not theft as far as burglary is concerned, making answer C incorrect.

Investigators' Manual, paras 2.2.1 and 2.2.3

MCQ 9.4 Answer **B** — Entry need only be 'effective' (*R v Brown* [1985] Crim LR 212).

Investigators' Manual, para 2.2.1

MCQ 9.5 Answer **C** — At points A and B, BURTOFT has already entered the bedroom and cannot become a trespasser, therefore she cannot commit burglary. Her intention to steal from the loft goes beyond a condition of entry and the moment she enters a separate part of the building she becomes a trespasser, making answer D incorrect.

Investigators' Manual, para 2.2.1

MCQ 9.6 Answer **C** — Rape is not one of the trigger offences for burglary under s 9(1)(a). All the other examples are burglaries under that section of the Theft Act 1968.

Investigators' Manual, para 2.2.3

MCQ 9.7 Answer **C** — An industrial freezer has been held to be a building (*B and S v Leathley* [1979] Crim LR 314).

Investigators' Manual, para 2.2.2

MCQ 9.8 Answer **B** — The rope is a weapon of offence as it is intended to incapacitate a person and comes within the **WIFE** mnemonic. WARREN actually has physical possession of the rope as well as an intention to use it to incapacitate a person and OAK has knowledge of its existence as well as access; so both men would be caught by the expression 'has with him' regarding this item. This means that both men commit an aggravated burglary in relation to the rope. Therefore, **WARREN and OAK commit the offence**.

While both men have the screwdriver 'with them', WARREN does not know of OAK's intentions regarding the sharpened screwdriver. The screwdriver is a weapon of offence to OAK (as he has sharpened it to use against HOLLAND, i.e. adapted and intends) but not to

WARREN, to whom this is just a screwdriver. Therefore OAK commits aggravated burglary in relation to the screwdriver but WARREN does not.

Option D says that both men commit the offence but OAK **only** commits it in relation to the screwdriver. This is wrong as he commits it in relation to the rope as well.

Option B is right as both men commit the offence but WARREN **only** commits it in relation to the rope (and not the screwdriver).

Investigators' Manual, para 2.3

MCQ 9.9   Answer **D** — Answer A is incorrect as the assault at point A takes place outside a building. Answer B is incorrect as the bin liner is used to incapacitate a CCTV and not a person. Answer C is incorrect as using fingers as an imitation firearm *would not* qualify (*R v Bentham* [2005] UKHL 18). Therefore, answer D is correct.

Investigators' Manual, paras 2.3 to 2.3.1

MCQ 9.10   Answer **A** — The defendant must at least know that they have the article with them. CO-HEN's lack of knowledge means the offence is incomplete.

Investigators' Manual, paras 2.3 and 2.3.1

MCQ 9.11   Answer **D** — FRANCIS has no intention to commit a s 9(1)(a) 'trigger' offence, making answer A incorrect. Although he entered as a trespasser, the weapon of offence was left outside so answer B is incorrect. Because he stole whilst inside and is a trespasser, answer C is incorrect.

Investigators' Manual, paras 2.3 to 2.3.1

10. Robbery and Blackmail

Answers to Multiple-choice Questions

MCQ 10.1   Answer **D** — For there to be a robbery there must be a theft. If FISHER honestly believes he has a right in law to the property then he is not dishonest. If he is not dishonest then there is no theft. If there is no theft then there is no robbery.

Investigators' Manual, para 2.4

MCQ 10.2   Answer **B** — If the force is applied, not to the person directly but to his/her property (such as pulling a shopping basket or handbag from a person's hand), this may still be robbery as the force has been applied, albeit indirectly (*R v Clouden* [1987] Crim LR 56, CA).

Investigators' Manual, para 2.4

MCQ 10.3   Answer **B** — Answer A is incorrect because this is a threat to use force at some time in the future (this would be a blackmail). The fact that RIHAN is deaf and blind is immaterial. LEWIN sought to put RIHAN in fear of being then and there subjected to force, and just because the threats are not heard or seen makes no difference. Therefore, answer C is incorrect as the threats were first made at point B.

Investigators' Manual, para 2.5

MCQ 10.4 Answer **C** — Answer A is incorrect as the force must be used or threatened 'immediately before or at the time' of the theft. Here force is threatened to be used the next day. Answer B is incorrect as to have a robbery there must be a theft. If one of the theft elements is missing (here there is no dishonesty) then there is no theft and therefore no robbery. Answer D is incorrect as the accidental application of force is not willed by the offender i.e. there is no voluntary conduct and therefore no *actus reus*. The fact that GREY (in answer C) is not actually in fear does not matter—it is the intent of the offender that is all important.

Investigators' Manual, para 2.5

MCQ 10.5 Answer **D** — A 'gain' and 'loss' relates to money and other property, making answer A incorrect. Answer B is incorrect because the demand can be made with a view to gain for 'himself or another'. Answer C is incorrect as the gain need not be permanent.

Investigators' Manual, paras 2.5 to 2.5.1

MCQ 10.6 Answer **D** — Blackmail is committed when the demand is actually made. It can be a written demand and in such a situation the demand is made when the letter is posted, making answers A and C incorrect. Answer B is incorrect as no special permission is required for a prosecution of blackmail.

Investigators' Manual, paras 2.5 to 2.5.3

11. Handling Stolen Goods

Answers to Multiple-choice Questions

MCQ 11.1 Answer **D** — When JONES obtained the lawnmower from HARDING he did not know it was stolen. To handle the goods the defendant must know or believe they are stolen and this is not the case at point A. If the only person 'benefiting' from the defendant's actions is the defendant himself/herself, the element of 'assisting/acting for another's benefit' will not be made out (*R v Bloxham* [1983] 1 AC 109). This makes answer C incorrect. At point B, JONES has not even tried to dispose of the mower. Merely finding out you have bought stolen property does not make you a handler if you bought the property in good faith.

Investigators' Manual, paras 2.7 and 2.7.4

MCQ 11.2 Answer **C** — Goods stolen outside England and Wales will be stolen goods where the stealing amounts to an offence in that country, making answer A incorrect. Stolen goods (apart from the original stolen goods) are those that represent the stolen goods in the hands of the thief and/or the handler. Therefore, the car will always be stolen goods. The £3,000.00 in the hands of ELLIOT represents the car, as does the watch he buys with the £3,000.00. This makes answers B and D incorrect.

Investigators' Manual, para 2.7.1

MCQ 11.3 Answer **B** — The purpose of admitting this evidence is for the purpose of proving that COWSER knew or believed the goods to be stolen goods.

Investigators' Manual, para 2.7.7

MCQ 11.4   Answer **A** — The correct answer is A. Section 27(3)(b) states that evidence that the defendant has, within the previous five years of the date of the offence charged, been convicted of theft or handling stolen goods.

Investigators' Manual, para 2.7.7

12. Criminal Damage

Answers to Multiple-choice Questions

MCQ 12.1   Answer **A** — This question relates to the case of *Jaggard v Dickinson* [1981] QB 527. ANSCOMBE will commit the offence but may have a defence because he believes that the property is his and therefore he can damage it if he likes. The fact that he makes a drunken mistake and damages his neighbour's door does not matter, because when he caused the damage his belief was honestly held.

Investigators' Manual, para 2.9.2.7

MCQ 12.2   Answer **D** — When a defendant is charged with this offence, it must be shown that it was the damage that caused the danger to life. In *R v Steer* [1988] AC 111, a defendant fired a gun through a window pane. The court felt that, although the defendant was clearly reckless as to the damage his actions would cause, the two people standing behind the window pane were not put in danger by the damage but by the missile. Therefore, the court held that the defendant was not guilty of this offence.

Investigators' Manual, para 2.9.3

MCQ 12.3   Answer **A** — Section 2 of the Act (threats to destroy or damage property) refers to the offence as one of *intention*. The key element is the defendant's intention that the person receiving the threat fears it would be carried out. It is immaterial whether the threat is believed (answer C), whether the threat was to commit damage in the future (answer B), or whether the defendant actually intended to carry out the threat.

Investigators' Manual, para 2.9.5

MCQ 12.4   Answer **C** — This is an offence of intent, i.e. the damage need not actually have been attempted or committed, making answer D incorrect. A conditional intent, that is, an intent to use something to cause criminal damage should the need arise, will be enough (*R v Buckingham* (1976) 63 Cr App R 159). The term used in the definition is 'custody or control', which is far wider than 'possession'; there is no need to show that the defendant actually had the item with him, making answer A incorrect.

Investigators' Manual, para 2.9.6

MCQ 12.5   Answer **C** — Criminal damage can be racially aggravated, making answer D incorrect. The fact that there was nobody in the shop to hear the remark is immaterial, making answer B incorrect. The words, 'bloody foreigners' stated immediately before a criminal damage were held by the Divisional Court to be capable of amounting to an expression of hostility based on a person's membership or presumed membership of a racial group, making answer A incorrect.

Investigators' Manual, para 2.9.2.1

13. Homicide

Answers to Multiple-choice Questions

MCQ 13.1 Answer **B** — The House of Lords ruled that the rule of doctrine of transferred malice does not fully apply to an unborn baby, making answer D incorrect. If Adrian's intention is to kill Joan this may support a charge of murder of the baby in these circumstances, making A incorrect. If the intention is to commit GBH to Joan and the baby is born alive, but later dies from injuries received in the womb, it is manslaughter, making answer B correct. Answer C is incorrect as a consequence of the above.

Investigators' Manual, para 3.1.2

MCQ 13.2 Answer **C** — If the victim of an alleged murder dies more than three years after receiving his/her injury, then the consent of the Attorney General or Solicitor General is needed before bringing a prosecution.

Investigators' Manual, para 3.1.2.2

MCQ 13.3 Answer **A** — The special defence of provocation can only be used when the defendant is charged with the offence of murder, *not* attempted murder. This makes answers B, C, and D incorrect. A consequence of a successful plea would be to reduce murder to manslaughter (not attempted murder to a s 18 wounding), making answer C further incorrect. The consent of the DPP is not required to raise the defence, making answer D further incorrect.

Investigators' Manual, para 3.1.3.2

MCQ 13.4 Answer **D** — The sentence for manslaughter is life imprisonment (not mandatory), making answer C incorrect. Answers A and B are incorrect, because to be guilty of manslaughter by unlawful act the defendant *must* have the required *mens rea* for the unlawful act. This question is based on the case of *R v Lamb* [1967] 2 QB 981, where the defendant was shown (in mirror circumstances to this question) not to have the required *mens rea* for assault and his conviction for manslaughter was quashed.

Investigators' Manual, para 3.1.4.1

MCQ 13.5 Answer **C** — Although the Act deals with deaths in custody, these provisions will not be brought into force for some time, making answer A incorrect. Answer B is incorrect as the offence is punishable by an unlimited fine and not imprisonment. Answer D is incorrect as there are exceptions to the relevant duty of care e.g. in operations for dealing with terrorism, civil unrest or serious disorder.

Investigators' Manual, para 3.1.4.3

14. Offences Against the Person

Answers to Multiple-choice Questions

MCQ 14.1 Answer **A** — The defendant commits an assault when he/she intentionally or recklessly causes another person to apprehend *immediate* unlawful violence, making answers B and D incorrect. Answer C is incorrect, as an assault can be committed by words alone.

Investigators' Manual, para 3.2.4

MCQ 14.2   Answer **B** — Answers A, C, and D are all examples of assault where consent by the person assaulted *cannot remove* liability for the defendant.

Investigators' Manual, para 3.2.6

MCQ 14.3   Answer **C** — Answers A, B, and D are all injuries that would amount to 'actual bodily harm'. A punch causing a tooth to puncture the cheek would be classed as a 'wound', even though in was caused internally.

Investigators' Manual, para 3.2.19

MCQ 14.4   Answer **D** — Remember that the word 'malicious' should be read as 'reckless'. JOHAL recklessly caused serious harm/injury to PC HARRIS intending to prevent his arrest, and this would constitute a s 18 wounding.

Investigators' Manual, paras 3.2.20 to 3.2.21

MCQ 14.5   Answer **B** — The injuries received by MATONI and the child will amount to an offence under s 39 of the Criminal Justice Act 1988 and not to a s 47 assault (Offences Against the Person Act 1861) making answers C and D incorrect. Answer A is incorrect as THEAKSTON is liable for the injuries the child receives. This is because a battery can be committed indirectly (as per *Haystead* v *Chief Constable of Derbyshire* [2000] 3 All ER 890).

Investigators' Manual, para 3.2.4

MCQ 14.6   Answer **B** — Belief in your own innocence, even if it is thoroughly merited, is no defence to this offence, making answer C incorrect. The offence is committed when a person assaults any person (including members of the public) with intent to resist or prevent their own or anothers arrest, making answers A and D incorrect.

Investigators' Manual, para 3.2.12

MCQ 14.7   Answer **A** — Provocation is only a defence to murder, making answer D incorrect. The offence has not been committed as WEST did not intend either CRAIG or SARTIN to believe the threat.

Investigators' Manual, para 3.2.17

15. Child Abduction

Answers to Multiple-choice Questions

MCQ 15.1   Answer **B** — The fact that COLETO is the father of all three children will not afford him a defence, as he has taken his children out of the United Kingdom without the consent of his wife who has lawful custody of all of the children, making answer D incorrect. The relevant age for an offence under s 1 of the Act is '*under the age of 16*'. This means that the offence is not committed with regard to Anthony who is 16 years old, but is committed with regard to Phillipa (aged 14 years) and Mark (aged 12 years), making answers A and C incorrect.

Investigators' Manual, para 3.3.1

MCQ 15.2   Answer **D** — The fact that the child has been taken out of the United Kingdom for less than a month is immaterial in these circumstances. This forms part of the defence under s 1(4) of the Act and only becomes relevant if the person who takes the child out of the country is a person in whose favour a residence order exists, and this is not the case with Andrea YOUNG. This makes answer B incorrect. Andrea YOUNG does require the consent of James PERSHORE to take her son out of the country, but the fact that she did not attempt to contact him does not mean she commits the offence, making answer C incorrect. Answer A is incorrect, as a defence under s 1(5)(a)(i) exists where the person believes the other would consent to the taking in the circumstances.

Investigators' Manual, paras 3.3.1 and 3.3.2

MCQ 15.3   Answer **A** — Answer B is incorrect, as there is no requirement that the removal of the child from a person's lawful control be accomplished by the use of force or physical constraint. Answer C is incorrect, as whether CURTIS has an ulterior motive for the removal is immaterial. In *R v Mousir* [1987] Crim LR 561 it was said that the phrase 'so as to' in s 2(1)(a) of the Act is concerned with the objective consequences of the taking or detaining, and not with the accused's subjective motives. Answer D is incorrect, as the consent of the victim is irrelevant.

Investigators' Manual, para 3.3.3

MCQ 15.4   Answer **B** — There are three defences available to an offence under s 2 of the Act.

(3) ... it shall be a defence for [the defendant] to prove—
    (a) where the father and mother of the child in question were not married to each other at the time of his birth—
        (i) that he is the child's father; or
        (ii) that, at the time of the alleged offence, he believed, on reasonable grounds, that he was the child's father; or
    (b) that, at the time of the alleged offence, he believed that the child had attained the age of 16.

As there are three defences, answer C is incorrect. Answer A is incorrect, as the fact that DAY is not the father of the child does not necessarily mean he commits the offence (because of the other defences). Answer D is incorrect, as PELL has removed the child from DAY's lawful control.

Investigators' Manual, paras 3.3.3 and 3.3.4

16. Public Order and Racially and Religiously Aggravated Offences

Answers to Multiple-choice Questions

MCQ 16.1   Answer **C** — Violent disorder requires three persons to use or threaten unlawful violence. The unlawful violence in this context includes violent conduct towards property as well as violent conduct towards persons.

Investigators' Manual, para 3.6.3

MCQ 16.2   Answer **B** — Where there are only three defendants to a charge of violent disorder and one of them is acquitted, unless you can prove there were others involved who were not charged, the remaining two defendants should be acquitted as well (*R v Worton* (1990) 154 JP 201).

Investigators' Manual, para 3.6.3

MCQ 16.3   Answer **D** — The House of Lords has held that in order to prove an affray, the threat of unlawful violence has to be towards a person(s) present at the scene (*I v DPP* [2002] 1 AC 285). If there is nobody present to whom the threat is directed then there is no affray.

Investigators' Manual, para 3.6.4

MCQ 16.4   Answer **A** — The offence of s 20 (grievous bodily harm, Offences Against the Person Act 1861) is the only offence that could be racially or religiously aggravated.

Investigators' Manual, para 3.7.1

MCQ 16.5   Answer **D** — Travellers are the only group of people who are identified as falling outside the definition of a racial or religious group.

Investigators' Manual, para 3.7.6

17. Kidnapping and False Imprisonment

Answers to Multiple-choice Questions

MCQ 17.1   Answer **A** — An offence of kidnapping can be carried out by the use of force or fraud. When NICKLIN's wife is moved from the front of POYNER's house towards NICKLIN's car, the offence is complete.

Investigators' Manual, para 3.5

MCQ 17.2   Answer **B** — Answer A is correct as the offence can be committed if the defendant either intends or is reckless as to whether a person's freedom is restrained. Answer C is incorrect as there is no time restraint in relation to the offence; keeping someone in a particular place for however short a time may amount to false imprisonment. Answer D is incorrect as false imprisonment is triable on indictment and carries an unlimited maximum penalty.

Investigators' Manual, para 3.4

MCQ 17.3   Answer **A** — The use of force is not required for the offence of false imprisonment, making answer B incorrect. Answer C is incorrect, as UDALL has moved ACTON from one point to another by the use of a fraud and the offence of kidnapping is complete at this point. There is no requirement for the victim to be taken to the offender's ultimate destination, making answer D incorrect.

Investigators' Manual, paras 3.4 and 3.5

18. Misuse of Drugs

Answers to Multiple-choice Questions

MCQ 18.1   Answer **B** — In order to be in possession of anything, the common law requires physical control of the object plus knowledge of its presence. If a drug is slipped into RUSH's pocket and he has no idea it is there, he is not in possession of it.

Investigators' Manual, paras 3.8.2 to 3.8.2.5

MCQ 18.2   Answer **C**—Possession with intent to supply to an undercover police officer is an offence under this section, making answer A incorrect. Answer B is incorrect as, although possession of this material is relevant to show that GARWOOD is an active dealer generally, it does not prove the offence. The presence of large sums of money can be used to prove the offence (*R v Wright* [1994] Crim LR 55).

Investigators' Manual, para 3.8.5.6

MCQ 18.3   Answer **B**—Possession of a Class C drug is an offence punishable by two years' imprisonment, making answer A incorrect. Answer D relates to the defence under s 5(4)(a), whereby a person takes possession of a drug to prevent another from committing or continuing to commit an offence in connection with the drug. DIXON has not taken possession of the drug for that reason and so the defence is unavailable, making answer D incorrect. Although DIXON's intentions at the time of finding the drug were noble, he must *as soon as possible after taking possession of it, take reasonable steps to hand it to a person entitled to possess it*. This makes answer C incorrect.

Investigators' Manual, paras 3.8.4.1 and 3.8.4.2

MCQ 18.4   Answer **C**—Answer A is incorrect, as the minimum period for such an order is two years (s 33(3) of the Act). Answer B is incorrect, as the offences covered by travel restriction orders include the production and supply of controlled drugs (therefore including an offence under s 4(3) of the 1971 Act). Answer D is incorrect, as an offender may apply to the court that made the restriction order to have it revoked or suspended (s 35 of the Act).

Investigators' Manual, para 3.8.6.3

Answers to Scenario-based Questions

SBQ 18.1   Section 37 of the Misuse Drugs Act 1971 defines 'cannabis'. It states that cannabis means any plant of the genus *Cannabis* or any part of any such plant, except that it does not include any of the following products after separation from the rest of the plant:

A) mature stalk of any such plant,
B) fibre produced from mature stalk of any such plant, and
C) seed of any such plant.

Mrs GRUNDY is only in possession of the seeds and commits no offence.

SBQ 18.2   Section 6 of the Misuse of Drugs Act 1971 simply says that it shall not be lawful to cultivate any plant of the genus *Cannabis*. Cultivation is not clearly defined, but some form of watering or feeding would be more than sufficient. You may also wish to consider the offence of producing a controlled drug under s 4(2) of the Act, as 'production' means producing by manufacture *or* by cultivation. The benefits of a charge under this section are simple; production is a drugs trafficking offence and if found guilty the offender can be made subject of a Drugs Profits Confiscation order, allowing the court to seize any assets from his/her production activities. Another example of production is found in the making of 'crack' cocaine from normal cocaine hydrochloride. The process removes the salt part of the compound, thus creating a more potent drug. If you were able to prove a person's involvement in this, you would be able to consider the offence of producing a controlled drug as production is by manufacture, cultivation, or *by any other method*.

SBQ 18.3   Mrs GRUNDY is fully aware that the cake contains a controlled drug. The fact that it has been prepared in some other way for consumption is irrelevant. Putting the cannabis in a cake for consumption is no different to the more common method of including it with tobacco in a rolled cigarette for consumption. The term 'supply' means more than a simple transfer of physical control and includes distribution of a substance. Mrs GRUNDY has distributed the substance and the fact that her friend does not know is irrelevant.

SBQ 18.4   Amphetamine (more recently being spelt 'Amfetamine') is a Class B controlled drug under the Misuse of Drugs Act 1971. However, when it is prepared for injection it is automatically reclassified as a Class A drug. Therefore, COLT is in possession of a Class A drug under MDA 1971. This goes some way to explaining why amphetamine is listed under Class A and Class B in your *Investigators' Manual*.

SBQ 18.5   COLT clearly possesses a controlled drug (morphine), as the tablets are issued to his mother and not to him. It does not matter whether the drug is illicitly produced or pharmaceutically produced; it remains a Class A drug under the Misuse of Drugs Act 1971.

SBQ 18.6   COLT would have a defence to possession under s 5(4)(b) in that 'knowing or suspecting it to be a controlled drug, he took possession of it for the purpose of delivering it into the custody of a person lawfully entitled to take custody of it and that as soon as possible after taking possession of it he took all reasonable steps to deliver it into the custody of such a person.' Therefore, as long as COLT had the authority of his mother to collect the tablets and he took them straight to her as soon as possible, he has a defence to possession.

SBQ 18.7   Under s 23(1) of the Misuse of Drugs Act 1971, a constable or other authorized person can enter the premises of a person carrying on the business of supplying controlled drugs, and demand the production of and to inspect any books or documents relating to the dealings in such drugs and to inspect any stocks of any such drugs.

SBQ 18.8   No. Section 23(3)(a) and (b) of the Misuse of Drugs Act 1971 only allows for a Justice of the Peace to grant a search warrant if he/she is satisfied that there are controlled drugs on the premises or documents relating to any transaction or dealing in those controlled drugs. Therefore, any application to search for this machine would not be granted (under this particular section of this Act)

19. Firearms and Gun Crime

Answers to Multiple-choice Questions

MCQ 19.1   Answer **A** — The firearm must be the means by which life is endangered and the fact that ROBE has possession of the firearm at the time of the offence is immaterial, making answer B incorrect. The fact that the victim of the offence is not injured makes no difference to the commission of this offence, making answer C incorrect. Answer D is correct insofar as the offence does not require the firearm to be produced, but option A supersedes this.

Investigators' Manual, para 3.9.6.1

MCQ 19.2   Answer **C** — Answers A, B, and D are all offences under Schedule 1. However, although the Schedule covers several types of assaults (s 47 and s 20), it does not cover s 18 wounding.

Investigators' Manual, para 3.9.6.4

MCQ 19.3   Answer **B** — This offence is 'absolute', but can only be committed if the defendant has with him a *loaded* shotgun, making answer A incorrect. This fact makes answer C incorrect as well. Answer D is incorrect because the offence is 'absolute' and knowledge is not required.

Investigators' Manual, para 3.9.6.7

MCQ 19.4   Answer **A** — Section 47 of the 1968 Firearms Act allows a constable who has reasonable cause to suspect a person has a firearm with him in a public place to require him/her to hand over the firearm for examination by the officer, making answers B and D incorrect. It does not matter whether the firearm is loaded or if the person who is requested to hand over the firearm has ammunition in his/her possession, making answer C incorrect.

Investigators' Manual, para 3.9.8

20. Sexual Offences

Answers to Multiple-choice Questions

MCQ 20.1   Answer **D** — Under the Sexual Offences (Amendment) Acts 1976 and 1992, victims of most sexual offences (including rape, incest, and indecency with children) are entitled to anonymity throughout their lifetime.

Investigators' Manual, para 4.1.3

MCQ 20.2   Answer **C** — The offence of rape can only be committed by a male, so answer A is incorrect. The offence can only be committed by penetration with the penis, so answer B is incorrect. The penetration by the penis can be to the mouth, anus, or vagina, making answer C correct and answer D incorrect as a consequence.

Investigators' Manual, para 4.3

MCQ 20.3   Answer **C** — The sex of the victim is immaterial, making answer B incorrect. Penetration can be committed with a part of the body or anything else, making answer D incorrect. Section 79(3) of the Act covers the fact that references to a part of the body (e.g. penis, vagina) will include references to a body part that has been surgically constructed, particularly if it is through gender reassignment. Therefore, the offence is committed when the surgically constructed vagina is penetrated by SUTTON.

Investigators' Manual, paras 4.3.1 and 4.4.1

MCQ 20.4   Answer **A** — If the activity would not appear to a reasonable person to be sexual then, irrespective of the sexual gratification the person might derive from the activity, it will not be 'sexual'. Therefore, weird or exotic fetishes that no ordinary person would regard as being sexual or potentially sexual will not be covered. As the activity is not 'sexual', WALTON does not commit the offence, making answers B and D incorrect. Answer C is incorrect, as a sexual organ or potentially sexual organ does not have to be touched for the offence to be committed.

Investigators' Manual, paras 4.2.1 to 4.2.2 and 4.4.2

MCQ 20.5   Answer **A** — The offence is committed when a person is forced to engage in sexual activity with another. Forcing OAKEY to masturbate JEVONS would mean the offence is committed, making answer B incorrect. Although the maximum sentence is ten years in normal circumstances, the fact that OAKEY was forced to penetrate JEVONS's anus means that the offence is punishable with life imprisonment, making answer A correct and answer C incorrect. The fact that JEVONS is a willing participant makes no difference to the offence being committed.

Investigators' Manual, para 4.4.3

21. Child Sex Offences

Answers to Multiple-choice Questions

MCQ 21.1   Answer **B** — The fact that LEENEY consented to the activity is irrelevant, making answer A incorrect. Answer C is incorrect as the offence can be committed by someone over the age of 18. If LEENEY were under 13 then the offence would be complete, but as she is under 14 years old the prosecution will have to show that COLCOUGH did not reasonably believe that LEENEY was over 16.

Investigators' Manual, para 4.5.1

MCQ 21.2   Answer **D** — Answer A is incorrect as the offender for the offence under s 11 of the Act must be aged 18 or over. Answer B is incorrect as sexual gratification is a required part of the definition. Answer C is incorrect as this offence applies to children who are under 16 years of age. D is correct as it is not necessary to show that the child was aware of the activity in every case.

Investigators' Manual, para 4.5.2

MCQ 21.3   Answer **B** — The fact that the images shown to a child are still or cartoons is immaterial (s 79(5)), making answer A incorrect. Although TURNER did not initially intend his nephew to see the images, he would commit the offence when he asked him if he wanted to stay (if TURNER were under 16 years old). TURNER falls outside the age group for this offence, making answer C incorrect.

Investigators' Manual, para 4.5.3

MCQ 21.4   Answer **A** — This offence applies to activities by which the defendant intends to commit a relevant child sex offence himself, or by which the defendant intends or believes another person will do so in any part of the world. This makes answers B and D incorrect. There is no need for TREVENA to have agreed to leave the country, making answer C incorrect.

Investigators' Manual, para 4.5.4

MCQ 21.5   Answer **C** — Up until this point no offence would be committed. Although JEFFERSON is classed as a 'child', i.e. under 18, the exceptions under s 1A of the Act would prevent an

371

offence taking place until HENSON shows the photographs to a frie.
the Act).

Investigato.

22. Preparatory Offences

Answers to Multiple-choice Questions

MCQ 22.1   Answer **D** — Answer A is incorrect, as this is a preparatory offence and there is no need for sexual activity to take place. Answer B is incorrect, as the offence is committed when the substance is administered to WALKER. Alcohol would be classed as a substance, making answer C incorrect.

Investigators' Manual, para 4.7.3

MCQ 22.2   Answer **A** — Virtually all sexual offences are 'relevant' offences other than those that exist under the Protection of Children Act 1978, making answer B incorrect. Answers C and D are incorrect as there is no limitation on the type of criminal offence committed. If the offence is one of kidnapping or false imprisonment, then the maximum sentence is increased from ten years to life.

Investigators' Manual, para 4.7.1

MCQ 22.3   Answer **B** — The defendant must intend to commit the relevant offence on the premises, i.e. in the house. Intending to commit the offence in the garden would not be enough.

Investigators' Manual, para 4.7.2